Divine Providence

A volume in the series

Cornell Studies in the Philosophy of Religion

EDITED BY WILLIAM P. ALSTON

A list of titles in this series is available at
www.cornellpress.cornell.edu.

Thomas P. Flint

DIVINE PROVIDENCE

The Molinist Account

Cornell University Press, Ithaca and London

First published 1998 by Cornell University Press
First printing, Cornell Paperbacks, 2006

Library of Congress Cataloging-in-Publication Data
Flint, Thomas P.
Divine providence : the Molinist account / Thomas P. Flint.
    p.   cm.—(Cornell studies in the philosophy of religion)
Includes bibliographical references and index.
ISBN-13: 978-0-8014-7336-4 (pbk. : alk. paper)
1. Providence and government of God—History of doctrines—16th century.
2. Molinism.   3. Catholic Church—Doctrines—History—16th century.
I. Title.   II. Series.
BT135.2.F274   1998
231'.5—dc21   97-36673

Cornell University Press strives to use environmentally responsible suppliers and materials to the fullest extent possible in the publishing of its books. Such materials include vegetable-based, low-VOC inks and acid-free papers that are recycled, totally chlorine-free, or partly composed of nonwood fibers. For further information, visit our website at www.cornellpress.cornell.edu.

Paperback printing   10   9   8   7   6   5   4   3

To JoAnn

Sì come eterna vita è veder Dio
né più si brama né brama più lice,
così me, Donna, il voi veder felice
fa in questo breve et fraile viver mio.
　　　　—Petrarch, *Rime sparse* 191.1–4

Contents

Acknowledgments

The number of people who have assisted me in one way or another in the composition of this book is huge. Among my colleagues at Notre Dame, three are particularly worthy of thanks. The seeds of the book were evident in my doctoral dissertation, written under the able guidance of Michael Loux and Alvin Plantinga; each of them has left an enormous and lasting impression upon me, and their influence on this work has been pervasive. Even more important has been Fred Freddoso. Ever since our collaborative endeavor to fashion a Molinist-inspired account of omnipotence in the early 1980s, he has been an invaluable critic and interlocutor on matters Molinist.

Other faculty at Notre Dame, both current and former, have also earned my gratitude for their help with this project. I especially thank David Burrell, Frederick Crosson, Cornelius Delaney, Richard Foley, Jorge Garcia, Gary Gutting, Ralph McInerny, Thomas Morris, Philip Quinn, William Ramsey, Eleonore Stump, Peter van Inwagen, and Fritz Warfield.

Visitors to the Notre Dame Center for Philosophy of Religion have also been subjected to much of this work, and it has benefited greatly from their responses. Though virtually every fellow has contributed to my thinking on this subject, special thanks are due to Robert Audi, Godehard Bruntrup, Andrew Cortens, Michael Griffin, Ken Konyndyk, Bruce Langtry, George Mavrodes, Scott Shalkowski, William Tolhurst, James Wetzel, David Widerker, Edward Wierenga, Nicholas Wolterstorff, and Linda Zagzebski. Extra-special thanks are due to two former Center fellows—David Hunt, whose careful comments on earlier versions of several chapters proved very helpful, and William Hasker, whose astute criticisms and generous discussions of many of my writings related to Molinism have left me greatly in his debt (as did his excellent reader's report for Cornell University Press).

Former graduate students at Notre Dame (most of them now well-established philosophers themselves) have also furthered my thinking on the issues addressed in this book. I am especially grateful to Douglas Blount, Michael Byron, William Davis, Scott Davison, Stewart Goetz, A. A. Howsepian, Trenton Merricks, Caleb Miller, Michael Murray, John O'Callaghan, Robert O'Connor, Charles Seymour, Christopher Taggart, David Vander-Laan, Jerry Walls, Mark Webb, Thomas Williams, and Keith Wyma. I also thank two colleagues from my graduate school days, David Kessler and Alven Neiman, who influenced my early thinking on these issues.

Among those few colleagues interested in Molinism who have *not* spent considerable time at Notre Dame, three are especially worthy of mention. I have benefited enormously from the writings of Robert Adams and William Craig on issues related to middle knowledge, and I am grateful to them for sending me several essays before their publication. Thanks are also due to William Alston, who, as editor of this series, made many excellent suggestions for alterations to the initial draft.

I also wish to acknowledge the invaluable assistance that Martha Detlefsen of the Notre Dame Center for Philosophy of Religion has provided over the many years during which this book was being written. Equally important at the end of the project was the generous support of the Notre Dame London Programme, under the able guidance of Anastasia Gutting, Paul Bradshaw, Sandra Berry, and the incomparable Kay Henderson. The wonderful staff at Cornell University Press, especially John Ackerman, have also earned my admiration.

Finally, my deepest expression of thanks goes to my wife, JoAnn Della-Neva. I have never ceased to view her entry into my life as the surest sign of divine providence I have been fortunate enough to receive. It is thus fitting that, with abundant gratitude, I dedicate this book to her.

Some material throughout the book is reprinted from Luis de Molina, *On Divine Foreknowledge: Part IV of the "Concordia,"* translated with an introduction and notes by Alfred J. Freddoso. Copyright © 1988 by Cornell University. Used by permission of the publisher, Cornell University Press.

Some material in Chapter 1 is reprinted from my "Providence and Predestination," in *A Companion to Philosophy of Religion*, edited by Philip L. Quinn and Charles Taliaferro (Cambridge, Mass.: Blackwell, 1997). Used by permission.

Some material in Chapter 2 is adapted from Thomas P. Flint, "Two Accounts of Providence," in Thomas V. Morris, ed., *Divine and Human Action:*

Essays in the Metaphysics of Theism. Copyright © 1988 by Cornell University. Used by permission of the publisher, Cornell University Press.

Some material in Chapter 6 is adapted from my "Hasker's *God, Time, and Knowledge,*" *Philosophical Studies* 60 (1990), 103–115, © 1990 Kluwer Academic Publishers, with kind permission from Kluwer Academic Publishers.

Some material in Chapter 8 is adapted from my "Middle Knowledge and the Doctrine of Infallibility," which appeared in *Philosophical Perspectives, 5, Philosophy of Religion, 1991,* edited by James E. Tomberlin (copyright by Ridgeview Publishing Company, Atascadero, CA). Reprinted by permission of Ridgeview Publishing Company.

Some material in Chapter 9 is adapted from my "Prophecy, Freedom, and Middle Knowledge," in *Our Knowledge of God,* edited by Kelly James Clark (Boston: Kluwer Academic Publishers, 1992), © 1992 Kluwer Academic Publishers, with kind permission from Kluwer Academic Publishers.

Some material in Chapter 11 is adapted from my "Praying for Things to Have Happened," in *Midwest Studies in Philosophy,* vol. 21, edited by Peter A. French, Theodore E. Uehling Jr., and Howard K. Wettstein, © 1997 by the University of Notre Dame Press. Used by permission.

T. P. F.

Introduction

1. The Senators and the Philosophers

In February 1964, Bobby Rowan, a member of the Georgia Senate, proposed that the following amendment be incorporated into the Georgia election code:

> No person may vote either in the Democratic primary or in the general election
> in the State of Georgia who has been deceased more than three years.

Needless to say, such a proposal immediately engenders questions (as well as smiles). At least two of these questions are especially pertinent. First, why let dead people vote at all? And second, why suspend their post mortem franchise after three years?

Supporters of the proposal apparently had answers to such questions. In general, they argued, the friends and relatives of the deceased would know full well how their dearly departed would have freely decided to vote in any proximate election. Why should the accident of death prevent a vote from being cast in the way everyone knows it would have been cast had said accident not occurred? Of course, since candidates and issues change as time moves on, our knowledge concerning how the deceased would have voted decreases the longer they have been dead. At some point, our confidence would be low enough that we would no longer have any idea just how to count the vote of the inanimate. The proposed amendment thus suggested three years as a reasonable statutory limit.[1]

[1] For a discussion of this fascinating incident, see Jimmy Carter, *Turning Point* (New York: Times Books, 1992), pp. 183–184.

Fortunately, the debate over this curious proposal was apparently not without humor. Equally fortunately, the debaters did not include contemporary philosophers of religion. For had such philosophers been present, the discussion might well have evolved into a debate over an issue that most politicians would find, as Alice (of Wonderland fame) might put it, even curiouser than the proposed amendment. On the surface, the advocates of the amendment seemed to be assuming that there are truths stating how a dead person would have freely voted had he or she lived until election day.[2] But, a philosophical Senator might have asked, *are* there any such truths? Can we, can even God, know how a person would freely act in a certain situation if they are in fact never placed in that situation? Is there any fact of the matter to be known in such cases?

Discussion of this question would no doubt have set many senators' heads spinning. But during the past twenty years or so, this issue has become one of the most hotly debated topics in the field of philosophical theology. Many philosophers have argued that there are truths of the sort described above, and that God would be both cognizant of such truths and able to utilize his knowledge of them in his creation and providential governance of the world. On the other hand, many have denied such claims; some have insisted that there are no such facts to be known, while others have argued that, even if there are such truths, they would be of no practical use to God.

The current debate on this issue, though, is hardly unique in the history of philosophy. The claim that God both knows and can use propositions of the requisite type was proposed and defended at length by Luis de Molina, a sixteenth-century Spanish Jesuit theologian whose views on divine providence and related issues were set forth in his *Liberi Arbitrii cum Gratiae Donis, Divina Praescientia, Providentia, Praedestinatione et Reprobatione Concordia*, known commonly by a less audacious but more mnemonic moniker—the *Concordia*. Molina's *Concordia* was attacked with great vehemence by a number of his contemporaries. The controversy his work engendered, perhaps the most fiery in the annals of late medieval philosophy, has simmered on the back burner of philosophical attention ever since, with intermittent trips to the front of the range. Among English-speaking philosophers, the heat was turned up again roughly two decades ago when Alvin Plantinga unknowingly presupposed the Molinist view in his response to the problem of evil.[3] Since that time, the dispute has reached the boiling point, and currently shows no sign of cooling. Alfred Freddoso's 1988 translation of Part IV of the *Concordia* has

---

[2] William Hasker would no doubt remind me that many of the bill's supporters may have believed only in truths about the *likely* voting behavior of the deceased!

[3] See Alvin Plantinga, *The Nature of Necessity* (Oxford: Clarendon Press, 1974), chap. 9; see also his *God, Freedom and Evil* (New York: Harper & Row, 1974), pp. 34–45.

only added to the contest by making the relevant section of Molina's work (augmented by Freddoso's excellent introduction and notes) more widely accessible.[4]

2. The Plan of This Book

In this book, I endeavor to contribute to this discussion in three ways: by explicating the picture of divine providence offered by Molinists, by defending that picture against what I see as its most powerful critics, and by applying the general Molinist picture to specific providential domains.[5] Not surprisingly, I have divided the work into three parts.

Part I offers the attempt at explication. The first chapter presents what I see as the two foundations of the Molinist edifice: the traditional theological claim that God is the all-knowing, sovereign, providential lord of the universe, and the metaphysical claim that, as those known as libertarians have insisted, freedom requires indeterminism. My aim in this chapter is both to elucidate these two claims and to suggest that the orthodox Christian would naturally be inclined to embrace both of them. Chapter 2 then gives a detailed account of the picture of providence fashioned by Molina, a picture designed to accord with the theological traditionalism and metaphysical libertarianism described in the first chapter.

In Part II, this Molinist account is defended against numerous attacks. Having (in Chapter 3) canvassed the major alternatives to Molinism and argued that the traditional Christian has solid prima facie reason to prefer the Molinist picture, I proceed in the next four chapters to consider whether this surface plausibility of Molinism can be undermined. Various objections to Molinism, from traditional Thomist objections to the contemporary criticisms of such philosophers as Robert Merrihew Adams and William Hasker, are examined in these chapters. Central to this part of the book is a discussion of the "grounding" objection, an objection which, in one form or another, crops up in most criticisms of Molinism. My conclusion is that none of the objectors offers a persuasive case against the Molinist. Since the burden of proof is, it

[4] See Luis de Molina, *On Divine Foreknowledge: Part IV of the Concordia*, tr. Alfred J. Freddoso (Ithaca: Cornell University Press, 1988). References to Molina in later notes are to this translation, and provide both the disputation and section numbers and the page number in the Freddoso translation; e.g., Molina, Disputation 51, section 14 (p. 153). References to Freddoso's introduction are given as, e.g., Freddoso, "Introduction," p. 49.

[5] Though references to Molina are frequent in the course of this book, the reader should note that my main concern is with the account of providence that Molina sketched—i.e., with the *object* pictured, not primarily with either the artist or his picture. For better or worse, this is a book in philosophical theology, not in the history of philosophy.

seems to me, on the critics here, the failure of their arguments suggests that the Molinist picture of providence is by far the most attractive one for the orthodox theist to endorse.

To suggest, though, is not to entail. For it could be that the general Molinist picture, though graced with the veneer of verisimilitude and resilient in the face of attack, would prove unenlightening or even distorting when we try to apply it to particular topics encompassed by the general Christian notion of providence. Part III looks at several attempts at applied Molinism. Questions connected with papal infallibility, prophecy, and petitionary prayer are addressed from an expressly Molinist point of view to see whether or not such a stance is of value to the Christian concerned with such issues. In each case, I will suggest, Molinism can indeed be applied fruitfully (though not nearly so easily as one might initially have conjectured). This result probably ought not astonish the reader; after all, as a confessed Molinist, I would hardly be expected to pick topics that are *not* susceptible to profitable Molinist analyses. Even so, since the issues addressed (even papal infallibility, if understood as evoking the larger issue of divine governance of the Church) are of central concern to most Christians, I think that both the value of the Molinist perspective and the plausibility of expecting that perspective to prove fertile relative to issues not investigated here (issues such as predestination, revelation, the Incarnation, and others) will have been firmly established if my efforts in Part III are successful.

Before embarking on this tripartite expedition, let me first identify my starting points.

3. Orthodox Christianity

In describing the plan of this book, I have made several references to traditional or orthodox Christianity, and the reader might well wonder what exactly this is. I have no simple (or even complex) definition to offer. As a Roman Catholic, I think I have a pretty clear grasp of what orthodox Catholicism amounts to.[6] But among Christians as a whole, nothing comparable to definitive papal or conciliar pronouncements, or to the consistent teaching of the magisterium, can be appealed to as a clear and unquestioned arbiter of disputed questions concerning Christian practice or belief.[7] And, of course,

---

[6] It might be argued that, were I better acquainted with the work of contemporary Catholic theologians, my sense of having a firm grasp would have dissolved by now. I doubt it. Still, it could be. And, of course, it could be that I have cause here to be grateful to a providential God.

[7] Needless to say, virtually all Christians look upon Scripture as authoritative. But I take it as an obvious truth that Scripture does not offer clear answers—answers that just anyone can see—to disputed questions; if it did, the questions would not be disputed.

the list of questions which have not been disputed over the last century or so, even among those who consider themselves Christians, is not all that long.

Still, I think that the notion of traditional or orthodox Christianity is not so vague as to be useless. And though propositional belief is only part (and arguably not the most important part) of Christian commitment, I think we can identify a number of theses which, if not definitive of what is usually meant by orthodox Christianity, are at least typical of such Christians.

Traditional Christians believe that God exists. And the God they believe in is not just a symbol of overarching truths, or an impersonal ground of being, or the life-force oozing throughout the universe, or anything of that sort. Orthodox Christians believe in a personal God, one who freely chose to create the universe we see around us and who sustains that universe in being. Unlike us, this God is perfect in all respects. He is infinite in knowledge, power, and goodness, and unencumbered by spatial or temporal limitations. Moreover, he doesn't just *happen* to be perfect; it couldn't have been the case that God failed to possess any of the perfections he actually exhibits. God has a plan for his universe, and his perfections guarantee that his plan shall succeed. Part of this plan involved God's saving fallen mankind by sending his only son among us. That son, Jesus, true God and true man, reconciled us to his father through his death and resurrection; through references to the Holy Spirit, he also led us toward a recognition of the Trinity—of three persons in one God. As Christians, we are united together with Christ and each other on earth, and look forward to the perfection of these relationships when Christ raises our bodies from the dead and leads us with him to paradise.

Perhaps enough has been said to give one a feel for what I mean by orthodox Christianity. If not, this might help: Think of those who are widely considered the towering figures in the history of Christian thought—figures such as Jerome, Boethius, Augustine, Anselm, Aquinas, Luther, Calvin, and Edwards. If a proposition is universally embraced (or nearly so) among such figures, then the proposition is part of orthodox Christianity. (My guess is that each of the claims listed in the previous paragraph would pass this test.)

I am painfully aware of just how inexact all this is. Still, my guess is that only the obstinate would deny that there is a genuine tradition of the sort I am alluding to within Christianity. More important, I feel confident that many of my readers will recognize this tradition as one that they themselves embrace. Since it is these readers whom I see as my principal interlocutors, perhaps enough has been said about what I mean by traditional or orthodox Christianity.[8]

[8] I refer in Chapter 1 to what I call the traditional view of providence. Hence, to avoid possible confusion, I shall henceforth generally use *orthodox* (rather than *traditional*) to designate the position I have outlined in this section.

4. A Passel of Philosophical Presuppositions

In addition to this theological presupposition, a number of philosophical assumptions will be made throughout this text.[9]

First, I will assume that there are *properties* (e.g., *being purple*), *propositions* (e.g., *No iguana is purple*), and *states of affairs* (e.g., *my iguana's being green*). I will assume that properties can exist if nothing has that property; that propositions can exist even if they are false; and that states of affairs can exist even if they are not *actual*, or do not *obtain*. One proposition will be said to *entail* another just in case it is not possible that both the first be true and the second be false. (Entailment will be symbolized by a double-line arrow; hence, where A and B stand for propositions, "$A \Rightarrow B$" will stand for "A entails B.") One state of affairs will be said to *include* another if and only if it is not possible that both the first obtain and the second not obtain; if it is not possible that both the first obtain and the second obtain, then the first will be said to *preclude* the second.

I will assume that there are individual substances, and that some of the properties exhibited by these substances are *essential* to them (i.e., such that it is not possible that the individual exist but not have that property) while others are *accidental*.

As several of the assumptions already mentioned imply, I will assume that there are modal facts—that some propositions are *necessary* (i.e., necessarily true), some *impossible* (necessarily false), and some *contingent* (neither necessary nor impossible). Analogous distinctions can be made among states of affairs.

I will also assume that there are *possible worlds*—states of affairs that both possibly obtain and are *maximal*, where a maximal state of affairs is one such that every other state of affairs is either included or precluded by it. Propositions will be said to be possible just in case they are true in some possible world, where to say that a proposition is true *in* a world is to say that it would have been true if that world had been actual. Necessary propositions will be those that are true in every possible world; impossible propositions, those that are true in no possible world. A proposition is true if and only if it is true in the *actual* world—the possible world which is in fact actual.

Finally, I will assume that there are some true *counterfactuals* (sometimes called subjunctive conditionals), and that a conditional of this "If it were the case that C, it would be the case that A" sort (symbolized by a single-line

---

[9] My reliance on Plantinga here should be evident. See *The Nature of Necessity*, especially the first six chapters. For a concise presentation of the core of this metaphysical picture, see Edward Wierenga, *The Nature of God* (Ithaca: Cornell University Press, 1989), pp. 6–11.

arrow: "$C \rightarrow A$") is true just in case there is some possible world in which C and A are both true which is closer (i.e., more similar) to the actual world than is any world in which C is true and A is false.[10]

None of these assumptions will be defended in this book, for three reasons. First, there is more than enough to say on the topic at hand without doubling the size of the book by discussing foundational matters. Second, I doubt that I would be up to completing a work thus doubled. And finally, I have little original to say in defense of these claims. Readers interested in debating them will find ample discussion in what we philosophers so charitably refer to as "the literature." I take it that most readers would at least recognize that the assumptions I have made are far from idiosyncratic. Furthermore, my guess is that many of the arguments given in the following chapters are not essentially dependent on the metaphysical assumptions listed here. Those assumptions may be, not the crucial foundation without which those arguments collapse, but rather like the ship, sails, and maps one relies on in sailing around an island: other ships, employing different rigging and charts, might afford one much the same view.[11]

---

[10] See David Lewis, *Counterfactuals* (Cambridge: Harvard University Press, 1973), chap. 1.

[11] I hope that no one will try to make relativistic nonsense out of this. My point is *not* that it makes no difference what assumptions one makes, or that all assumptions are equally valid (any more than a sailor would claim that it makes no difference what ship one takes, or that all maps are equally accurate). The point is only that, having used one set of assumptions to reach a certain conclusion, I have no right to presume that others, using what I see as inferior assumptions, would not end up in the same place, just as, having used one ship and map to reach a certain destination, I have no right to presume that others, using what I see as inferior ships or less accurate maps, would not reach the same place.

Part I

AN EXPLICATION OF THE
MOLINIST ACCOUNT

The Twin Bases of Molinism:
Providence and Freedom

You who are living consider every cause
  as originating in the heavens
  as if they determined all, of necessity.

If this were so, free will would be destroyed,
  and there would be no justice,
  no joy for good nor sorrow for evil.

The heavens initiate your impulses—
  I do not say all, but granting I did say so,
  a light is given to you to distinguish good from evil,

and free will which, if it is severely tested
  in its first battles with the heavens,
  afterward, rightly nurtured, conquers all.
     —Dante, *The Divine Comedy (Purgatory)*, tr. H. R. Huse, 16.67–78

The Molinist picture of providence constitutes an attempt to blend together two distinct notions which are independently attractive to the orthodox Christian. The first of these is the strong notion of divine providence typically affirmed by Christians through the centuries; the second is the libertarian picture of freedom. Before looking at the Molinist picture which develops from their combination, let us in this chapter examine each of the two notions independently. My goal here is to provide a clear (albeit brief) sketch of the two ideas and explain why the orthodox Christian would naturally find them extremely appealing.

1. The Traditional Notion of Providence

As we saw in the Introduction, one central element of orthodox Christian belief is the claim that God, our creator, is perfect in every respect. The notion

of divine providence that orthodox Christians have typically come to endorse—a notion I shall refer to as the *traditional notion* (or *traditional picture*) of
providence—is essentially a picture of how a God who is perfect in knowledge, love, and power exhibits those perfections through the detailed control
he exercises over his creation.[1] Being omniscient, God has complete and detailed knowledge of his world—its history, its current state, and its future.
Being omnipotent, God has complete and specific control over that world, a
world which has developed and will continue to evolve in accord with his
sovereign and never-failing will. Being omnibenevolent, God has used his
knowledge and power to fashion and execute a plan for his world that manifests his own moral perfection and the inexhaustible love he bears for his
creation. According to this traditional picture, then, to see God as provident
is to see him as knowingly and lovingly directing each and every event involving each and every creature toward the ends he has ordained for them.

Though God's providential control of individuals' lives is clearly central in
the traditional picture, that control is just as clearly seen as extending to various
groups. For example, God can have providential plans for families or nations
as well as for individuals. Similarly, Christians have traditionally seen the
Church as the beneficiary of specific divine care and guidance. The tradition
has also insisted on the special place of humans (as opposed to other species)
in creation, and has sometimes even suggested that individuals of other species
are divinely provided for merely as a means to some end, not for their own
sake.[2]

Two elements of the traditional picture of providence are worth emphasizing, since they will play significant roles in ensuing discussions. First, the
tradition maintains that God has complete and certain *foreknowledge.*[3] That is,
there is no event still to occur of which God is ignorant or uncertain. God
never has to "wait and see" how things develop; he never has to fashion a
horde of contingency plans and prepare to execute them depending upon
how things turn out; he never has to make do with only probabilities, or

---

[1] It is perhaps worth noting that at least many of these orthodox Christians would also insist
that the danger of distortion is very real if we assume that terms such as *knowledge, love, power,*
and *control* can be used in a strictly univocal sense when speaking of the human and divine
realms.

[2] See, for example, Aquinas, *De Veritate,* question 5, article 7. It should be noted that, in
recent years, many traditionalists, while not denying that providence may well single out certain
groups, have attempted to downplay what might be seen as exaggerations of this truth, and
have instead emphasized the universality of God's providential care.

[3] In speaking of foreknowledge here, I mean only that God has knowledge of what is in
our future, whether or not such events are future to him. No assumption is being made
concerning the (interminably) disputed questions concerning God's relation to time.

likelihoods, or best guesses concerning the future. Second, God exercises *sovereignty* over his world in a very strong and specific sense. God doesn't simply give his first creatures their initial powers and arrangement and then, like the deity of the deists, sit back and let things develop on their own. Nor does his control extend only to certain general features of the world, the specifics being out of his hands. (For example, advocates of the traditional notion would frown on those who might suggest that God sees to it that animals come into existence, but does not determine which species in particular come to be. Similarly, it would reject the claim that God ensures only that some people or other are saved, but not that any particular person is among those saved.) Rather, traditionalists insist that God is sovereign in the sense that every event, no matter how large or small, is under God's control and is incorporated into his overall plan for the world.

It is easy to see why such a picture would naturally appeal to orthodox Christians.[4] Clearly, a God who exercised *no* control over or knowledge of his creation would be a far cry from the loving Father in whom orthodox Christians believe. If God is perfect in knowledge, power, and goodness, then he surely must be lovingly involved with and cognizant of the lives of his creatures. But why, the orthodox Christian would naturally wonder, diminish this involvement and knowledge unnecessarily? Isn't it natural (for the orthodox) to think that God knows, not just *some* things about his world, but *everything* about it? Isn't it natural to think that he has arranged it so that, not just *some* things, but *everything* fits together in such a way that his love is made manifest? Isn't it natural to think that *nothing* is left to chance, that nothing haphazard or unexpected from the divine perspective occurs—that "Oops!" is an interjection God need never employ? In the absence of strong arguments to settle for something weaker, the appeal of the picture of providence described above seems evident.

In fact, it is fairly easy to portray a God who lacks this type of strong providential control as a rather comical figure. Consider, for example, the following dialogue from Avery Corman's novel *Oh, God!*, where the first speaker is the title character.

> "It's better that I shouldn't meddle. What am I going to do—get into favorites? So I come up with the concepts, the big ideas—the details can take care of themselves."

---

[4] Of course, aspects of this picture might simultaneously frighten, or at least unsettle, some Christians. God's control, for example, might seem so extensive as to threaten human initiative and dignity. Much philosophical reflection on what is largely an appealing picture of providence might well be the fruit of fears such as these.

"Then the way things happen on earth . . ."

"They happen. Don't look at me."

"And there's no plan, no scheme that controls our destinies?"

"A lot of it is luck. Luck and who you know."

I was staggered. He just went zipping along.

"Looking back, of course I made a few mistakes. Giraffes. It was a good thought, but it really didn't work out. Avocados—on that I made the pit too big. Then there are things that worked pretty good. Photosynthesis is a big favorite of mine. Spring is nice. Tomatoes are cute. Also raccoons."

"But what about *Man*?" I was trying to rise to the responsibility. "What about his future? The future of the planet?"

"It's a good question."

"And?"

"I couldn't tell you."

"Don't you know?"

"Well, like I say, I don't get into that. Of course I hope you make it. I mean, I'm a real fan. But it's like in a ball game. If you're in the stands, you can root, but that's about all."

"You're God. You can protect our future, alleviate suffering, work miracles!"

"I don't do miracles. They're too flashy and they upset the natural balance. Oh, maybe I'll do a miracle now and then, just for fun—if it's not too important. The last miracle I did was the 1969 Mets and before that the 1914 Boston Braves and before that I think you have to go back to the Red Sea."[5]

Needless to say, humorous constructions of this sort cut little philosophical ice. Still, from the orthodox Christian's perspective at least, the very fact that there *is* humor here is due in large part to the incongruity between the deity Corman depicts and the God of the tradition. The prima facie case for an orthodox Christian's embracing the traditional notion of providence thus seems strong.

Not surprisingly, those we have called orthodox Christians have (with rare exceptions) in fact historically embraced this traditional notion of providence. Virtually all of the major Christian voices through the centuries, from such early figures as Justin Martyr, Origen, and Augustine, through such great medieval thinkers as Anselm, Aquinas, Scotus, and Ockham, to Reformers such as Luther and Calvin, would firmly embrace this traditional picture.[6]

[5] Avery Corman, *Oh, God!* (New York: Simon & Schuster, 1971), pp. 20–21.

[6] I have resisted the urge to offer voluminous references at this point. After all, even critics of this picture have not denied its traditional status, and some of them have gone to great lengths to explain why they think so many giants in the history of Christianity have been led astray in this regard. See, for example, William Hasker, "Response to Thomas Flint," *Philosophical Studies* 60 (1990), 123. See also Richard Rice, "Biblical Support for a New Perspective," and John Sanders, "Historical Considerations," both in *The Openness of God: A Biblical*

Councils and catechisms are equally explicit in their endorsements. Take, for example, the following passage from the Westminster Confession of 1647:

> God, the great Creator of all things, doth uphold, direct, dispose, and govern all creatures, actions and things, from the greatest even to the least, by his most wise and holy providence, according to his infallible foreknowledge, and the free and immutable counsel of his own will, to the praise of the glory of his wisdom, power, justice, goodness, and mercy.[7]

Or consider the equally explicit statement from the First Vatican Council:

> By his providence God protects and governs all things which he has made, "reaching mightily from one end of the earth to the other, and ordering all things well" [Wisdom 8:1]. For "all are open and laid bare to his eyes" [Hebrews 4:13], even those things which are yet to come into existence through the free action of creatures.[8]

That there is a solid Christian tradition here, then, seems evident.

Equally clear is the support within that tradition for the two elements of providence—foreknowledge and sovereignty—highlighted above. Explicit affirmations of God's foreknowledge even of free human actions can be found in such early Christian writers as Justin Martyr, Origen, Tertullian, Damascene, Chrysostom, Jerome, Augustine, and Cyril.[9] Medieval and Reformed thinkers were equally explicit. Aquinas, for example, in various places considers the question whether God knows future contingents (i.e., truths about future events which are not physically determined by present events), and gives various reasons for concluding that he does know them.[10] Specific sovereignty is likewise repeatedly affirmed. Calvin is typically enthusiastic and eloquent in this regard:

Challenge to the Traditional Understanding of God, ed. Clark Pinnock, Richard Rice, John Sanders, William Hasker, and David Basinger (Downers Grove, Ill.: InterVarsity Press, 1994).

[7] Quoted in Paul Helm, *The Providence of God* (Downers Grove, Ill.: InterVarsity Press, 1994), p. 42. Note as well this earlier passage from the Confession: "God from all eternity did, by the most wise and holy counsel of his own will, freely and unchangeably ordain whatsoever comes to pass; yet so, as thereby neither is God the author of sin, nor is violence offered to the will of the creatures, nor is the liberty or contingency of second causes taken away, but rather established" (ibid., p. 87).

[8] Vatican Council I, *Dei Filius;* tr. in *Catechism of the Catholic Church* (Washington, D.C.: United States Catholic Conference, 1994), p. 80.

[9] For Tertullian, see *Adversus Marcionem,* ed. and tr. Ernest Evans (Oxford: Clarendon Press, 1972), II, 5. For the rest, see Molina, Disputation 52, sections 21–27 (pp. 181–183).

[10] See, for example, *De Veritate,* question 2, article 12, and *Summa Theologiae,* Ia, question 14, article 13.

After learning that there is a Creator, [faith] must forthwith infer that he is also a Governor and Preserver, and that, not by producing a kind of general motion in the machine of the globe as well as in each of its parts, but by a special Providence sustaining, cherishing, superintending, all the things which he has made, to the very minutest, even to a sparrow. . . . the providence of God, as taught in Scripture, is opposed to fortune or fortuitous causes. . . . And truly God claims omnipotence to himself, and would have us to acknowledge it,—not the vain, indolent, slumbering omnipotence which sophists feign, but vigilant, efficacious, energetic, and ever active,—not an omnipotence which may only act as a general principle of confused motion, as in ordering a stream to keep within the channel once prescribed to it, but one which is intent on individual and special movements. . . . Let him, therefore, who would beware of such unbelief, always bear in mind, that there is no random power, or agency, or motion in the creatures, who are so governed by the secret counsel of God, that nothing happens but what he has knowingly and willingly decreed.[11]

That there is, then, a traditional notion of providence, a notion with obvious appeal to those who believe in a perfect creator, cannot reasonably be denied. Still, to recognize the presence of such a concept within the Christian community is not to explain its origin. Where, one might wonder, did this notion arise? Is it a discovery of Christian thought, or do we find it (or the rudiments of it) in earlier sources?

2. Roots of the Tradition

What we are calling the traditional notion of providence clearly has both biblical and classical roots. Though the word "providence" is nowhere found in the Bible,[12] Scripture seems to speak clearly and repeatedly of a God who knowingly and lovingly exercises detailed control over his creation. God is presented as a sovereign who knows everything about his world:

> The Lord looks down from heaven;
> he sees all humankind.
> From where he sits enthroned he watches

---

[11] John Calvin, *Institutes of the Christian Religion*, tr. Henry Beveridge (London: James Clarke, 1949), bk. I, chap. 16, pp. 172–175. In denying that chance or fortune has any place in a world ruled by God, Calvin is also speaking for the tradition. For a concurring opinion, see Aquinas, *Summa Theologiae*, Ia, question 22, article 2, ad 1. For a defense (as enthusiastic and eloquent as Calvin's) of the opposite view, see Peter van Inwagen, "The Place of Chance in a World Sustained by God," in Thomas V. Morris, ed., *Divine and Human Action* (Ithaca: Cornell University Press, 1988), pp. 211–235.

[12] Or so, at least, says Helm; see *Providence of God*, p. 16.

> all the inhabitants of the earth—
> he who fashions the hearts of them all,
> and observes all their deeds.
>
> (Psalm 33:13–15)[13]

Future as well as past events are fully known to God:

> Even before a word is on my tongue,
>   O Lord, you know it completely. . . .
> Your eyes beheld my unformed substance.
> In your book were written
>   all the days that were formed for me,
> when none of them as yet existed.
>
> (Psalm 139:4, 16)

And these events are foreknown to God because it is his will that they occur:

> "For you have done these things and those that went before and those that
> followed. You have designed the things that are now, and those that are to
> come. What you had in mind has happened; the things you decided on pre-
> sented themselves and said, 'Here we are!' For all your ways are prepared in
> advance, and your judgment is with foreknowledge." (Judith 9:5–6)

The fate of whole nations, we are told, is in God's hands:

> The word that came to Jeremiah from the Lord: "Come, go down to the
> potter's house, and there I will let you hear my words." So I went down to
> the potter's house, and there he was working at his wheel. The vessel he was
> making of clay was spoiled in the potter's hand, and he reworked it into another
> vessel, as seemed good to him.
> Then the word of the Lord came to me: Can I not do with you, O house
> of Israel, just as this potter has done? says the Lord. Just like the clay in the
> potter's hand, so are you in my hand, O house of Israel. (Jeremiah 18:1–6)

God's plan may at times leads to the downfall of nations, but it also, we are
assured, provides for the needs of his children:

> Look at the birds of the air; they neither sow nor reap nor gather into barns,
> and yet your heavenly Father feeds them. Are you not of more value than they?

[13] All Scriptural quotations are from *The New Revised Standard Version* (New York: Oxford
University Press, 1989).

And can any of you by worrying add a single hour to your span of life? And why do you worry about clothing? Consider the lilies of the field, how they grow; they neither toil nor spin, yet I tell you, even Solomon in all his glory was not clothed like one of these. But if God so clothes the grass of the field, which is alive today and tomorrow is thrown into the oven, will he not much more clothe you—you of little faith? Therefore do not worry, saying 'What will we eat?' or 'What will we drink?' or 'What will we wear?' For it is the Gentiles who strive for all these things; and indeed your heavenly Father knows that you need all these things. But strive first for the kingdom of God and his righteousness, and all these things will be given to you as well. (Matthew 6:26–33)

 Even seemingly chance events, we hear, are actually determined by God:

> The lot is cast into the lap,
>   but the decision is the Lord's alone.
>   (Proverbs 16:33)

Whether these and the many other Scriptural passages cited by advocates of the traditional notion entail the view of providence they favor may be debated. Still, that they can cite an impressive body of biblical support for their position seems evident.

Equally clear is the fact that classical sources anticipated in many ways the development among Christians of the traditional picture of providence. The impact of the Greek philosophical tradition on this development has often been noted (sometimes with pleasure, sometimes with regret). While no classical Greek philosopher could honestly be deemed a proponent of the full-blooded Christian notion of providence, many can properly be seen as providing building blocks for its construction. Among the Presocratics, Xenophanes is perhaps most noteworthy for his rejection of the anthropomorphism of conventional ancient polytheism and his insistence that there is "one god, greatest among gods and men, in no way similar to mortals either in body or in thought," a god who, though himself motionless, "shakes all things by the thought of his mind."[14] Much like Xenophanes, the Socrates of Plato's dialogues rejected the popular ascription of human failings to Zeus and the other gods, and insisted (after being sentenced to death) that his supporters "keep this one truth in mind, that a good man cannot be harmed either in

---

[14] See G. S. Kirk and J. E. Raven, *The Presocratic Philosophers* (Cambridge: Cambridge University Press, 1957), p. 169.

life or in death, and that his affairs are not neglected by the gods."[15] Plato himself seems to have believed in an unchanging God, a God who is "in every way in the best possible state"[16] and who acts, not simply as (to repeat Calvin's phrase) "a general principle of confused motion," but as the agent of that specific sovereignty we identified as included in the traditional Christian account:

> We are never, then, to fancy God the inferior of human workmen. The better they are at their work, the more exactly and perfectly do they accomplish their proper tasks, small or great, in virtue of one and the same skill, and we must never suppose that God, who is at once supremely wise and both willing and able to provide, makes no provision for the small matters, which we have found it easier to care for, but only for the great, like some idle fellow or faintheart who shirks his work from fear of exertion.[17]

Many later Greek philosophers, especially among the Stoics, also expounded views amenable to the developing Christian picture. Epictetus, for example, emphasizes the divine determination of our place in life:

> Remember that you are an actor in a play, which is as the playwright wants it to be: short if he wants it short, long if he wants it long. If he wants you to play a beggar, play even this part skillfully, or a cripple, or a public official, or a public citizen. What is yours is to play the assigned part well. But to choose it belongs to someone else.[18]

The power and goodness of the divine is similarly underscored by Epictetus:

> The most important aspect of piety toward the gods is certainly both to have correct beliefs about them, as beings that arrange the universe well and justly, and to set yourself to obey them and acquiesce in everything that happens and to follow it willingly, as something brought to completion by the best judgment.[19]

[15] Plato, *Apology*, in *The Trial and Death of Socrates*, tr. G. M. A. Grube (Indianapolis: Hackett, 1975), 41c–d, p. 42. For Socrates's rejection of traditional stories concerning the moral failings of the gods, see Plato, *Euthyphro*, 6a.

[16] See Plato, *Republic*, tr. Paul Shorey, in Edith Hamilton and Huntington Cairns, eds., *The Collected Dialogues of Plato* (Princeton: Princeton University Press, 1961), 381b, p. 628.

[17] Plato, *Laws*, tr. A. E. Taylor, in Hamilton and Cairns, *Collected Dialogues of Plato*, 902e–903a, p. 1459.

[18] Epictetus, *Handbook*, tr. Nicholas White (Indianapolis: Hackett, 1983), section 17, p. 16.

[19] Ibid., section 31, p. 21.

This confidence in the control over human affairs of just and good supernatural powers was equally emphasized by many nonphilosophical classical figures, most notably perhaps during the golden age of imperial Athens.[20] Herodotus, in his *Histories*, repeatedly sees God as intervening in human affairs to punish unruly humans or to teach a moral lesson, and while he praises Athens as more responsible than any other Greek state for the defeat of the Persian invasion, he ascribes the primary responsibility for the Greek victory not to any human, but to God.[21] The great Greek tragedians also give evidence of similar convictions. For example, in his *Oresteia*, Aeschylus presents us with an illustration of how it is that "From the gods who sit in grandeur / grace comes somehow violent."[22] After Clytaemestra kills her victorious husband Agamemnon and defends her act as just, the Chorus, wondering how God could have allowed such events to happen, is near despair:

> Surely it is a huge
> and heavy spirit bending the house you cry;
> alas, the bitter glory
> of a doom that shall never be done with;
> and all through Zeus, Zeus,
> first cause, prime mover.
> For what thing without Zeus is done among mortals?
> What here is without God's blessing?[23]

Yet, by the end of the trilogy, we see that Zeus has indeed been acting through the gory events described, bringing his people to a recognition of the futility of individual acts of vengeance and bestowing upon them the blessing of an enlightened system of justice. So propitious an outcome might have seemed unlikely, but, as Athene assures us at the end of the trilogy,

---

[20] In referring to such figures as nonphilosophical, I mean not that the writers in question reveal no interest in philosophical issues, but only that they are usually thought of primarily as something other than philosophers—as historians, dramatists, poets, and the like.

[21] Herodotus, *The Histories*, tr. Aubrey de Selincourt, rev. A. R. Burn (New York: Penguin Books, 1972). See, e.g., Herodotus's judgments concerning Croesus (p. 54), the Trojans (pp. 173–174), Pheretima (pp. 338–339), and Cleomenes (p. 417). For Herodotus's view on God's responsibility for the defeat of Xerxes's invasion, see p. 487; see also p. 529.

[22] Aeschylus, *Agamemnon*, in *The Oresteia*, tr. Richmond Lattimore (Chicago: University of Chicago Press, 1953), ll. 182–183.

[23] Aeschylus, *Agamemnon*, ll. 1481–1488.

"Zeus, who guides men's speech in councils, was too / strong; and my ambition / for good wins out in the whole issue."[24]

It would, of course, be fatuous to see these classical figures as subscribing to the fully developed traditional Christian picture of providence, or as consciously paving the way for the composition of that picture. Indeed, it would be misleading to pretend that there was a single homogeneous classical view here, for many Greek and Roman thinkers rejected central elements of that picture. (For example, Aristotle, like Euripides before him and the Epicureans after him, implied that divine beings are unconcerned with the affairs of earthly individuals, while Cicero suggested that divine foreknowledge of free actions is impossible.[25]) Even so, our fear of repeating past mistakes—of "baptizing" Socrates and other classical figures by anachronistically reading Christian interpretations into their words—ought not lead us to err in the opposite direction. The fact of the matter is that a significant number of classical authors expressed views which Christians could and did see as corroborating the picture of providence they embraced.

For the orthodox Christian, then, what we have called the traditional notion of providence is attractive indeed. It is a picture that seems a natural accompaniment to a belief in a perfect creator, that has been endorsed by virtually all of the giants of Christendom, that appears to be repeatedly implied by Scriptural passages, and that receives substantial support from that non-

----

[24] Aeschylus, *The Eumenides*, ll. 973–975. Though the *Oresteia* may offer the most blatant affirmation of something akin to divine providence by the Athenian playwrights, similar sentiments are suggested in many other works. In Sophocles's *Oedipus the King*, for example, after Jocasta has expressed her disdain for the oracles (and, implicitly, for the gods themselves), the Chorus calls for a divine response to such insolence: "O Zeus, if you are rightly called / the sovereign lord, all-mastering, / let this not escape you nor your ever-living power!" (Sophocles, *Oedipus the King*, tr. David Grene [Chicago: University of Chicago Press, 1954], ll. 903–905.) Of course, the events that transpire later in the play suggest that Zeus is indeed the sovereign, all-mastering god in whom the Chorus trusts, though it must be acknowledged that the moral qualities of Sophocles's god are difficult to discern.

[25] For Aristotle, see *Nichomachean Ethics* 1178b and *Eudemian Ethics* 1249b. For Cicero, see *De divinatione*, II, 5, 7. Euripides's doubts concerning providence are evident in many of his plays, but are nowhere expressed more eloquently than in the words Talthybius speaks when he first spies the abject figure of Hecuba:

> O Zeus, what can I say? That you look on man
> and care? Or do we, holding that the gods exist,
> deceive ourselves with unsubstantial dreams
> and lies, while random careless chance and change
> alone control the world?

(Euripides, *Hecuba*, tr. William Arrowsmith [Chicago: University of Chicago Press, 1958], ll. 488–492.)

biblical intellectual tradition which Christians have often seen as perhaps the greatest nonrevealed repository of human wisdom. With all this going for it, the traditional notion of providence is surely one that an orthodox Christian should be most reluctant to jettison.

3. Three Accounts of Freedom

As noted at the start of this chapter, the second base of the Molinist picture of providence is the notion of freedom commonly referred to as libertarianism. To see what libertarianism amounts to, and to appreciate its distinction from the other two positions on freedom commonly endorsed, let us consider three theses concerning freedom and determinism.

First, consider

(1)   Some human actions are free.

Such a thesis seems quite plausible at first glance. Indeed, some might wish to expand (1) in various ways—for example, by insisting that all human actions are free, or by contending that freedom is conceptually inseparable from the very notion of an action, or by suggesting that at least some nonhuman activity should be considered free. But the more cautious (1) is a claim that few of us initially would doubt, for our experience suggests to us that we often act in situations where doing otherwise is genuinely open to us.

Next, consider

(2)   All human actions are ultimately causally determined by events not under the causal control of their agents.[26]

Proposition (2) may have less initial appeal than (1), but many who have carefully considered it have found it difficult to reject. The most common line of argument for (2) goes as follows. Human actions cannot be random occurrences; if they were, they would not be the kind of thing which we consider free, or for which we hold agents responsible. Actions, then, must have causes, and the most plausible causes to which we can point are the reasons which the agent has for acting—her beliefs, desires, and the like. But

---

[26] Causal determination here is to be understood in the (more or less) standard sense, such that one event A causally determines (or is a sufficient causal condition for) another event B just in case, though the occurrence of A does not entail the occurrence of B, it is not logically possible, given the laws of nature, that A occur but B fail to occur. To say that an event E is not under an agent's causal control is to say that E occurs and that there is no action within the agent's power such that the performance of that action would have causally determined the nonoccurrence of E.

beliefs and desires, it seems, are not the sorts of things which simply pop into existence; they too are generated causally. The causal chain to which we thus seem committed cannot plausibly be thought of as originating within the agent, but must be seen as extending beyond her, to other agents or events over which she has no causal control. That is, the mediate causal determiners of her action are such that there is nothing she has the power to do such that her so acting would cause those determiners not to be.

As with (1), some advocates of (2) would see it as a specific instance of a more general truth. For instance, some would claim that every event is causally determined by prior events—that, for any event E occurring at time t, the causal history of the world H prior to t and the laws of nature L are such that the conjunction of H and L entails the occurrence of E. The plausibility of such a thesis of universal causal determinism has, of course, been called into question by (among other things) the development of microphysics during this century, and probably has a smaller percentage of adherents among the academically informed now than it did a century ago. Still, a significant core of true believers hold out hope that universal causal determinism will regain its position of dominance within the scientific community. More significantly, though, even many of those who are dubious of this resurrection cannot see how genuine human actions could occur without determining causes, and hence are attracted to (2).

Finally, consider

(3)   It is not possible that a free human action be ultimately causally deter-mined by events not under the causal control of its agent.

Such a claim strikes most people initially as quite plausible. For my act to be free, one is inclined to think, it has to be *my* action, not someone else's. Self-determination lies at the very heart of freedom; to say that an act of mine was free, but was ultimately determined by someone or something other than me, someone or something whose determining activity was utterly beyond my power to control, is to speak nonsense.

Each of (1) through (3), then, is a claim which exerts considerable prima facie pull on many people. The problem, of course, is that the three are manifestly inconsistent; the conjunction of any two entails the falsity of the third. By looking at the ways in which one might reject one of the three claims so as to maintain the other two, we can in effect identify the three general positions open to us concerning freedom and determinism.

Take first the possibility of rejecting (1) so as to retain (2) and (3). In doing so, one would be (to put it simply) holding on to the claims that human actions are determined and that free actions cannot be determined, and concluding that there are in fact no free human actions. This view is commonly known as *hard determinism*.

Second, consider the possibility of retaining (1) and (3), and hence abandoning (2). What one would be saying here is that, since there are free human actions, and since such actions cannot have ultimate external determinants, it follows that some human actions do not in fact have such determinants. Typically, this stance is called *libertarianism*.

Finally, there is also the possibility of rejecting (3) but affirming (1) and (2). That is, one could argue that, because some of our actions are free but all of our actions are determined externally, it follows that there is no incompatibility between such determination and freedom. The standard name for this position, appropriately enough, is *compatibilism*.

Clearly, each of the three positions outlined here could be developed in any of a number of different ways. For example, compatibilists could (and do) differ among themselves concerning precisely what type of causal chain needs to be present in order for an action to be free. Hence, the three positions we have identified are really more starting points than they are worked-out philosophical theories. Still, so long as we realize that a term such as "libertarianism" really refers to a family of views, a family all of whose members look alike in certain crucial respects (though some members are markedly more attractive than others!), we ought not go astray in continuing (for now) to speak of only three positions here.

4. The Lure of Libertarianism

What is the orthodox Christian to make of this variety of metaphysical options? Are all of these positions open to her? Is any definitively closed? Is there one which, if not entailed by her Christian commitment, still seems to fit in most easily with her theological convictions?

Hard determinism seems a hard position for any orthodox Christian to take seriously. For in completely rejecting the existence of human freedom, hard determinism seems at odds both with our ordinary beliefs about ourselves as human agents and with the testimony of Scripture. The Pentateuch, for example, offers numerous stories that seem to make sense only if we assume that the human characters involved—Adam and Eve, Cain and Abel, Abraham and Isaac, and so on—are free. Implicit affirmations of human freedom are also evident in the Bible. For example:

> See, I have set before you today life and prosperity, death and adversity. If you obey the commandments of the Lord your God that I am commanding you today, by loving the Lord your God, walking in his ways, and observing

his commandments, decrees, and ordinances, then you shall live and become numerous, and the Lord your God will bless you in the land that your are entering to possess. But if your heart turns away and you do not hear, but are led astray to bow down to other gods and serve them, I declare to you today that you shall perish; you shall not live long in the land that you are crossing the Jordan to enter and possess. I call heaven and earth to witness against you today that I have set before you life and death, blessings and curses. Choose life so that you and your descendants may live, loving the lord your God, obeying him, and holding fast to him. (Deuteronomy 30:15–20)

New Testament ascriptions of freedom are also plentiful. For example, in the Gospel of Matthew, Jesus bemoans the intransigence of his people:

> Jerusalem, Jerusalem, the city that kills the prophets and stones those who are sent to it! How often have I desired to gather your children together as a hen gathers her brood under her wings, and you were not willing! (Matthew 23:37)

Similarly clear are deuterocanonical works such as Sirach:

> Blessed is the rich person who is found blameless,
>   and who does not go after gold.
> Who is he, that we may praise him?
>   For he has done wonders among his people.
> Who has been tested by it and been found perfect?
>   Let it be for him a ground for boasting.
> Who has had the power to transgress and did not transgress,
>   and to do evil and did not do it?
> His prosperity will be established,
>   and the assembly will proclaim his acts of charity.
>   (Sirach 31:8–11)

Sirach also contains the following, even more explicit (and, even among orthodox Christians, more controversial) passage:

> Do not say, "It was the Lord's doing that I fell away";
>   for he does not do what he hates.
> Do not say, "It was he who led me astray";
>   for he has no need of the sinful.
> The Lord hates all abominations;
>   such things are not loved by those who fear him.
> It was he who created humankind in the beginning,
>   and he left them in the power of their own free choice.
> If you choose, you can keep the commandments,

and to act faithfully is a matter of your own choice.
He has placed before you fire and water;
   stretch out your hand for whichever you choose.
Before each person are life and death,
   and whichever one chooses will be given.
                    (Sirach 15:11–17)

Given these and the many other Scriptural examples which might be offered, the case against an orthodox Christian's embracing hard determinism seems impressive.

The choice between libertarianism and compatibilism is far less clear. After all, each of these positions insists upon the reality of human freedom, and hence each has no problem accommodating biblical professions of such freedom. Furthermore, though hard determinists have been scarce in the history of Christianity, the same cannot be said of either libertarians or compatibilists; today as in the past, both Christian libertarians and Christian compatibilists abound. Finding a decisive reason for a Christian to embrace one of these positions and reject the other is not, one would guess, going to be easy.

In fact, my own guess is that it is not going to be possible. There are, I suspect, no considerations that will compel all reasonable Christians in one of these directions as opposed to the other. Here, as in so many areas of philosophy, the evidence is simply inconclusive, and the rationality of dissenting opinions ought to be acknowledged by even the most fervent proponents of either side.

Yet tolerance is not indifference; recognizing that other reasonable people see things differently need not eliminate one's confidence that those others see things wrongly. Like many orthodox Christians, I find libertarianism by far the more attractive of the two remaining positions, and feel strongly that it is the view most in consonance with Christian belief. Though, as noted, I doubt that there are any demonstrative arguments in favor of this conclusion, let me note three lines of reasoning which seem to lend it considerable support. The first of these arguments appeals solely to secular considerations; the second might appeal (in slightly different ways) both to believers and to nonbelievers, while the third is directed exclusively to Christians.

The first pro-libertarian argument is basically an attempt to expand upon the libertarian intuitions which undergird (3). Why exactly should we think that causal determinism is incompatible with human freedom? Because, the argument goes, external causal determination would mean that my actions were not genuinely up to me. Suppose some action of mine (call it *A*) were ultimately causally determined by events beyond my control. Then the occurrence of those events (call them *E*) would be *necessary*, or *unalterable*, or *unavoidable* for me. Letting *U* stand for this notion of unavoidability, we could thus use

(4) $U(E)$

to represent the claim that the occurrence of *E* was beyond my control. Of course, by hypothesis, *E* causally determines *A*. Since I have no control over the laws of nature, I have no control over what would cause what; hence, if it is a law of nature that, if *E* occurs, then *A* occurs, the conditional in question is one over which I have no control. That is,

(5) $U(E \supset A)$

also seems warranted by our assumption. But, the argument goes, if the occurrence of certain events is unavoidable for me, and the fact that the occurrence of those events implies my performance of a certain action is equally unavoidable for me, then surely my performance of that action is unavoidable for me. That is, surely it follows from (4) and (5) that

(6) $U(A)$.

But (6) seems clearly incompatible with *A*'s being a free action. For surely no free action is one that is unavoidable for me, one over which I have no control. Assuming *A* to have external causal determinants, then, is inconsistent with assuming *A* to be free. Free actions, then, cannot be ultimately caused by external events not under the agent's control. And so (3), the characteristic libertarian thesis, has been demonstrated.

An argument of this sort has been explicitly proposed by a number of libertarians in recent years.[27] But such an argument has undoubtedly been at least half-consciously embraced by libertarians for centuries—as I see it, with good reason, for this argument (or at least a close relative of it) strikes me as

---

[27] See especially Peter van Inwagen, *An Essay on Free Will* (New York: Oxford University Press, 1983), chap. 3. See also: Carl Ginet, "Might We Have No Choice?" in Keith Lehrer, ed., *Freedom and Determinism* (New York: Random House, 1966), pp. 87–104; James Lamb, "On a Proof of Incompatibilism," *Philosophical Review* 86 (1977), 20–35; and David Wiggins, "Towards a Reasonable Libertarianism," in Ted Honderich, ed., *Essays on Freedom of Action* (London: Routledge & Kegan Paul, 1973), pp. 31–61.

a sound and impressive one.[28] In all honesty, I doubt that one ought to bestow upon it such lofty titles as proof or demonstration, for I think there are reasonable responses to it that the die-hard compatibilist can make.[29] Still, arguments can be powerful even if they are acknowledged to be less than compelling, and this anti-compatibilist argument seems to me to be cogent indeed.

A second reason for rejecting compatibilism is based on the belief that we are at least sometimes morally responsible for our actions. Almost everyone unencumbered with philosophical baggage thinks that this claim is true. But Christians are especially big on moral responsibility—especially, some might say, on moral guilt. Without such notions as sin and guilt, the complete Christian story of salvation makes little sense; and, of course, Christianity without salvation is about as coherent as Darwinism without natural selection. Orthodox Christians, then, on religious as well as nonreligious grounds, will share with many of their secular colleagues the conviction that moral responsibility sometimes attaches to our deeds.

But moral responsibility seems hard to square with the kind of external determination countenanced by compatibilists. The type of argument that most readily comes to mind here is reminiscent of our first argument against compatibilism. Suppose once again that my action A is ultimately causally determined by events E over which I have no causal control. It seems evident that my impotence with respect to E entails that I have no moral responsibility for its occurrence, a fact which we might symbolize as

(7) $\sim MR(E)$.

But surely I bear no moral responsibility for the causal laws which guarantee my performing A if E occurs. Thus,

---

[28] It might be that a bit of tinkering with the argument as usually presented is necessary. For example, an argument which moves to (6) via

(4*) $U(E \ \& \ L)$,

where L stands for the laws of nature, and

(5*) $(E \ \& \ L) \Rightarrow A$

might well be impervious to objections that tend to deflate the argument as presented here. My thanks to Fritz Warfield for bringing this point to my attention.

[29] See my "Compatibilism and the Argument from Unavoidability," *Journal of Philosophy* 84 (1987), 423–440. I argue here that, if viewed as a refutation of compatibilism, the argument falters because there are various ways in which the notion of unavoidability might be understood, and the only interpretations I can see that would make the argument from (4) and (5) to (6) clearly valid, sound, and relevant to the question of freedom are ones that presuppose a principle which compatibilists can reasonably reject.

(8) $\sim MR(E \supset A)$.

Yet, if I am morally responsible neither for E nor for the fact that E causes A, I can hardly be responsible for A. So, from (7) and (8), we can conclude that

(9) $\sim MR(A)$.

If our actions were all determined in the way the compatibilist alleges, then, we would be morally responsible for none of them. To believe coherently in moral responsibility, it seems, we need to reject compatibilism.

As with the first argument to which it is so patently related, this line of reasoning strikes me as a suggestive if nondemonstrative one. Whether or not this precise argument does the trick, many philosophers would agree that there is some argument in the neighborhood here which offers powerful reasons for thinking that libertarianism is far preferable to any compatibilist alternative.[30]

Experience suggests to me that the power of such arguments is especially great for Christians who accept the traditional doctrine of hell. Many (though, as we shall see, not all) such Christians find it inconceivable that a good and loving God could consign to eternal punishment those whose sinful actions were the ultimate causal consequences of conditions for which they bore no moral responsibility. For these Christians, it seems, the case against compatibilism is forged as much in the heart as in the mind.

The third line of reasoning for preferring libertarianism to compatibilism is, I think, a tad less common and a bit less precise than the first two, but seems influential nevertheless. The argument I have in mind is basically a response to certain questions that compatibilist objectors frequently raise to the intelligibility of the libertarian position. Suppose one assumes the existence of the God of orthodox Christianity and begins with the inclination (perhaps shaped by our first two arguments) to prefer libertarianism to compatibilism. Yet, our imaginary objector proceeds, isn't there something right about the compatibilist claim that all actions must ultimately be accounted for via a chain of causes which extends outside the agent? Wouldn't an act that was free in the libertarian sense be a random occurrence, something that takes place for no rhyme or reason? Wouldn't we insist that such out-of-the-blue happenings are hardly the sort of thing for which an agent can be held responsible? For

---

[30] For an excellent tour of the neighborhood, see van Inwagen, *An Essay on Free Will*, chap. 5. For the special attraction many Christians would feel to such arguments, see Alvin Plantinga, "Advice to Christian Philosophers," *Faith and Philosophy* 1 (1984), 265–266.

true moral responsibility, mustn't an agent's action be the consequence of the agent's character at the time of the action? In sum, whatever the surface allure of libertarianism, mustn't our infatuation with it fade once we consider such questions?

The heart of our third argument is to suggest that, whatever responses a secular libertarian may or may not be able to give to such challenges, their force is greatly diminished for the Christian philosopher who recalls that God is viewed by the tradition as our *free* creator. God is a free agent par excellence. But can God's freedom be plausibly understood in a compatibilist way? Is God causally determined to create as he does by causes over which he has no control? Of course not. There *are* no causes external to God which could, so to speak, set him in motion, for God is the free creator of all causal agents. Nor is it plausible to think that internal factors (relating to his nature or character, say) over which he has no control fully determine his creative activity. For if they did, this world would be the only genuinely possible world, and all true distinctions between necessity and contingency would collapse, as would the gratuitousness both of God's creation and of our existence. But if God is not determined to create as he does, should we conclude that God's creative actions are random, haphazard, irrational occurrences? By no means. God is the epitome of rationality for the Christian. Is God rendered unworthy of moral praise if we say, as the tradition affirms, that his character was compatible with the creation of worlds very different from ours? Certainly not. The possibility of such worlds lessens not at all the goodness of God's act of creating this world.

 The thrust of this third argument should now be clear. God is a free creator. Yet it seems that the typical compatibilist complaints against the libertarian notion of a free action are (from an orthodox Christian's perspective) not applicable to God's actions. But then, if God's actions can be rational and appropriate, actions for which he is properly seen as morally praiseworthy, even in the absence of any ultimate causes beyond his control, then there clearly can be no *conceptual* problem with the notion of free, rational, responsible, but undetermined actions. And if there is no such conceptual problem, then there seems to be no conceptual problem with viewing ourselves as agents with libertarian freedom as well.[31]

The three arguments sketched here seem to me to offer powerful reasons for the orthodox Christian to favor the libertarian view. Though nondemonstrative, they elicit in many Christians who encounter them a strong incli-

---

[31] For comments suggestive of this line of reasoning, see Plantinga, "Advice to Christian Philosophers," 266–267.

nation to reject the compatibilist alternative. For these Christians, libertarianism, like the traditional notion of providence, seems eminently plausible, and the burden of proof will be squarely on the shoulders of those who would countenance its denial.

5. The Varieties of Libertarianism

While a detailed examination of libertarianism lies beyond the scope of this book, a few words concerning the variety of libertarian positions are probably in order, for a couple of reasons. First, noting these options should serve to remind us that libertarians constitute less a monolithic force than a frequently feuding family, whose barbs are aimed at one another as often as at those outside the tribe. Second, considering the various alternatives within libertarianism might well show us that certain types of libertarianism would probably appear quite unattractive to the orthodox Christian.

As we have seen, libertarians insist that (1) is true—that some of our actions are free. But, one might ask, how many? Are they all free? Almost all? Only a few? Here libertarians can and do differ. Some would insist that it is the very nature of an action to be free; where determinism reigns, activity may occur, but not genuine action. Others would contend that, provided the proper cognitive and volitional aspects are present, true (albeit unfree) action can take place even in the presence of ultimate external determination. Some would think of such determined actions as rare phenomena; others would see them as the norm, with free actions being (as Peter van Inwagen once put it) reserved for state occasions—for example, for fundamental choices which will be among the crucial determining antecedents of subsequent actions.[32] While my own preference would be for the middle position here, orthodox Christians would seem to be free to adopt virtually any position on this matter.

Related to this question on the extent of freedom is the question whether freedom applies only to means or to ultimate ends as well. For example, is the desire for happiness something that we can reject, or is it part of our very nature, so that to speak of us as "choosing" happiness, as opposed to choosing the means to it, makes no sense? Here, I think, most orthodox Christians would find the latter view far more attractive. To think of ourselves as free is not to think of ourselves as denatured, as free to decide upon the ultimate ends for beings of our kind. Indeed, Christians who would extend freedom even to ends would have a difficult time accepting the traditional picture of

[32] See Peter van Inwagen, "When Is the Will Free?" in James E. Tomberlin, ed., *Philosophical Perspectives*, vol. 3 (Atascadero, Calif.: Ridgeview, 1989), pp. 399–422.

the beatific vision as imperdible, for if one can freely reject even one's ultimate good, then surely even the blessed in heaven would retain the freedom to reject God.

Libertarians concur in rejecting the causal determination of free actions. But they differ among themselves concerning what type of causation, if any, is present in free actions. Many libertarians have been attracted to the theory of agent causation, according to which the ultimate cause of a free action is not some set of prior conditions but the agent herself who performs the action.[33] Others, while reluctant to see causal relations as holding between anything other than events, have suggested that the notion of causation should be separated from those of determination or necessitation; hence, we might say that my reasons for acting caused me to perform the free act I did perform even though that act was not causally determined by those reasons (or by any other set of events).[34] Still other libertarians have argued that causal language should be expunged entirely from our account of free acts: when we act freely, we *perform* actions, or *do* things, but to speak of either us or our reasons as *causing* our actions is to enmesh us in conceptual nets which can and should be avoided.[35] Though many Christians have been attracted toward the theory of agent causation, it's not clear that one's Christian commitment is truly decisive in choosing among these options.

Finally, libertarians differ regarding the notion of influence. Any reasonable libertarian will agree that events can influence an agent, can incline her toward or away from a particular action. Dante seems to be acknowledging this fact in the quotation with which we began this chapter; the stars do not determine all of our actions (for that would eliminate freedom), but they might conceivably incline us in certain directions, and resisting such inclinations could be quite difficult. Even those of us not bedazzled by the possibility of astrological influences can hardly deny the general point here. For example, suppose you and I were visiting the famed Vatican cattle ranch in Montana, and your flashing a copy of Mao's Little Red Book were to raise the hackles of one of the resident bulls. My hearing your cries for help as you flee the enraged papal bull would presumably influence my subsequent action, even

[33] Two of the major recent defenses of the theory of agency are found in Richard Taylor, *Action and Purpose* (Englewood Cliffs, N.J.: Prentice-Hall, 1966), and in Roderick Chisholm, *Person and Object* (LaSalle, Ill.: Open Court, 1976).

[34] Such a position is considered (though not advocated) by van Inwagen. See his *Essay on Free Will*, especially pp. 138–140. See also G. E. M. Anscombe, *Causality and Determination* (Cambridge: Cambridge University Press, 1971); reprinted in Ernest Sosa, ed., *Causation and Conditionals* (Oxford: Oxford University Press, 1975), pp. 63–81.

[35] See Stewart Goetz, "A Noncausal Theory of Agency," *Philosophy and Phenomenological Research* 49 (1988), 303–316.

if no particular action on my part were determined. But though the existence of such influence is evident, what is less clear is exactly how this notion is to be understood.

Roderick Chisholm has suggested two ways in which such influence might be understood in terms of familiar causal notions, ways that can be illustrated via our taurine example.[36] First, your cries may influence in the sense that, given the circumstances, they provide a *necessary condition* for my acting as I do. Suppose that I courageously (or foolishly) respond to your cries by instantly charging forward, taking the bull by the horns, and returning him to his pen. Assuming that such matadorial ministrations are not everyday matters for me, it may well be that, had I not heard your terrified cries, I would have been literally unable to act in so uncharacteristic a manner. Hence, your cries influenced me in the sense that they provided a necessary condition for my being able to perform the act I ultimately performed. Second, it may be that your cries influence me by *limiting my options*. Perhaps, before I heard your cries, there were various things I could have done—for instince, drive off calmly listening to a Haydn string quartet—which, given my formed character, I no longer can do having heard your cries. Your cries may leave me with various options (wrestling the bull, using the car to divert it, getting you into the car and escaping, and so on), but doing nothing to help you may not be among them. If so, then hearing you has influenced my action in the sense that it has limited my options.[37]

While it seems evident that some cases of influence can be understood in one or the other of the two ways Chisholm suggests, it is less clear whether every case of influence can be so analyzed.[38] Here, I think, libertarians can differ, and Christian libertarians could end up on either side of the dispute. Similarly, Christians could disagree over the extent to which influences are present in our lives, or over the degree of freedom with which we are left. (Obviously, if the influences upon me leave me with but two options, my freedom is not present in as robust a sense as it would have been had they left me with those two options and more besides.)

Despite these disagreements, virtually all orthodox Christians would presumably insist upon the reality of divine influence in our lives, an influence greater in degree and different in type from the more mundane influences we have thus far been discussing. Most Christians see God not only as having

---

[36] Chisholm himself explicitly endorses what seems to me a rather implausible account of inclination. See *Person and Object*, p. 69.

[37] Ibid., pp. 67–68.

[38] For a thoughtful examination of this question, see William Rowe, "Two Criticisms of the Agency Theory," *Philosophical Studies* 42 (1982), 363–378.

created us, but also as conserving us and our causal powers in being from one moment to the next. Many also insist that any action of ours requires concurrent divine activity to occur.[39] And clearly, all Christians see grace as a fundamental and crucial supernatural influence. Christians may differ regarding the precise nature of such grace, or over the degree (if any) of freedom to resist which the recipient of grace retains, but no orthodox Christian can plausibly minimize its beneficent role in our lives. Christian libertarians, then, will be reluctant to embrace suggestions that the free human agent is, like God, an unmoved mover.[40] On the contrary, it seems more accurate to think of our free actions as invariably reactive—as responses to divine initiatives. Our movements may not be determined by the natural and supernatural influences to which we are subject, but the presence and power of such influences can hardly be gainsaid.[41]

6. Conclusion

My goal in this chapter has been a simple one: to describe the traditional notion of providence and the libertarian account of freedom to which many orthodox Christians feel naturally drawn. I have not argued that utterly unavoidable pathways from orthodox Christianity to either traditional providence or libertarianism exist. But neither have I meant to suggest that either of these positions is just one of many equally reasonable ones the Christian might adopt. It seems to me that the prima facie case made here in favor of the Christian's endorsing both the traditional notion of providence and the libertarian account of freedom—that is, for embracing what I shall call *libertarian traditionalism*—is a potent one. Absent insurmountable problems which its acceptance might engender, libertarian traditionalism seems, if not the only, then at least by far the best game in town.

---

[39] For an excellent discussion of the issues surrounding concurrence, see Alfred J. Freddoso, "God's General Concurrence with Secondary Causes: Why Conservation Is Not Enough," in James Tomberlin, ed., *Philosophical Perspectives*, vol. 5 (Atascadero, Calif.: Ridgeview, 1991), pp. 553–585.

[40] Chisholm, alas, once used this misleading image. See his "Freedom and Action," in Keith Lehrer, ed., *Freedom and Determinism* (New York: Random House, 1966), p. 23.

[41] I am grateful to David Burrell for conversations that have helped me state the points being made here with greater precision.

The Molinist Account
of Providence

Unless we want to wander about precariously in reconciling our freedom
of choice and the contingency of things with divine foreknowledge, it is
necessary for us to distinguish *three* types of knowledge in God.
—Molina, Disputation 52, section 9

1. Prima Facie Problems with Providence

As we have seen, there seem to be solid reasons for orthodox Christians to
embrace libertarian traditionalism—that is, to endorse both the traditional
notion of providence and the libertarian conception of freedom outlined in
the preceding chapter. Yet there appear to be a couple of problems here,
problems which at first glance suggest that the theist needs to choose between
providence (traditionally conceived) and libertarianism. Thinking about these
problems offers us a useful way of introducing the Molinist picture of providence, for, from the Molinist perspective, it is only by adopting that picture
that these problems can be adequately resolved.

The problems I have in mind have to do with the two elements of providence outlined in Chapter 1 (divine foreknowledge and divine sovereignty)
and their relationship with undetermined events—in particular, with free human actions. Suppose we humans are free in the way that the libertarian says
we are. How, then, is God to have foreknowledge of our free actions? He
cannot foreknow them by knowing that we are in, or even are going to be
in, situations which determine our actions, because, according to libertarianism, we just are not in such situations when we are acting freely. Similarly,
he cannot foreknow our free actions by knowing his own intentions to cause
us to act in certain ways, for such external causation is, according to the
libertarian, incompatible with freedom. God can, perhaps, cause us to act in
certain ways, but if he does so, those actions are not free. So how can God

have complete foreknowledge if we are free in the way libertarians say we are?

This problem with foreknowledge seems serious enough. But the one with sovereignty seems, if anything, even more severe. If we are free in the libertarian sense, then what we do is, in a very strong sense, up to us. Nobody other than me, and no conjunction of prior or concurrent events, causes me to act in a particular way if the circumstances I am in leave me free. But then, how is God to have any control over free creatures? If what I do *is* up to me, doesn't it just follow that it is *not* up to God? God could, presumably, refrain from creating free creatures; but, in creating them, doesn't he surrender the kind of universal control which we saw as essential to the traditional notion of providence?

Faced with these problems, orthodox Christians might go in a number of directions. Some might be led to abandon the libertarian account of freedom. Others might argue that the traditional picture of a provident God as one with foreknowledge and sovereignty needs to be rejected. As Molina saw it, though, neither of these responses is tolerable, either philosophically or theologically. But fortunately, he thought, neither is it necessary for us to take one of these unsavory alternatives. The problems we have outlined can be solved without surrendering either libertarianism or a strong traditional concept of providence.

To understand Molina's distinctive means of reconciling freedom and providence, let us first note in more detail the large degree of common ground he shares with other traditionalists—that is, with other advocates of the traditional notion of providence. Doing so should help both to remind us of the similarities between, for example, even the most strident Thomist and Molinist combatants, and to identify precisely the point at which consensus dissolves.

2. Common Ground in Explicating Providence

Consider again the first two elements we noted as essential to providence—foreknowledge and sovereignty. Clearly, the first of these must in some sense follow from the second. That is, God's knowledge of what will happen must be dependent upon his decision as to what he himself will do. If it were not so dependent—if his decisions made no difference to his foreknowledge—then the notion of God's being in control of his world would clearly be a sham.

Let me make this point a bit more precisely. Consider what we might call God's *creative act of will*—his decision to create a certain order of creatures in a certain set of circumstances, an unchanging decision that leads to a multitude of successive temporal acts or effects (e.g., the creation of Cuthbert in this

time and place, the bestowal of this grace at this time to this person, and so
on) which together can be thought of as constituting God's *complete creative
action*.[1] That there is such an act of the divine will seems clearly to follow
from the picture of providence outlined previously. What seems equally obvious is that, if God's sovereignty is to be taken seriously, this act of will must
be thought of as prior to, and at least partially determinative of, God's foreknowledge. For example, God knows that Cuthbert will come to be at a
certain time *because* he has *decided* that Cuthbert will come to be at that time.
Were this not the case (were his creative act of will determined by his foreknowledge, or were foreknowledge and will utterly independent of one another), then to speak of God as in control of Cuthbert's coming to be would
clearly be out of place.

So it is only subsequent to his performing his creative act of will that God
has foreknowledge as to how things actually will be. In other words, his
knowledge of which possible world is actual is posterior to his decision concerning which of the various possible creative acts of will open to him he will
in fact perform.

It should be noted that, in speaking of priority and posteriority, the traditionalist is not to be thought of as speaking of *temporal* notions. Whether or
not one thinks of God as being eternal, there clearly can never be a time
when a provident God is ignorant of what he will do, or of what world is
actual. Still, since there seems to be a clear analogy between the process of
practical reasoning on the human level (where foreknowledge and action temporally follow choice, which in turn temporally follows deliberation) and that
on the divine level, talk of priority seems appropriate here.[2]

Of course, we ought not think of God as performing his creative act of
will in a state of total ignorance. Foreknowledge may not guide his action,
but clearly his act of will must be based on *some* knowledge already present
to him. To guide his act of will, such knowledge would have to be prior to
that act—that is, it would need to be *prevolitional*. And the kind of knowledge
that most readily pops to mind here is knowledge of *necessary truths*. For it

---

[1] Whether *temporal acts* are to be ascribed to God, or whether we should instead view, e.g.,
Cuthbert's creation at a certain place and time as a *temporal effect* of an *eternal* divine act, is a
question on which the Molinist, I think (or is it hope?), need not take sides. In any event, no
commitment to either side is being assumed in this work. It should also be noted that I am
thinking of God's complete creative action as equivalent to what Plantinga refers to as God's
actualizing the largest state of affairs that he strongly actualizes (i.e., that he causes to be the
case). See Alvin Plantinga, *The Nature of Necessity* (Oxford: Clarendon Press, 1974), pp. 173,
180–181.
[2] For Molina's brief discussion of this point, see Disputation 53, Part I, section 20 (pp. 211–
212).

seems eminently reasonable to think of such propositions as beyond God's control. Since such propositions are true independent of any free choice on God's part, and since God is (according to orthodox Christianity) essentially omniscient, it would seem to be part of his very nature to know such truths. It is hardly unnatural, then, for Molina to label God's *prevolitional* knowledge of *necessary* truths as *natural knowledge*.[3] Now, in knowing what is necessary, God also knows what is possible. For if something *is* possible (in the sense of metaphysical possibility at issue here), then the fact that it is possible is itself necessary. So, by his natural knowledge, God knows all possibilities. And from this it follows that natural knowledge provides God with knowledge of which worlds are possible.

Hence, God can be thought of as moving from knowledge of which worlds are possible to knowledge of which world is actual, and this movement is mediated by his free creative act of will. Knowing which world is actual adds to God's knowledge by informing him as to which contingent propositions that he might have rendered false (e.g., that Cuthbert comes into existence at *t*) are in fact true in the wake of his free activity. As Molina saw it, then, we can appropriately call God's *postvolitional* knowledge of *contingent* truths his *free knowledge*.[4]

Though the terminology of natural and free knowledge is Molinist, it is important to remember that we have thus far said nothing with which any traditionalist could reasonably take issue. No sensible proponent of that view could deny that some truths are necessary, and hence not such that God could choose to make them false; therefore, no such proponent could deny that some of God's knowledge is natural. Nor could any such advocate plausibly deny that some truths are contingent, and that their truth is dependent upon God's having freely chosen to act in a certain way; hence, no such advocate could deny that some of God's knowledge is free. Our employment of Molinist language, then, though preparatory for a thesis that *will* divide the ranks of the proponents of divine providence, should not mislead one into thinking that anything thus far affirmed would be controversial within the traditionalist camp.

Though noncontroversial, the picture thus far sketched is incomplete. For how, one might wonder, does it provide God with *complete* foreknowledge or control of events which are contingent? More precisely, how does it assure him knowledge or sovereignty with respect to those events involving non-divine beings that are not only logically contingent, but causally contingent as well—that is, with respect to events that are not naturally necessary? Events

---

[3] Molina, Disputation 52, section 9 (p. 168).
[4] Ibid.

that are physically determined, of course, would pose no obstacle to divine providence, since their occurrence would follow with necessity from elements of his complete creative action—that is, from divine volitions concerning which beings with which powers to create in which situations, along with further volitions concerning conserving and concurring divine activity. But with events that do not occur by a necessity of nature, no such simple link between God's volitions and their occurrence exists, and thus the means by which divine providence might extend to them thus far remain opaque.

Perhaps an example will help to illustrate this opacity. Molina argued that events of many different types would be contingent in the relevant sense— free angelic actions and their consequences, free human actions and their consequences, free actions of other animals and their consequences, the undetermined activities (and their consequences) of creatures lacking the type of cognitive ability needed for an ascription of action (e.g., the types of microphysical entities postulated by contemporary physics),[5] and free divine actions which presuppose contingent events of one of the aforementioned types (e.g., God's curing a victim of demonic possession). For our purposes, though, let us focus upon the kind of contingent event which is generally of most interest to us—a free human action.

Suppose that Cuthbert is at some point *t* in the future placed in a situation C which leaves him free with respect to the act of buying a certain iguana. If so, then Cuthbert will at *t* have the power to buy the iguana freely and the power to refrain from buying it freely, for without such powers, Cuthbert's act would not be free. But then it follows that there are two distinct sets of possible worlds that share the same Cuthbertian iguana-buying circumstances: the set of B-worlds, in which Cuthbert buys the iguana freely; and the set of R-worlds, in which he freely refrains. Now, it would appear that God, by his natural knowledge, would know that worlds of both types are possible; and let us further suppose that, by a creative act of will, he could directly bring it about that C obtains. How would this knowledge and this act of will allow him to know whether a B-world or an R-world will become actual, since either type of world is fully compatible with that knowledge and that act of will?[6] How can God have *free* knowledge, how can he exercise genuine providence, if he creates free (or at least undetermined) beings?

---

[5] I am assuming here that a being possessing no mental properties (one which could not reason, believe, desire, etc.) would not properly be referred to as being free or as performing actions.

[6] Can we think of God's creative act of will as simply including his willing that Cuthbert buy the iguana, and hence as entailing that some B-world be actual? No. For this act of will is to be thought of as extending only to those states of affairs that God strongly actualizes; see note 1 above. Because God doesn't (indeed, can't) strongly actualize Cuthbert's freely buying

The answer to these questions is evident: <u>providence can be exercised,</u> free <u>knowledge can be present, only if God knows how his creatures would act</u> if placed in various nondetermining circumstances. For example, suppose God knew that, if he *were* to place Cuthbert in *C*, Cuthbert would freely buy the iguana. Given his knowledge of that counterfactual concerning Cuthbert, God would know that, should he bring about *C*, a *B*-world would result. To know *which B*-world—in other words, to have the complete and perfect free knowledge called for by the tradition—he would have to know infinitely many other counterfactuals of the same sort, counterfactuals about Cuthbert and about other undetermined beings. And since God's providential activity is not limited to Cuthbert, and since there can be no time at which his decision concerning a complete creative action has not been made, he must have known from eternity how *any* undetermined creature he might create would act in *any* situation in which it might be placed. Though acknowledging that some of these conditionals might refer to unfree but undetermined beings, let us follow the recent tradition and call any such counterfactual whose antecedent is complete—that is, one that, like *C*, specifies the complete set of nondetermining circumstances in which the creature is placed—a *counterfactual of creaturely freedom*. Provided that God has knowledge of all the true counterfactuals of creaturely freedom, there is no problem with either his exercise of providential control over his world or his possession of free knowledge.

It is vital once again to recognize that, for the traditionalist, nothing we have said so far is genuinely negotiable. On the modern philosophical scene, the contention that God knows counterfactuals of creaturely freedom is sometimes equated with Molinism. As we have just seen, though, no such equation in fact exists. *No* traditionalist can consistently deny either that there are true counterfactuals of creaturely freedom or that God employs his knowledge of such counterfactuals in his providential activity.[7]

So God's knowledge of these counterfactuals is *not* the point at which controversy among the traditionalists arises. But it is easy now to identify that

---

the iguana (since God's will doesn't cause Cuthbert to act as he does), his creative act of will can't be thought of as including his willing that Cuthbert buy the iguana.

[7] Many anti-Molinist traditionalists have recognized that their position commits them to an acceptance of counterfactuals of creaturely freedom. For an especially clear Thomist example, see Franz Diekamp, *Theologiae dogmaticae manuale*, vol. 1 (Paris: Society of St. John the Evangelist, 1932), p. 204. It is perhaps worth noting that, when discussing his Catholic critics such as Bañez (in Disputation 50) and Zumel (in Disputation 53), Molina never seriously alleges that his opponents deny that there are true counterfactuals of creaturely freedom. Had he felt that they did, it seems unlikely that he would have concealed the fact, since the thesis that God knows counterfactuals of creaturely freedom, while not quite an article of faith for Roman Catholics, comes close. See Ludwig Ott, *Fundamentals of Catholic Dogma*, ed. James Bastible, tr. Patrick Lynch (St. Louis: B. Herder, 1964), p. 42.

point. For consider those counterfactuals of creaturely freedom that God knows. In which of the two categories of divine knowledge so far identified—natural knowledge or free knowledge—are they to be included? Molina's answer is that knowledge of counterfactuals of creaturely freedom is part neither of God's natural knowledge nor of his free knowledge, but instead is part of a third category of knowledge which lies between the other two. As we shall see in later chapters, many theists (both traditionalists and nontraditionalists) have rejected this Molinist answer. For the present, though, let us bracket their objections and attempt to explain why Molina feels this answer is required.

3. The Molinist Account in Brief

As we have seen, Molina thinks of natural knowledge as differing from free knowledge in two crucial respects: the former is prevolitional knowledge of necessary truths, while the latter is postvolitional knowledge of contingent truths. This double distinction can be graphically displayed as follows:

	Natural knowledge	*Free knowledge*
Truths known are:	Necessary	Contingent
	Independent of	Dependent on
	God's free will	God's free will

Given such a display, Molina's response to the question whether God's knowledge of counterfactuals of creaturely freedom should be considered natural or free should hardly come as a surprise:

> To this question it must be replied, first, that such knowledge should in no way be called *free*, both because it is prior to any free act of God's will and also because it was not within God's power to know through this type of knowledge anything other than what He in fact knew. Second, it should likewise not be said that this knowledge is *natural* in the sense of being so innate to God that He could not have known the opposite of that which He knows through it. For if created free choice were going to do the opposite, as indeed it can, then God would have known *that very thing* through this same type of knowledge, and not what He in fact knows. Therefore, it is not more natural for God to know through this sort of knowledge one part of a contradiction that depends on created free choice than it is for Him to know the opposite part.[8]

[8] Molina, Disputation 52, section 9 (pp. 168–169).

For Molina, then, true counterfactuals of creaturely freedom, being contingent propositions not under God's control, belong neither to natural nor to free knowledge, but rather to the middle ground between these two, a middle ground which, when added to our previous display, yields the following picture:

	Natural knowledge	Middle knowledge	Free knowledge
Truths known are:	Necessary	Contingent	Contingent
	Independent of	Independent of	Dependent on
	God's free will	God's free will	God's free will

Counterfactuals of creaturely freedom, then, will form part of God's middle knowledge. But it is important to note that they do not necessarily form the *only* part. Clearly, any contingent, prevolitional truth will have to be placed by Molina in God's middle knowledge, and it is conceivable that some such propositions are not counterfactuals about undetermined creaturely activity. For example, suppose God knows by middle knowledge that, if he were to create Adam in circumstances C, circumstances which include God's assuring Adam that eating the fruit of a particular tree would lead to immediate expulsion from the garden, Adam would in fact freely eat the forbidden fruit. Letting D stand for a proposition describing Adam's dastardly deed of disobedience, then, middle knowledge would tell God that $(C \rightarrow D)$. Of course, given that C includes God's warning, and given that divine assurances of this sort cannot be offered in vain, God would also know that expulsion would have to follow were Adam to disobey in C—that is, he would know that $[(C \& D) \Rightarrow E]$, where E describes God's act of expelling Adam. But from $(C \rightarrow D)$ and $[(C \& D) \Rightarrow E]$, it follows that $(C \rightarrow E)$; so God would know this truth as well. That is, he would know a proposition of the form "If I were to create Adam in circumstances C, I would expel him from the garden." Such a proposition would clearly be contingent (since Adam was free not to act in such a way as to merit expulsion), but just as clearly would not be under God's control, for it follows from a counterfactual of creaturely freedom about Adam (over which truth God has no control) and a necessary truth about God's doing what he has promised to do (over which truth he likewise has no control).[9] So $(C \rightarrow E)$ would be part of God's middle knowledge. Yet this counterfactual clearly is not a counterfactual of creaturely free-

---

[9] Here and elsewhere in this chapter, I will be assuming that "not under God's control" is closed under entailment—i.e., that if A is not under God's control, and A entails B, then B is not under God's control. Such an assumption seems safe enough, since to say that some

dom: it states what God would do in a certain situation, not what some undetermined creature would do. It seems evident, then, that middle knowledge might encompass much more than counterfactuals of creaturely freedom.[10]

Though more needs to be said to ward off other common misconceptions about middle knowledge, it is vital that we not miss the forest for the trees. As we are now in a position to explain briefly how Molina sees God's creative and providential activity as occurring and why he thinks his picture frees us from the problems with foreknowledge and sovereignty that seemed to beset the traditionalist, let us examine these crucial points first.

On the Molinist view, the knowledge of a providential God can be thought of as in a sense growing through four logical moments. First, God has natural knowledge—he knows all necessary truths. Second, he has middle knowledge—he knows all contingent truths over which he has no control. As we have seen, given this natural and middle knowledge, God knows what world would in fact result from any creative act of will he might perform.[11] In the third logical moment, God decides upon a particular creative act of will—he decides which beings to create in which circumstances. From this divine decision and the knowledge which precedes it flow not only all the contingent creaturely events ultimately precipitated by God's creative action, but also (and immediately) the fourth logical moment, in which God knows all the contingent truths under his control—that is, in which he has free knowledge. This picture of God's "growth" in knowledge might be illustrated as follows:

First moment	Second moment	Third moment	Fourth moment
Natural knowledge	Middle knowledge	Creative act of will	Free knowledge

---

truth is not under God's control, in the sense of that phrase which I am using here, is to say that he has no *counterfactual power* over that truth—i.e., it is to say that every creative act of will which God has the power to perform is such that, were he to perform it, the proposition in question would still have been true. The reader should note, though, that to say that powerlessness *so understood* is closed under entailment does *not* imply that powerlessness *understood differently* is similarly closed. For more on this issue, see my "Compatibilism and the Argument from Unavoidability," *Journal of Philosophy* 84 (1987), 423–440; see also the discussion of Hasker below in Chapter 6.

[10] For another example, see Chapter 8, section 8.

[11] If what I will call Maverick Molinism in section 9 below were a tenable position, this claim would need to be modified. Since I will argue that Maverick Molinism is *not* a tenable view, no such modification is in my opinion required.

The problems of foreknowledge and sovereignty are solved on this picture due to the fact that God's foreknowledge of contingent events flows from a combination of knowledge beyond his control and decisions under his control. Because he has middle knowledge and makes free choices concerning which creatures will exist in which circumstances, God has both complete foreknowledge concerning how those creatures will act and great control over their actions, in the sense that any act they perform is either intended or permitted by him. Yet because the knowledge which generates this foresight and sovereignty is not itself a product of free divine activity, our actions remain genuinely free, not the robotic effects of divine causal determination.

For example, take Cuthbert's free action of buying the iguana in C. On the Molinist picture, God does have foreknowledge of and control over this action. Prior to creation, God first (by his natural knowledge) knew infinitely many necessary truths concerning Cuthbert—for example, that it is possible that Cuthbert buy an iguana. By middle knowledge, he knew that Cuthbert would indeed freely buy the iguana if placed in situation C. Such knowledge, of course, left God with innumerable options prior to his creative act of will. He could presumably place Cuthbert in C. He could place Cuthbert in other sets of circumstances, some of them leaving him free, others not. In some of these alternative circumstances, God might see, Cuthbert would still freely buy the iguana; in others, he might see, Cuthbert would freely eschew iguanoid purchases. Finally, God might decide not to create Cuthbert at all. Whichever of these many options he might choose with respect to Cuthbert (and others), God would know via middle knowledge exactly how the world would turn out should he adopt that option. So God will exercise immense control over Cuthbert. Whatever Cuthbert does (assuming, of course, that there is a Cuthbert to do anything in the first place) he will do only because God knowingly put him in a situation in which that very action was divinely foreseen. Weighing these many options, let us assume, God performs his creative act of will, an act which includes Cuthbert's being created and put in C. This act on God's part has, as its immediate noetic effect, God's foreknowledge that Cuthbert will buy the iguana; as its remote temporal offspring, God's act results in Cuthbert's being in C, which in turn leads to his freely buying the iguana. Middle knowledge, then, affords God both foreknowledge of and control over Cuthbert's free action.

It is important to note that, on this Molinist picture, God's foreknowledge is neither the effect nor the cause of our free actions. Foreknowledge follows immediately from God's conjoining his creative act of will to his prevolitional knowledge; he has no need to observe or to be causally impacted in any way by the events he foreknows in order to know them. Even so, that foreknowledge should not be seen as in any sense the cause of that which is foreknown.

God's foreknowledge and the contingent event foreknown are, in effect, two separate consequences of the creative act of will God selects. Indeed, foreknowledge is virtually epiphenomenal, in the sense that it is the causally impotent byproduct of a causally cornucopian act of divine will. As Molina saw it, recognizing this causal impotence of foreknowledge helps free us from the fear that such knowledge compromises our freedom:

> the knowledge by which God knew *absolutely* that such-and-such things would come to be is not a cause of the things, but rather, once the order of things that we see has been posited by the free determination of the divine will, then (as Origen and the other Fathers observe) the effects will issue forth from their causes—naturally from natural causes, freely and contingently with respect to both parts from free causes—just as if God had no foreknowledge of future events. From this it clearly follows that no prejudice at all is done to freedom of choice or to the contingency of things by God's foreknowledge.[12]

God's creative act of will, then, along with the exercises of causal power by God's creatures that follow it, are the only causal forces needed to account for any event that occurs. In terms of explanation or causation, foreknowledge is a fifth wheel, and we can truly say, as Molina does, that the contingent events that follow upon God's creative act of will would still have occurred even if (*per impossibile*) God had not foreknown them.

Free knowledge, then, is neither causally nor explanatorily prior to the true future contingent foreknown. Indeed, in the sense that the truth of a proposition must be thought of as prior to the fact that someone knows that truth, it seems evident that the true future contingent should be seen as explanatorily prior to God's knowledge of it. Hence, from a Molinist standpoint, we can indeed say with Molina that "it is not because [God] knows that something is going to be that that thing is going to be. Just the opposite, it is because the thing will come to be from its causes that He knows that it is going to be."[13] So God knows that Cuthbert will buy the iguana because Cuthbert will buy the iguana—not in the sense that Cuthbert's future action *causes* God's prior knowledge, but in the sense that God's knowledge, though flowing from that same divine act which gives rise to Cuthbert's buying the iguana, is logically posterior to that Cuthbertian action.[14]

Such, then, is the essence of the Molinist account. Having thus surveyed this forest as a whole, let us now pause to look more closely at a few of its

---

[12] Molina, Disputation 52, section 29 (p. 184).
[13] Molina, Disputation 52, section 19 (p. 179).
[14] For more on the notion of priority at issue here, see Chapter 7, section 8.

trees.[15] In doing so, our language will go beyond that employed by Molina. The goal, however, is simply to understand that position better, not to alter it.

4. Counterfactuals of Creaturely Freedom and World-Types

As noted above, middle knowledge cannot be equated with knowledge of counterfactuals of creaturely freedom. Still, it can hardly be denied that such counterfactuals comprise the part of middle knowledge most important for God's providential activity. Let us look at such counterfactuals a bit more carefully.

What precisely is the form of such a counterfactual? Clearly, a number of factors need to be kept in mind if we are to avoid some common contemporary mistakes. Four such factors seem especially worthy of mention.

First, the antecedent of such a conditional needs to be stated in such a way that no assumption is made that the agent being described is a genuinely free, action-performing creature. For as we have seen, it is at least possible that there be nonfree but undetermined beings, and if there are, God would by middle knowledge know how they would react in various nondetermining situations.

Second, we need to make it clear in the antecedent that only counterfactuals involving creaturely activity are being considered. Presumably, there are counterfactuals of *divine* freedom—counterfactuals indicating what God would freely do in various different situations—which God knows. But, as we shall see, such counterfactuals would clearly be part of God's free knowledge, not his middle knowledge, since their truth would evidently be dependent upon God's free will; the fact that God has no say in how *we* would freely react to different circumstances gives us no reason to think he has no say in how *he* would freely react.

Third, the counterfactuals in question need to be such that no assumption is made concerning the existence of the creature being discussed. To (continue to) put this point rather loosely: middle knowledge needs to include not only counterfactuals about actual free creatures, but also conditionals about merely possible but nonactual creatures. This is so because such counterfactuals, on the Molinist picture, are known by God prior to his creative act of will, and

---

[15] The remainder of this chapter is, in a sense, a detour from the main road of this book, and thus might be skipped by those sorry souls whose time demands dictate their abstaining from all diversions. The reader should be cautioned, though, that some terminology introduced in the following sections (especially concerning world-types, galaxies, and feasibility) is employed in later chapters.

thus are true prior to any decision by God as to which creatures to create. Were God prevolitionally aware *only* of counterfactuals concerning those beings who turn out to be actual, there would *be* no free decision on God's part to create them. Hence, to maintain God's status as a free creator, and to safeguard the action-guiding status of his middle knowledge, the Molinist needs to affirm that, prior to his creative act of will, God has middle knowledge concerning the actions that would be performed by creatures who never in fact will be created. Of course, speaking or even thinking about beings that do not exist is notoriously difficult, but most of the problems here can be avoided if we think of the counterfactuals of creaturely freedom as making reference, not directly to *creatures*, but rather to the *individual essences* of such creatures, where the essence of a creature is simply the set of properties essential to it.[16] Since such *creaturely essences* could exist whether or not any being which instantiates the essence exists, the counterfactuals which God is considering when making his creative decisions are best thought of as conditionals which refer to such essences. Though we will often continue to speak as if these counterfactuals refer directly to creatures, such locutions should be recognized as sacrificing a bit of accuracy for stylistic grace and dexterity.

Finally, Molinists can and should think of the circumstances in which an action is performed as being *complete*. That is, what God would know is how a free being would act given all, not just some, of the causal factors affecting her activity. Obviously, the safest thing to do here is to think of the circumstances as including all of the prior causal activity of all agents along with all of the simultaneous causal activity by all agents other than the agent the counterfactual is about. Circumstances which are all-inclusive in this way will be said to be *complete* circumstances.

Keeping all of these points in mind, let us say that a counterfactual of creaturely freedom is to be thought of as a counterfactual of the following form:

> If creaturely essence *P* were instantiated in nondetermining complete circumstances *C* at time *t*, the instantiation of *P* would (freely) do *A*.[17]

---

[16] See Plantinga, *Nature of Necessity*, pp. 70–77. Note that I am assuming here that among the properties essential to a creature will be some (e.g., certain world-indexed properties) which are unique to it.

[17] A couple of explanatory notes are in order here. First, in saying that the circumstances are nondetermining, I mean that they neither logically nor causally determine the activity of *P*'s instantiation. Second, the "freely" has been put in parentheses because, as we saw, it is at least conceivable that some counterfactuals of creaturely freedom are about beings that are undetermined but not, properly speaking, free.

If God has middle knowledge, then he clearly knows all true counterfactuals of creaturely freedom, and knows them prior to his creative act of will. Which counterfactuals he knows, though, clearly will *limit* the type of world God can make. For example, if God knows a counterfactual of creaturely freedom which we might symbolize as $(C \rightarrow A)$, then he knows that he cannot make a world in which circumstances C are actual but action A is not performed. For to make such a world, he would have to bring it about that C is actual; but, since $(C \rightarrow A)$ is prevolitionally true, God knows that his bringing about C would as a matter of fact lead to A's being performed. Hence, since any complete set of counterfactuals of creaturely freedom which God might know to be true would restrict God to making a certain type of world, let us refer to such a set as a *creaturely world-type*. For God to have middle knowledge, then, he must know prevolitionally which creaturely world-type is *true*, where to say that such a set is true is just to say that each member of it is true.[18]

Though the notion of a creaturely world-type and its connection to the claim that God has middle knowledge is intuitively clear enough, saying precisely what constitutes a world-type is somewhat more difficult. At one point, I suggested that the following would do the trick:

(CWT1) T is a creaturely world-type iff T is a set such that, for any proposition s,
    (i) s is a member of T only if either s or $\sim s$ is a counterfactual of creaturely freedom, and
    (ii) if s is a counterfactual of creaturely freedom, then either s or $\sim s$ (but not both) is a member of T.[19]

Though initially plausible, such an account suffers from a crucial drawback: It does not guarantee that God has any *positive* knowledge of what his creatures would do. If middle knowledge consists primarily in God's knowing which counterfactuals of creaturely freedom are true and using this knowledge to direct the course of worldly affairs, then (CWT1) will not quite do, since it allows a creaturely world-type to contain solely negations of counterfactuals of creaturely freedom.

How can we take care of this problem? Two possibilities suggest themselves. First, we might simply add a third condition to (CWT1) so as to assure

[18] World-type terminology was first introduced in my dissertation, "Divine Freedom" (University of Notre Dame, 1980); see also my "Problem of Divine Freedom," *American Philosophical Quarterly* 20 (1983), 255–264.
[19] See "Problem of Divine Freedom," pp. 256–257.

that knowledge of the true creaturely world-type would afford God the positive knowledge left in limbo by (CWT1). One way to do this would produce the following:

(CWT2) T is a creaturely world-type iff T is a set such that, for any proposition s,
  (i) s is a member of T only if either s or $\sim s$ is a counterfactual of creaturely freedom, and
  (ii) if s is a counterfactual of creaturely freedom, then either s or $\sim s$ (but not both) is a member of T, and
  (iii) if s is a counterfactual of creaturely freedom and s is not a member of T, then there exists a counterfactual of creaturely freedom $s\star$ such that
     (a) $s\star$ has the same antecedent as s, and
     (b) $s\star$ is a member of T.

While (CWT2) seems adequate to our purposes, one might suspect that it is unduly complex. Perhaps this is so; and perhaps the complexity can be traced to the motivation which triggered our initial account. For (CWT1) was constructed in an attempt to evade the dispute over the law of conditional excluded middle—the claim that, for any counterfactual, either $(A \rightarrow B)$ or $(A \rightarrow \sim B)$ is true.[20] With just (i) and (ii) in our analysis of creaturely world-types, we do evade this dispute, but we do not get an account that neatly relates the notion of a creaturely world-type with the Molinist notion of middle knowledge. By adding (iii), I think we do get such an account. But to endorse (iii) is implicitly to endorse conditional excluded middle anyway—or at least to say that it holds in the limited area under discussion (i.e., with respect to counterfactuals of creaturely freedom). So why not just bring this endorsement out into the open from the start?

If we do thus lay our modal cards on the table, we might propose something on the order of:

(CWT3) T is a creaturely world-type iff for any counterfactual of creaturely freedom $(C \rightarrow A)$, either $(C \rightarrow A)$ or $(C \rightarrow \sim A)$ is a member of T.

Are there still any problems with (CWT3)? Perhaps. For it might be thought that even this account does not guarantee God *positive* knowledge: What if

---

[20] For a classic discussion of the law of conditional excluded middle, see David Lewis, *Counterfactuals* (Cambridge: Harvard University Press, 1973), pp. 79–83.

only counterfactuals of the latter sort, counterfactuals with negative consequents, were members of T? I suspect that any creaturely world-type of this
sort would be an *impossible* world type—that is, one such that it is not possible
that all of its members be true—and thus such that it could not possibly be
the creaturely world-type of which God is aware. So perhaps this is a problem
we need not worry about. If one could not help worrying, though, one might
want to move to the following, more explicit account:

(CWT4) T is a creaturely world-type iff for any counterfactual of creaturely
         freedom $(C \to A)$, either $(C \to A)$ is a member of T or there exists
         a proposition A^* such that $(C \to A^*)$ is a counterfactual of creaturely
         freedom and $(C \to A^*)$ is a member of T.

Whichever of (CWT2) through (CWT4) we end up preferring—and my
guess is that it does not make a lot of difference which—several points concerning world-types are worth noting. First, since infinitely many sets of propositions will satisfy our conditions, there will be infinitely many world-types.
Not all of these, though, will be possible; some will include conditionals
which are incompatible. (Consider, for example, the world-type which contains both the counterfactual saying that if Cuthbert were in C, he would buy
exactly one iguana and the counterfactual saying that if Cuthbert were in C,
he would buy exactly two iguanas.) Furthermore, as we have already noted,
among the possible creaturely world-types (which henceforth will be called
simply creaturely world-types, the impossible ones being of no concern to
us), one has the privilege of being true—that is, of being such that every
member of it is true. Finally, since a counterfactual of creaturely freedom is,
if true at all, only contingently true (there being no necessity to, say, Cuthbert's freely buying an iguana if in C), the true creaturely world-type is true
only contingently.

The concept of a world-type allows us to re-express the central Molinist
claim. To say that God has middle knowledge is virtually equivalent to saying that God has prevolitional knowledge of the true creaturely world-
type.[21]

---

[21] The "virtually" here is required because, as noted in the last section, there may be
elements of middle knowledge which *aren't* counterfactuals of creaturely freedom and which
thus are not included in any creaturely world-type. This complication will be ignored in what
follows both for ease of presentation and because it seems plausible to think that counterfactuals
of creaturely freedom are the basic components of middle knowledge; elements of middle
knowledge that aren't themselves such counterfactuals would seem to be derivable from them
combined with the necessary truths that make up God's natural knowledge.

5. World-Types, Galaxies, and Feasibility

As we have seen, a creaturely world-type is at best only contingently true. In terms of possible worlds, this implies that each creaturely world-type is true only in certain worlds. Suppose T is the true creaturely world-type. Since it is only contingently true, T is true in only some possible worlds (call them T-worlds). So the truth of T entails that some T-world is actual, and that no $\sim T$-world is. Now God, via middle knowledge, knows that T is true. But God has no control whatsoever over the truth of T; there is no complete creative action God has the power to perform such that, were he to perform it, T would not be true. From this it follows that God has no control over the fact that some T-world is actual. Middle knowledge tells God that his creative options as a matter of fact extend only to those worlds in which T is true. So there are many possible worlds which, given his middle knowledge, God knows he is not in a position to actualize. Regardless of which complete creative action within his power he were to perform, no $\sim T$-world would result.

Let us call the set of possible worlds in which a creaturely world-type is true the *galaxy* of worlds determined by that world-type. We can then say that a particular world is *feasible* just in case it is a member of the galaxy determined by the true creaturely world-type; a world that is not a member of that galaxy would be *infeasible* for God.[22] By extension, a galaxy itself could be referred to as feasible or infeasible, depending upon whether the worlds which compose it are feasible or infeasible. In this terminology, to say that God has middle knowledge is to say that he knows which worlds are feasible and which ones are not. That is, God knows prevolitionally that his creative options are limited by the true world-type to the set of worlds determined by it. Within that galaxy, God can actualize whichever world he pleases; worlds outside of that galaxy, however, are not even contenders for actuality.[23]

Speaking of worlds and galaxies, of course, easily leads us (or at least those of us with a bit of astronomical interest) to forming certain mental images of physical things spread out in space and arranged in relatively stable clusters. Such pictures, I think, can be helpful in getting a firmer grasp on the Molinist

---

[22] The terminology of galaxies and feasible worlds was also first introduced in my "Divine Freedom" and "Problem of Divine Freedom."

[23] Could it be the case that, even within the feasible galaxy, there are certain worlds which God cannot actualize—because, e.g., doing so would be morally abhorrent? I think not. The Molinist will insist that, if a certain world is so atrocious that actualizing it would be inconsistent with God's moral perfection, then the world in question is not genuinely possible, and so is not a member of the feasible galaxy in the first place.

position. Possible worlds and galaxies are not, pace David Lewis, material things.[24] But worlds do differ from one another to varying degrees much as physical objects are separated from one another by varying spatial distances, and galaxies do consist of intricately related worlds much as the galaxies of the astronomers consist of intricately related planets, stars and the like.

Consider, then, the set of possible worlds as being represented by an infinite set of circles located at various distances from one another, the distances to be thought of as representing the varying relationships of similarity among the worlds. As we have seen, the Molinist will insist that these worlds differ with regard to which creaturely world-type is true, and hence will be grouped into various different galaxies. In some worlds, world-type $T1$ will be true; those worlds constitute galaxy $G1$. Other worlds boast the truth of world-type $T2$; such worlds make up galaxy $G2$. And so on. The set of possible worlds, along with the galactic divisions among worlds based upon differing world-types, might then be partially represented as in Diagram 1.

Diagram 1

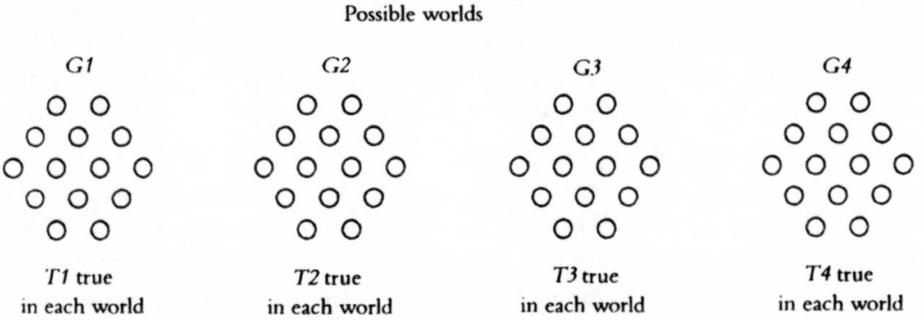

Possible worlds

$G1$	$G2$	$G3$	$G4$
O O	O O	O O	O O
O O O	O O O	O O O	O O O
O O O O	O O O O O	O O O O	O O O O
O O O	O O O	O O O	O O O
O O	O O	O O	O O
$T1$ true	$T2$ true	$T3$ true	$T4$ true
in each world	in each world	in each world	in each world

A word or two on the limitations of such a diagram seems in order here. First, since any world-type is presumably true in an infinite number of worlds, Diagram 1 offers only a partial representation of each galaxy. Furthermore, since there would seem to be an infinite number of world-types, the number of galaxies in fact far exceeds the four represented in our illustration. Diagram 1, then, offers a very selective and incomplete picture of the possible worlds and their galactic divisions.[25] So long as this fact is kept firmly in mind, Di-

---

[24] See Lewis, *Counterfactuals*, pp. 84–91; see also Lewis, *On the Plurality of Worlds* (Oxford: Basil Blackwell, 1986), esp. pp. 1–5.

[25] Indeed, more fine-grained representations of galactic arrangements would depend upon one's answers to a number of questions involving, among other things, the degree of heterogeneity possible within a galaxy. For example, must every member of a galaxy be more similar to every other member of its galaxy than it is to any world not in the galaxy? Could

agram 1 (and its successors below) can help us to visualize how the Molinist
sees worlds as arranged.

Of course, the Molinist believes that these galaxies are not all on a par,
because the world-types which determine them are not all on a par. One of
these galaxies (the one determined by the true world-type) happens to be
feasible, and so only those worlds which are members of this galaxy are feasible
for God—only they are genuine candidates for him to actualize. Suppose that
T_1 is the true world-type and G_1 the feasible galaxy. Since all the worlds not
in this galaxy exist, so to speak, in the shadow of unactualizability, we might
fittingly represent the distinction between feasible and infeasible worlds by
shading in the region of infeasibility. Our picture would then be that shown
in Diagram 2.

Diagram 2

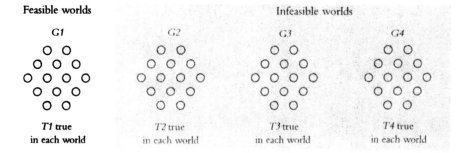

Feasible worlds   Infeasible worlds

G1   G2   G3   G4

T1 true   T2 true   T3 true   T4 true
in each world   in each world   in each world   in each world

It is important to remind ourselves that, even if God were presented with
such an arrangement of feasible and infeasible worlds, the arrangement might
easily have been different. Even if T_1 is the true world-type, it need not have
been, for the counterfactuals which constitute it are only contingently true.
T_2 or T_3 or any other creaturely world-type might have been true instead.
And, of course, had any of them been true, then the worlds in G_1, which
we are assuming to be in fact feasible, would not have been feasible. Feasibility, then, is a contingent feature of a world or of a galaxy. Any feasible

---

a world in one galaxy be more similar to some world in some other galaxy than it is to any
other world in its own galaxy? For what it is worth, I am inclined to think that the answer
to each of these two distinct questions is no. But I have no way of proving that this position—
that galaxies are, we might say, genuinely clustered, but not widely separated—is true. Nor
do I think that much hangs on it. On these as on many questions, reasonable Molinists can
disagree.

world or galaxy might have been infeasible, and any infeasible one might have been feasible.

Even so, a certain galaxy (G_1, we are supposing) *is* in fact feasible, and God's choice is restricted to that galaxy. God's creative act of will results in the actuality of one of the many worlds in G_1; one of those worlds, we might say, escapes the status of mere possibility and receives the fullness of actuality. Representing this actual world by a filled circle, we can augment our illustration so as to depict the result of God's creative decision via Diagram 3.

Diagram 3

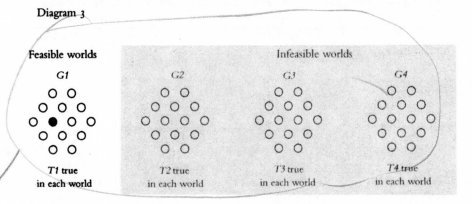

Feasible worlds   Infeasible worlds

$G1$	$G2$	$G3$	$G4$
$T1$ true in each world	$T2$ true in each world	$T3$ true in each world	$T4$ true in each world

It would be tempting for the Molinist to think of our diagrams as giving us graphic illustrations of the "growth" in divine knowledge discussed previously. Diagram 1, we might think, shows God's position at the first logical moment, when only natural knowledge is present. Diagram 2 represents his knowledge at the second moment, when middle knowledge is brought on stage. Finally, Diagram 3 illustrates his position at the fourth moment, when, because of his creative act of will made at the third moment, free knowledge arrives.

Thinking of our diagrams in this way is indeed tempting. And there is a grain (really a boulder) of truth to it. God's movement through the four logical moments *can* be thought of as a progression from knowledge of which worlds are possible, to knowledge of which worlds are feasible, and finally to knowledge of which world is actual, and our diagrams do represent this progression fairly well. But only *fairly* well, for our third diagram leaves out an element which Molina thought of as central to God's creative act of will and to the free knowledge which results from it. To see what this added element is, we need to consider a group of conditionals different from those that constitute creaturely world-types. We need to think about counterfactuals of *divine* freedom.

6. Counterfactuals of Divine Freedom and Chosen Worlds

Counterfactuals of creaturely freedom tell us what undetermined creatures would have done in various different situations. If Christianity is correct, though, creatures do not constitute the only undetermined beings. On the contrary, their creator is to be thought of as the free source of their very freedom. Needless to say, God's freedom may not be unlimited, at least not under some understandings of the word "free"; orthodox Christians would not, for example, think of God as "free" to break a promise. Still, the reality of divine freedom is a nonnegotiable part of orthodox belief.

Creatures, we are inclined to think, could have been in situations which are different from their actual situations but which still would have left them free. The same, it seems clear, is true with respect to God, though identifying the varying circumstances in which God might have been placed is a tad trickier. For example, Genesis tells us that Adam freely ate the apple in the Garden, and shows us how God reacted to this act of disobedience. As a free creature, though, Adam could have been obedient to God's command, and had he been, we are inclined to think, God would have been in a different situation which would have elicited a different free response on his part. Clearly, we might say, there is *some* sense in which Adam presents God with different situations here. Nevertheless, from a Molinist perspective, it might not be best to think of the situations as including the action of Adam itself. After all, for the Molinist, God does not have to wait until Adam is actually in the Garden, shamefully hiding from his creator, to decide how to react. On the Molinist picture, God's decision as to what he will do is a single, all-encompassing one which follows upon his middle knowledge and precedes his free knowledge. By eating the apple, then, Adam does not cause God to be in a certain decision-making situation, a situation other than the one he would have caused God to be in had he not eaten the apple. To think of things as working in that way is to think too anthropomorphically about divine activity.

Nevertheless, the sense in which God *can* be in diverse situations should be evident from our discussion of Adam. Were it the case that Adam would remain obedient if placed in the Garden, then the counterfactuals of creaturely freedom about him that are in fact true would not have been true. This means that some other creaturely world-type would have been true. And this, of course, means that God would have been presented with a galaxy of feasible worlds distinct from the galaxy he was in fact presented with. So God can be in different situations in the sense that he could have been presented with a different true creaturely world-type and a different set of feasible worlds. Of course, it seems reasonable to think that, whatever world-type God had been presented with, he would have remained free with respect to what creative act of will he would have performed. So it seems plausible to think that there are counterfactuals of divine freedom that state, for any creaturely world-type with which God might have been presented, what creative act of will he would have freely performed had he been so presented.

Molina saw clearly that such counterfactuals, being contingent truths subject to God's free will, would have to be part of God's free knowledge. As he puts it:

> even though (i) God does not know through the knowledge that *precedes* the free determination of His will which determinations of His will would have existed on hypotheses of the sort in question, and even though (ii) there is thus in God no *middle* knowledge concerning those determinations of His own will as there is concerning the determination of any created faculty of free choice given any hypothesis involving it, still He does know these determinations through the *free* knowledge that *follows upon* the free act of his will. For that free act regarding the things that are able to be done by God—an act in itself infinite, unlimited, and lacking any shadow of alteration—freely determined itself to one part of a contradiction with respect to all possible objects at once, not only (i) by freely establishing those things that He decided to bring about or to permit and by freely deciding not to bring about or permit the rest, but also (ii) by freely deciding which things He *would have* willed on any hypothesis that *could have* obtained and did not obtain.[26]

---

[26] Molina, Disputation 52, section 13 (p. 173). Molina seems to have felt that there was an additional reason why counterfactuals of divine freedom cannot be prevolitional, a reason having to do with a notion which later came to be known as *supercomprehension*. Roughly, to comprehend a being is to (as Freddoso puts it) "[grasp] the metaphysical modality of every state of affairs involving it" (Freddoso, "Introduction," p. 51). Comprehension thus amounts, in essence, to knowing the essential properties of a being. Since (pace Jonathan Kvanvig; see *The Possibility of an All-Knowing God* [New York: St. Martin's Press, 1986], pp. 124–125) counterfactuals of freedom, whether creaturely or divine, express only nonessential properties of a free being, comprehending a being will not afford one prevolitional knowledge of the counterfactuals of freedom which are true of it. For such knowledge, one must supercomprehend the being in question, and one can supercomprehend a being only if one "surpass[es] that being] in perfection by an infinite distance" (Molina, Disputation 52, section 13 [p. 174]). Since God doesn't surpass *himself* in perfection by an infinite distance, he doesn't supercomprehend himself, and thus (the argument concludes) doesn't have prevolitional knowledge of counterfactuals of divine freedom.

Though I have no desire to discredit this argument, I would surely sympathize with those readers who might see it as a classic case of employing the obscure to prove the obvious. Supercomprehension strikes me as a rather murky and unhelpful concept, one which the

God's creative act of will, then, is more all-encompassing than we have thus far indicated. Not only does he freely decide what creative act of will he *will* perform given the world-type which is true; he also freely decides what creative act of will he *would have* performed given any world-type which *could have* been true. His single act of will, then, makes infinitely many counterfactuals of divine freedom true.[27]

Suppose we continue to think of T_1 as the true creaturely world-type. Suppose we also think of V_1 as the creative act of will God as a matter of fact performs given T_1. Action V_1 obviously makes it true that God would perform V_1 if in T_1—that is, it makes it true that $(T_1 \rightarrow V_1)$. But V_1 also determines infinitely many other counterfactuals concerning what creative acts of will God would have performed had other world-types been true. Perhaps V_1 includes God's decision that, had T_2 been true, he would have performed V_2; had T_3 been true, he would have performed V_3; and so on. Then V_1 would have determined $(T_2 \rightarrow V_2)$, $(T_3 \rightarrow V_3)$, and so on.

The fact that God's creative act of will determines infinitely many coun-

---

Molinist needn't invoke to make a solid case for the postvolitional status of counterfactuals of divine freedom.

[27] *Could* a Molinist think of these counterfactuals as prevolitional? Clearly the conditional which indicates what God would do given the *true* creaturely world-type *cannot* be true independent of God's free act of will. But what of the others? Could a Molinist say that God *knows* but doesn't actually *decide* what he would have done had some false creaturely world-type been true? Such a position would surely be an odd one for a Molinist to take, and that for a number of reasons. For example, presumably there are world-types very close to the true one, each of which differs from it only with respect to a single counterfactual concerning some uninstantiated essence. It seems plausible to think that, had such world-types been true, God would have performed the same creative act of will V_1 which he performed in the actual world. So the Molinist in question would have us believe that, *prior* to deciding upon a creative act of will, God knew that, had the true world-type been different in any of these minor ways, he would have performed V_1. Isn't that rather hard to swallow? Doesn't it make far more sense to think of God as deciding upon V_1, and deciding that V_1 *still* would have been his choice had the world-type been infinitesimally different?

Thinking of counterfactuals of divine freedom as true prevolitionally also seems hard to square with certain biblical passages. For example, in chapter 18 of Genesis, Abraham gets God successively to commit himself to sparing Sodom should he find 50, or 45, or 40, or 30, or 20, or 10 righteous inhabitants of the city. This surely gives the appearance of God's deciding what he would do in various (as it turns out) counterfactual situations. It hardly looks like a case of his revealing certain truths over which he has no control.

Still, I know of no way (outside of appealing to supercomprehension) to *prove* that a Molinist would be inconsistent in holding some counterfactuals of divine freedom to be prevolitional. Indeed, some (such as Suarez) who traditionally have been considered Molinists have done precisely this; see William Craig, *The Problem of Divine Foreknowledge and Future Contingents from Aristotle to Suarez* (Leiden: E. J. Brill, 1988), pp. 225–233. Such Molinists, though, would have to alter our diagrams by including in Diagrams 2 and 3 indications of what will be referred to below as the chosen infeasible worlds.

terfactuals of divine freedom helps us to see why Diagram 3 offers an inadequate picture of God's cognitive state when he possesses free knowledge. Take
any true counterfactual of divine freedom—say, ($T_2 \rightarrow V_2$). Since V_2 includes
all of God's causal activity, God would know precisely what world would
result (given the truth of T_2) were he to perform V_2. If we call this world
W_2, then God knows that $[(T_2 \ \& \ V_2) \Rightarrow W_2]$. But from ($T_2 \rightarrow V_2$) and
$[(T_2 \ \& \ V_2) \Rightarrow W_2]$, it follows that ($T_2 \rightarrow W_2$). So God would know by his
free knowledge that ($T_2 \rightarrow W_2$). And the same, of course, would go for any
creaturely world-type; God by his free knowledge would know which world
would have been actual had that world-type been true. If we call such conditionals *counterfactuals of world-selection*, what this implies is that God by his
creative act of will makes infinitely many counterfactuals of world-selection
true.

For each galaxy, then, there is one world which God would have freely
chosen to be actual had that galaxy been feasible. Suppose we refer to a world
of this sort as the *chosen* world of that galaxy. By free knowledge, then, God
knows the chosen world of each galaxy. For the galaxy determined by the
true creaturely world-type, of course, the chosen world just is the actual
world—the world represented in Diagram 3 by a filled circle. The problem
with Diagram 3 can now be stated succinctly: it represents only one of the
chosen worlds, and thus represents only part of God's free knowledge. To
repair this deficiency, suppose we agree to represent each chosen world by a
filled circle. Our picture would then become as in Diagram 4.

Diagram 4

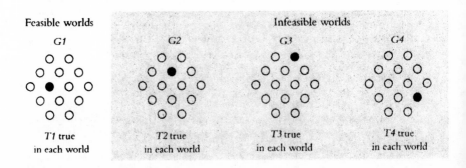

If we assume that God has comprehensive knowledge of each possible
world represented in this picture, then Diagram 4 offers a reasonably accurate

partial portrayal of God's state at the fourth logical moment, when he possesses free knowledge.

Diagram 4 suggests that worlds can be thought of as divided into four categories, depending upon whether or not God *could* actualize them (i.e., depending upon whether or not they are feasible) and whether or not he *would* actualize them if he could. In the first category are worlds which God could actualize and would actualize if he could. Clearly, speaking in the plural here is a bit misleading, for there is only one world that matches this description—the actual world. The second category would consist of worlds God could actualize, but wouldn't—the unchosen worlds of the feasible galaxy. Third, we have the worlds God couldn't actualize, but would have actualized if he could. These, of course, would be the chosen worlds in the infeasible galaxies. Finally, we have those sorry worlds which God couldn't have actualized, but wouldn't have actualized even if he could. The infeasible and unchosen worlds are the unfortunate inhabitants of this fourth category.

7. Two Questions about Chosen Worlds

A couple of questions concerning chosen worlds—one with an easy answer, one much tougher—are perhaps worth mentioning at this point.

First, one might wonder, could the chosen worlds have been different? If W_2 is a chosen world, is this a necessary truth about it, or only a contingent fact? Little reflection is needed to see that no chosen world is necessarily chosen. For which world is chosen in a particular galaxy is dependent upon which counterfactual of divine freedom is true—that is to say, it is dependent upon what complete creative action God would have performed had the world-type determining that galaxy been true. Since God could have decided differently, a different counterfactual of divine freedom could have been true, and so a different world could have been chosen. That a certain world is a chosen world, then, is a contingent fact.

Our second question is a bit more challenging. Given that a certain world is a chosen world, would it still have been a chosen world if a creaturely world-type *other than the one which is in fact true* had been true? Suppose, for example, that W_1 and W_2 are both chosen worlds; W_1 would have been actual had world-type T_1 been true, while W_2 would have been actual had world-type T_2 been true. In other words, suppose that

(1) $T_1 \rightarrow W_1$

and

(2) $T_2 \rightarrow W_2$

were both true. Would W_1 still have been chosen had T_2 been true? That is, would

(3) $T_2 \rightarrow (T_1 \rightarrow W_1)$

have been true as well? Or could it be the case that, even though W_1 in fact *is* the chosen member of the galaxy G_1 determined by T_1, some other world (say, W_5) *would have been* the chosen member of G_1 had T_2 been true? In other words, could

(4) $T_2 \rightarrow (T_1 \rightarrow W_5)$

be true even though (1) was true?[28]

Perhaps we should first make clear just what we would be saying in embracing both (1) and (4). Proposition (1) tells us that W_5 is not a chosen world; had the counterfactuals of creaturely freedom true in W_5 been true, God would have decided to actualize W_1, not W_5. Proposition (4), on the other hand, asserts that W_5 does have a rather special status. It is what we might call a culled world, where a world X is a *culled* world just in case there is a world-type such that, had God been presented with that world-type, part of his complete creative action would have been to decide that he would have chosen X if the counterfactuals of creaturely freedom true in X had been true. The advocate of (1) and (4) would be saying in effect that even a world such as W_5 which is not chosen may be culled. And since it would be odd to think of W_5 as being the only culled-but-unchosen world, the advocate of (1) and (4) would presumably be arguing that, among worlds, many are culled, but (comparatively) few are chosen.

It should be noted that no formal fallacy would be committed were one to say that (1) and (4) were both true. Counterfactuals which are themselves true very often would have been false given a certain hypothesis. Things being as they are in the actual world, if you were to ask me for a $10,000 contribution to a worthy charity, I would do two things: try to stifle the urge to laugh, and politely say no to your request. However, were I a billionaire

---

[28] Note that the issue under discussion here is distinct from the question considered in the preceding paragraph. There, our concern was whether $\square(T_1 \rightarrow W_1)$ follows from $(T_1 \rightarrow W_1)$. Here, the question is whether it follows from $(T_1 \rightarrow W_1)$ that, for any world-type T_n, $[T_n \rightarrow (T_1 \rightarrow W_1)]$.

instead of a philosopher, that counterfactual would no longer be true: if I were a billionaire, then, if you were to ask for the $10,000, I would agree to make the contribution. So no evident formal mistake would be involved in endorsing (1) and (4).

Even so, it seems odd to think that there could be culled-but-unchosen worlds, for it is difficult to imagine what might motivate God to perform the strange creative act of will needed to make both (1) and (4) true. If God has freely decided to make W_1 a chosen world (which is what (1) tells us), what possible reason could he have to decide by that very same act of will that he would alter W_1's status if he knew that T_2 were true? Perhaps this point can be made more forcefully if we note that God's creative act of will can be thought of as having two parts. Part of that act is *unconditional*; it involves God's deciding which beings *are* to be created and what situations they *are* to be placed in. The other part of that creative act of will is *conditional*; it involves God's deciding which beings *would have been* created and what situations they *would have been* placed in if a certain creaturely world-type had been true. It is obvious that the unconditional component of God's creative act of will might change as we move from galaxy to galaxy, for the creation of certain beings and situations which are conducive to God's providential aims given the true creaturely world-type might well not have been so conducive had other counterfactuals of creaturely freedom been true. But it is hard to see why the conditional part of God's creative act of will would similarly fluctuate from one galaxy to the next. If, given the true creaturely world-type (call it Tx), God has decided that he would actualize W_1 if T_1 were true, what reason could he possibly have to alter this decision if T_2 rather than Tx were true?

Indeed, if we are willing to grant what seems to me to be a very plausible principle, we can demonstrate that there can be no culled-but-unchosen worlds. The principle I have in mind states that, whatever the deliverances of the conditional part of God's creative act of will might be, they are at least logically compatible with the truth of any creaturely world-type. More formally, this principle might be presented in this manner:

(P)   Necessarily, if Vc is the set of true propositions determined by the conditional part of God's creative act of will, then for any creaturely world-type Tn, $\Diamond (Vc \ \& \ Tn)$.

Such a principle seems one which even the advocate of culled worlds should have no trouble endorsing, at least initially. For, with respect to the example discussed above, (P) does not say that a counterfactual such as (1) would *have to* still be true if T_2 were true; indeed, it does not so much as say that (1) *would* still be true if T_2 were true. It implies only that (1) *could* still be true if

T2 were true—that is, only that the truth of *T2* is compatible with the truth of (1). And that, on the surface, seems a modest claim indeed.

As noted, though, this concession is sufficient to show that there are no culled-but-unchosen worlds. For suppose there were such worlds. Suppose, to stick with our earlier example, that God had decided, via the conditional part of his creative act of will, to make not only (1) and (2) true, but (4) true as well. That is, suppose he had decided that he would actualize world *W1* if creaturely world-type *T1* were true; that he would actualize world *W2* if world-type *T2* were true; and that, if *T2* had been true, he would have decided to actualize *W5* (rather than *W1*) if *T1* had been true. Letting *Vc* represent the set of propositions determined by the conditional part of God's creative act of will, we would thus be supposing that

$$(5) \quad Vc \Rightarrow (T1 \rightarrow W1)$$

$$(6) \quad Vc \Rightarrow (T2 \rightarrow W2)$$

and

$$(7) \quad Vc \Rightarrow [T2 \rightarrow (T1 \rightarrow W5)]$$

were all true. But from (7) it follows that

$$(8) \quad (Vc \;\&\; T2) \Rightarrow (T1 \rightarrow W5).^{29}$$

Since *W5* is distinct from *W1*, we can deduce from (5) that

$$(9) \quad Vc \Rightarrow \sim(T1 \rightarrow W5).$$

---

[29] The inferential principle being employed here is *If [X $\Rightarrow$ (Y $\rightarrow$ Z)], then [(X & Y) $\Rightarrow$ Z]*. To see the validity of this principle, suppose that
  (a) $X \Rightarrow (Y \rightarrow Z)$.
Since antecedents of entailments can be strengthened, it follows from (a) that
  (b) $(X \;\&\; Y) \Rightarrow (Y \rightarrow Z)$.
Clearly,
  (c) $(X \;\&\; Y) \Rightarrow Y$.
From (b) and (c) it follows that
  (d) $(X \;\&\; Y) \Rightarrow [Y \;\&\; (Y \rightarrow Z)]$.
But
  (e) $[Y \;\&\; (Y \rightarrow Z)] \Rightarrow Z$.
And from (d) and (e) we can deduce the desired
  (f) $(X \;\&\; Y) \Rightarrow Z$.

But (8) and (9) together entail

(10) $(Vc \ \& \ T2) \Rightarrow \sim Vc,$

which in turn entails

(11) $\sim \Diamond (Vc \ \& \ T2).$

But (11), of course, cannot be true if (P) is accepted, for (P) implies that Vc is at least compatible with the truth of any creaturely world-type. So the assumptions required for there to be culled-but-unchosen worlds lead to a contradiction if the truth of (P) is granted. And since I think the truth of (P) should be granted, I think we have good reason to conclude that, if a world *is* a chosen world, then that world still *would have been* chosen had any other world-type been true.

Such considerations strike me as extremely persuasive. Still, some Molinists may find them less than compelling, especially since it would still be open to the champion of the culled-but-unchosen to reject (P). Such a rejection seems unwarranted to me, but, in the absence of a decisive argument for (P), I suppose I ought not deny others the right to renounce it. And so, while acknowledging that some Molinists might want to make room for culled-but-unchosen worlds, my own inclination is to reject the alleged distinction between the culled and the chosen.[30]

8. A Fifth Moment?

The distinction we have just noted between the conditional and the unconditional parts of God's creative act of will might suggest to some that the division into four logical moments in the "growth" of divine knowledge is both oversimplified and misleading. Recall the picture which, as we noted above, Molina seems to be endorsing:

First moment	Second moment	Third moment	Fourth moment
Natural knowledge	Middle knowledge	Creative act of will	Free knowledge

Once we realize the complexity of the creative act of will, one might argue, a new and more appealing alternative to this picture emerges. As we argued

---

[30] My colleague Fred Freddoso has indicated to me in conversation that his inclinations diverge from mine on this point.

in the last section, it is plausible to think that God's conditional creative act of will would not be affected by his knowledge as to which creaturely world-type happens to be true. What this implies, one might suggest, is that this part of God's creative act of will should be seen as prior to his middle knowledge. Clearly, the unconditional component of that act of will could not similarly be thought of as independent of God's middle knowledge; for the Molinist, at least, God's knowledge of the true counterfactuals of creaturely freedom plays a crucial action-guiding role in his decision concerning which beings to create in what situations. So God's unconditional creative act of will clearly needs to be seen as posterior to God's middle knowledge. The upshot, such a Molinist might conclude, is that we need to see the two parts of God's creative act of will as occurring at different logical moments, and hence we need to add a fifth moment to our account. The revised picture which is being promoted might be represented as follows:

First moment	Second moment	Third moment	Fourth moment	Fifth moment
Natural knowledge	Conditional creative act of will	Middle knowledge	Unconditional creative act of will	Free knowledge

What ought the Molinist to say about this alternative? On the whole, I see no reason to prefer it to that offered by Molina. Molina's picture has the advantage of preserving the unity of God's act of will. Why think of this as an advantage? For a number of reasons. Many advocates of Molinism might also be attracted toward the claim that God is absolutely simple, and simplicity would seem easier to endorse if we do not sanction distinct divine acts of will framing his middle knowledge. Furthermore, even those Molinists not enamored of simplicity might feel some inclination to keep God's act of will undivided. Why, they might ask, think of God as making *any* creative decision prior to his possession of *all* the knowledge prevolitionally available to him? Finally, isn't it possible that the revisionist's picture would actually be even messier than suggested above? Isn't it at least conceivable that many of God's unconditional creative decisions—say, his decision to create Alpha Centauri— are in fact independent of his middle knowledge and hence, using the revisionist's criteria, should occur prior to the third moment? Are we to push them into the second moment, along with God's conditional creative act of will? Or are we to fashion yet another moment for them to inhabit?

As with the dispute concerning culled and chosen worlds discussed in the last section, I find these reasons to retain Molina's picture of an undivided, single divine act of will to be telling, but less than demonstrative. Here, too, it seems to me, we ought to acknowledge that there are reasonable variations available within Molinism.

9. Maverick Molinism

Toleration, though, has its limits. Some purported variations constitute, not reasonable alternatives within the Molinist family, but an implicit betrayal of the familial heritage. For one example, consider what have come to be called *counterfactuals of world-actualization*—counterfactuals specifying, for any complete creative act of will God has the power to perform, what possible world would in fact become actual were God so to will. No Molinist, I think, would deny that there are such truths, and that God would be aware of them. But it may not be immediately apparent where in God's knowledge such conditionals are to be found. Since God's creative act of will is to be thought of as compatible with the existence of many different possible worlds, counterfactuals of world-actualization would have to be contingent, and so could not be part of God's natural knowledge. But in which of the remaining two categories do they belong? Are they part of God's middle knowledge, or part of his free knowledge? Are they prevolitional or postvolitional truths?

The typical Molinist response, it seems to me, would be to say that such counterfactual truths are part of God's middle knowledge. For which world would result from a complete creative action on God's part is simply a function of which creaturely world-type is true, and since the latter is not under God's control, neither is the former. Still, some who are otherwise favorably disposed toward Molinism might be tempted to challenge the alleged prevolitional status of such truths.[31] That is, they might want to say that a Molinist can hold that, whichever truth-value a counterfactual of world-actualization has, there nevertheless were things God had the power to do such that, had he done them, that counterfactual would have had the opposite truth-value. Is this type of position—call it *Maverick Molinism*—tenable for a Molinist?

Consider a counterfactual of world-actualization such as

(M)   If God were to perform creative act of will V_1, then world W_1 would be actual.

---

[31] Such a challenger might cite Plantinga in support; see his "Replies" in *Alvin Plantinga*, ed. James E. Tomberlin and Peter van Inwagen (Dordrecht: D. Reidel, 1985), pp. 375–377. It should be noted, though, that Plantinga never actually endorses what I am calling Maverick Molinism in this or any other published piece, and has in fact rejected the view in conversation. For something much closer to an endorsement of the view, see Jonathan Kvanvig, *The Problem of Hell* (New York: Oxford University Press, 1993), pp. 88–96.

In keeping with our usual practice, let us agree to simplify the symbolization of this conditional to

(M) $V_1 \rightarrow W_1$

Suppose that (M) is in fact false; hence,

(12) $\sim(V_1 \rightarrow W_1)$.

Suppose furthermore that, as the Maverick alleges, (M) is not false prevolitionally. In other words, suppose that there is some act of will S which God had the power to perform such that, had he performed it, then (M) would have been true. So, not only is (12) true, but

(13) $S \rightarrow (V_1 \rightarrow W_1)$

is true as well. Now, had S been actualized by God, either S itself would have been God's creative act of will or it would have been part of that act. So, for some creative act of will Vx,

(14) $S \rightarrow Vx$

and

(15) $Vx \Rightarrow S$.

From (14), (15), and (13) it follows that

(16) $Vx \rightarrow (V_1 \rightarrow W_1)$.[32]

So, the Maverick Molinist is committed to saying that (16) is true as well.[33]

Is (16) to be thought of as prevolitional? I think so. For if it isn't, then the Maverick seems to be trotting down a vicious infinite regress. The Maverick begins by saying that a simple counterfactual such as (M) is not prevolitional.

---

[32] The inferential principle being employed here is If $(X \rightarrow Y)$, $(Y \rightarrow X)$ and $(Y \rightarrow Z)$, then $(X \rightarrow Z)$.

[33] As Thomas Williams pointed out to me, this argument could be streamlined if we simply stipulated at the start that S is the largest state of affairs God strongly actualizes. While most Mavericks would probably see this stipulation as unobjectionable, the less discerning among their number might ask why they should be expected to accept it. Hence, I decided to leave the argument in this slightly more complicated but more clearly demonstrative form.

As we have seen, this commits him to saying that a more complex counter-factual—a counterfactual with a counterfactual consequent—is also true. If *this* counterfactual were also, though true, such that its truth was up to God, then the Maverick would be saying that an even more complex counterfac-tual—a counterfactual whose consequent is the negation of a counterfactual with a counterfactual consequent—would also be true. As should be clear, there would be no plausible place to stop this regress of counterfactuals. As should also be clear, the regress generated would indeed be a vicious one. For God would have, so to speak, no firm prevolitional ground to stand on. He could render one counterfactual true or false only by strongly actualizing a certain state of affairs; but the fact that that state of affairs *would* render that counterfactual true or false would not be a matter which was settled, but one which depended on some *prior* divine decision. Since one can't, I take it, plausibly think of every divine decision of this kind as depending upon a distinct and prior decision, the Maverick would presumably want to avoid the regress. And so, I think, we have to view (16) as a prevolitional truth.

Of course, even if (12) is true, it isn't (according to the Maverick) true prevolitionally; rather, it is true as a result of some divine activity. So there is some state of affairs V which God had the power to actualize such that, were he to actualize V, (12) would be true; that is,

(17) $V \rightarrow \sim(V_1 \rightarrow W_1)$.

Now, just as (16) follows from (13), so it would follow from (17) that, for some creative act of will V_z which God has the power to perform,

(18) $V_z \rightarrow \sim(V_1 \rightarrow W_1)$.

And since the reasons given for thinking that (16) is prevolitionally true would hold here as well, it follows that the Maverick is committed to thinking of (18) as prevolitional.

If (16) and (18) are both prevolitional, then it would seem that the Maverick can indeed say that the truth of (M) was up to God. He could have chosen V_x as his complete creative action, and had he done so, (M) would have been true. On the other hand, it was open to him to choose V_z instead, and had he so chosen, (M) would have been false.

Note, though, that there is no reason to think of V_x and V_z as exhausting God's creative options. Presumably there are other creative acts of will God could have strongly actualized. And, presumably, the Maverick will want to say that some of these are such that (M) would have been true had he actu-alized them, and others such that it would have been false. Indeed, it is hard to see how any creative act of will God might possibly have performed could fail to fall into one or the other of these categories. After all, the whole point of Maverick Molinism is not that counterfactuals of world-actualization lack truth values, but rather that their truth values are consequent upon God's creative action. Hence, it would seem that any such action must counterfactually imply either the truth or the falsity of any such counterfactual.

So the creative acts of will within God's power are of two types relative to (M). Some are what we might call (M)-actions; these are actions, such as actualizing Vx, which would have resulted in (M)'s being true. Others, such as Vz, are what we might call ∼(M)-actions—actions which would have resulted in (M)'s being false. And, for the reasons already sketched in connection with (16) and (18), the fact that a particular creative action would have the result it would have vis-à-vis (M) will be known by God prevolitionally.

So far, so good? I think not. For problems appear for the Maverick when we ask about V_1. Is this creative act of will to be thought of as an (M)-action or a ∼(M)-action?

Suppose it is an (M)-action. This means that God knew prior to any creative action on his part that, were he to perform V_1, (M) would be true. That is,

(19) $V_1 \rightarrow (V_1 \rightarrow W_1)$

is prevolitional. But (19) entails

(20) $V_1 \rightarrow W_1$.

So, (20) would be prevolitional as well. But, of course, the Maverick cannot accede to this, for (20) simply is (M), and the very essence of the Maverick's position is the claim that the truth of (M) is up to God. So it looks as though the Maverick must deny that V_1 is an (M)-action.

Could V_1 be a ∼(M)-action? If it were, then

(21) $V_1 \rightarrow \sim(V_1 \rightarrow W_1)$

would be true prevolitionally. Now, it seems to me that even the Maverick, being a Molinist, would agree that, if it weren't the case that W_1 would be actual were God to bring about V_1, then if God were to bring about V_1, some world other than W_1 would be actual. Even the Maverick, then, would agree that

(22) $\sim(V_1 \rightarrow W_1) \Rightarrow (V_1 \rightarrow \sim W_1)$.

Now, (21) and (22) entail

(23) $V_1 \rightarrow (V_1 \rightarrow \sim W_1)$.

So (23) would be prevolitional as well. But (23) in turn entails

(24) $V_1 \rightarrow \sim W_1$,

which means that (24) is also a prevolitional truth. Surely, though, the Maverick would grant that (24) entails

(25) $\sim(V_1 \rightarrow W_1)$,

and hence would be committed to saying that (25) is prevolitional too. But (25), note, just is (12), the very proposition which the Maverick has been insisting is *not* prevolitional. So it looks as though the Maverick cannot say that V_1 is a $\sim$(M)-action either.

What follows, it seems to me, is that the Maverick's position is not a coherent one for a Molinist to assume. The Maverick, as we saw, has to say that any creative act of will which God might perform is either an (M)-action or a $\sim$(M)-action. But if V_1 is an (M)-action, then (M) turns out to be prevolitional, which the Maverick denies; on the other hand, if V_1 is a $\sim$(M)-action, then $\sim$(M) turns out to be prevolitional, which the Maverick also denies. What, then, is the Maverick to say? That V_1 is not a possible creative act of will? But this course also is not open, for we began by assuming that (M) is a counterfactual of world-actualization, which means that we began by assuming that V_1 is indeed a creative act of will within God's power. The Maverick, I think, has been corralled; the clear-thinking Molinist will insist that counterfactuals of world-actualization are not under God's control.

It is perhaps worth noting, though, that there is a position superficially similar to Maverick Molinism which most any Molinist would probably accept. Suppose some counterfactual of creaturely freedom $(C \rightarrow A)$ is in fact true. Could there be some complete creative action on God's part V_1 such that $[V_1 \rightarrow \sim(C \rightarrow A)]$? The answer, I think, is yes. Suppose, for example, that V_1 includes all of the following:

> God promises not to do X if S freely does A in C.
> S is free in C.
> God does X.

If V_1 includes all of these states of affairs, then it seems clear to me that it would presuppose the truth of $\sim(C \rightarrow A)$. Since V_1 would thus entail $\sim(C \rightarrow A)$, it would of course be the case that $[V_1 \rightarrow \sim(C \rightarrow A)]$ would be not only true, but prevolitional as well. But does this mean that $\sim(C \rightarrow A)$ would also have to be prevolitionally true? I don't think so. Why couldn't it be the case that

(26) $[V_1 \rightarrow \sim(C \rightarrow A)]$

and

(27) $C \rightarrow A$

were both prevolitionally true? Of course, if they were both prevolitional, it would follow that

(28) $\sim V_1$

is prevolitional as well. But why should that bother us? It doesn't entail that God has any power over counterfactuals of creaturely freedom, for, though it does grant that some such counterfactuals which are in fact true would have been false had God acted in a certain way, it also says that God didn't in fact have the power to act in that way. Should the Molinist be reluctant to agree that there *are* some complete creative actions that God lacks the power to perform? I can't see why. For complete creative actions are indeed very complex critters, ones which (as the example above suggests) may well presuppose the truth of certain counterfactuals of creaturely freedom. Since those counterfactuals may or may not be true, and since their truth is not under God's control, it follows that a complete creative action may or may not be such that God can perform it.

As I see it, then, the Molinist can, and probably should, concede that some counterfactuals are such that, though true, they wouldn't have been true had God acted in a certain way. But this is not to endorse Maverick Molinism. Maverick Molinism holds that the counterfactuals which are thus counterfactually related to what God does are *not* prevolitionally true, and hence *are* under God's control. The position we have just been examining, however, says that the counterfactuals which are counterfactually related to what God does *are* prevolitionally true, and thus are *not* under God's control. So the tenability of this position should not remove our confidence in the conclusion we reached that Maverick Molinism is an untenable stance.

10. Conclusion

As we saw in Chapter 1, an orthodox Christian has good reason to want to hold on to both the traditional notion of divine providence and the libertarian analysis of freedom. The Molinist picture of providence presented in this chapter clearly offers one way of doing so. But is Molinism the *only* way for the Christian? Do we, as Molina implies in the quotation with which we began this chapter, "wander about precariously" if we attempt to remain orthodox Christians while denying middle knowledge? Or are there alternative pictures of providence available which any Christian ought to find equal or superior to the Molinist account? These are the questions to which we shall turn in the next chapter.

Part II

A DEFENSE OF THE MOLINIST ACCOUNT

3

Alternative Accounts
of Providence

If you are committed to a "strong" view of providence, according to which, down to the smallest detail, "things are as they are because God knowingly decided to create such a world," and yet you also wish to maintain a libertarian conception of free will—if this is what you want, then Molinism is the only game in town.
— William Hasker, "Response to Thomas Flint"

1. The Only Game in Town?

As we saw in Chapter 2, Molinism offers the libertarian traditionalist a very attractive route of escape from the two problems outlined in the beginning of that chapter, problems that initially seemed to call for a renunciation of either the traditional notion of providence or the libertarian conception of freedom. But, one might well ask, is it the only route of escape? Are there other paths down which the libertarian traditionalist might venture that would be just as salubrious as the Molinist one? Or is the libertarian traditionalist stuck (so to speak) with Molinism—is it, to switch to Hasker's terminology, the only game in town?

A brief recapitulation of the line of thought developed in Chapter 2 should suffice to convince us of the aptness of Hasker's metaphor. As we saw in section 2, one can uphold the traditional notion of providence only if one acknowledges that there are true counterfactuals of creaturely freedom that guide God's creative decisions. Diminish or dismiss this knowledge and one diminishes or dismisses the robust providential control over his world which the tradition proclaims. So, to be a genuine traditionalist, the libertarian traditionalist has no choice but to grant that there are true counterfactuals of creaturely freedom. But to be a genuine libertarian, she can hardly view such counterfactuals as under divine control, for if God were to determine the truth or falsity of such conditionals, they could not rank as conditionals of freedom, at least not of the sort of freedom that libertarians cherish. The libertarian traditionalist, then, is committed to believing that there are true counterfactuals of creaturely freedom whose truth value is prevolitional, not a result of divine determination. But to embrace the prevolitional status of these counterfactual truths is to embrace Molinism.

For the consistent libertarian traditionalist, then, the path to Molinism is inescapable. It is indeed the only game in town.

2. A Very Fine Game Indeed

Some of the language used in the previous section might suggest that the libertarian traditionalist's marriage to Molinism is of the shotgun variety—i.e., less a matter of love and volition than a matter of force and necessity. On the whole, it seems to me that this is a misleading way of viewing this union. While there are, as we shall see, serious objections that can be raised against the theory of middle knowledge, the Molinist outlook is not one that should initially strike the libertarian traditionalist as strange or distasteful. On the contrary, Molinism is most properly viewed as the philosophical development of prephilosophical beliefs which are widely shared both within the Christian community and beyond it.

As we saw (or at least as I asserted) in Chapter 1, belief in a strong, robust notion of providence has long been dominant among orthodox Christians. Adherence to a libertarian account of freedom, though not so widespread, has also been common within this community. As we have seen, the inevitable offspring of this coupling is Molinism. But the inevitability here is of a sort well known to philosophers. Many orthodox Christians who would, if informed of the options and asked their preferences, unhesitatingly embrace both the traditional notion of providence and the libertarian account of freedom have given precious few of their waking hours to extensive ruminations concerning either providence or freedom; their traditionalism (with respect to providence), like their libertarianism (with respect to freedom), is more dispositional than occurrent. And what holds for traditionalism and libertarianism holds even more, it seems to me, for Molinism. Few Christians would even know what the term "Molinism" stands for, let alone label themselves Molinists. But fewer still, upon encountering the theory of middle knowledge, find the position at first glance outlandish or patently unacceptable (unless, of course, they are among those benighted believers who find *any* explicit philosophical reflection upon their religious commitments outlandish or unacceptable). Far more common, at least in my experience, is the reaction that Molinism is but an elaboration of a view which they have held implicitly all along.[1]

---

[1] On a personal note, I have vivid memories of several nuns who taught me during ele-

Indeed, it seems evident to me that the Molinist stance regarding the existence of true counterfactuals of creaturely freedom has an initial plausibility to most people who hear of it, not just to informed Christians. Most of us come to our philosophical armchairs thinking that there are answers to "What would have happened if . . ." questions, even when we have hardly an inkling as to what those answers are. ("What would have happened if I'd accepted his proposal of marriage? How would our life together have proceeded? I wish I knew!") Often enough we find such questions impossible to answer, and thus pointless to ask. But equally often, I think, we find them vital to consider in assessing our past or planning our future, whether or not we have much confidence concerning the answers we end up endorsing.

Furthermore, we frequently *are* quite confident concerning the answers to such questions, and thus quite confident concerning the truth of certain counterfactuals of creaturely freedom. To take Adams's celebrated example:

> There does not normally seem to be any uncertainty at all about what a butcher, for example, would have done if I had asked him to sell me a pound of ground beef, although we suppose he would have had free will in the matter. We say he would certainly have sold me the meat, if he had it to sell.[2]

Many of our everyday actions in life (and most involving premeditated intercourse with other people) seem to be predicated on the assumption that there are indeed truths of this sort. Hence, Molinism (or at least this element of Molinism) appears to lie at the foundation of nearly everyone's life.

Critics of Molinism have questioned whether such examples are as telling as we have suggested. Adams himself, though finding the example of the butcher perplexing, ends up endorsing the view that all we are entitled to say is that the butcher *probably* would have sold him the meat, since this is all that is truly grounded by the character and psychological dispositions of the butcher.[3] Were there solid reasons for denying that there are true, nonprobabilistic counterfactuals of creaturely freedom, I think we would have to settle for the probabilistic conditionals Adams admits. But it seems evident to me that this should be a fallback position to which we retreat only if forced, much

---

mentary school attempting to explain the apparent "failure" of some prayers along lines which I now recognize to be Molinist, lines which will be developed in Chapter 10. I am fairly confident that none of these sisters had ever heard of Molina.

    [2] Robert M. Adams, "Middle Knowledge and the Problem of Evil," in Adams, *The Virtue of Faith and Other Essays in Philosophical Theology* (New York: Oxford University Press, 1987), p. 88.

    [3] Ibid., pp. 88–89. Adams's conclusion has been seconded by Hasker, who seemingly shares none of Adams's hesitation on the matter; see William Hasker, *God, Time, and Knowledge* (Ithaca: Cornell University Press, 1989), p. 31.

as the man who claims that he sees a tree in the courtyard would reasonably pull back to the more modest "Well, at least there *appears* to be a tree in the courtyard" only if forced to by evidence disconfirming his straightforward initial claim. On the face of it, what all of us seem to assume in our everyday lives is that there are genuine, full-blooded counterfactuals of creaturely free-dom, many of which are such that we are fairly confident of their truth or falsity. In asking us to accept the conditionals contained in middle knowledge, then, Molinism is not asking most of us to make any significant alteration in our prephilosophical doxastic practice.

Indeed, though the probabilistic alternative forwarded by Adams and others has a tinge of plausibility in certain contexts, there are many others in which it seems evident that what most of us are inclined to endorse are nonproba-bilistic conditionals of freedom, not just the probabilistic ones. This is made evident, for example, by the predispositions which are assumed in certain artistic works. Consider two of the classics of Christmastime, Charles Dick-ens's story *A Christmas Carol* and Frank Capra's film *It's a Wonderful Life*.

In Dickens's work, after the Ghost of Christmas Yet to Come has accom-panied Scrooge through several sobering scenes of his and others' futures, and as the Ghost beckons him to look upon the gravestone which, as we soon discover (had we not already guessed), bears his name, Scrooge pauses to ask the Ghost a question:

> "Before I draw nearer to that stone to which you point," said Scrooge, "answer me one question. Are these the shadows of the things that Will be, or are they shadows of things that May be, only?"[4]

In other words, Scrooge is asking, are the dismal "shadows" he has per-ceived—the indifference to his death exhibited by his business associates, the disdain shown by those who had pilfered his belongings, the desolation of the Cratchit family in the wake of Tiny Tim's death—events which *will* take place, or only ones which *might* occur? Having asked, and received no reply, Scrooge hints at a third possibility—that the shadows portray what *must* occur unless Scrooge changes his ways:

> "Men's courses will foreshadow certain ends, to which, if persevered in, they must lead," said Scrooge. "But if the courses be departed from, the ends will change. Say it is thus with what you show me?"[5]

---

[4] Charles Dickens, *A Christmas Carol* (1843; Roslyn, N.Y.: Walter J. Black, 1965), Stave 4, pp. 85–86.

[5] Ibid., p. 86.

The Spirit, of course, remains silent. But the reader surely must wonder if Scrooge hasn't gotten it wrong with each of his three guesses. Clearly the shadows don't depict what *will* be, for the remainder of the story shows us much happier events transpiring. Nor is it plausible to think of the shadows as showing us only what *might* be, for there are infinitely many ways in which the future *might* go; why should the Ghost's showing Scrooge one of this myriad of mere possibilities have frightened him (or us)? Finally, it seems unlikely that what we have seen is how things *must* be unless Scrooge changes. Why think that those businessmen, or Scrooge's charwoman and laundress, or the Cratchits would have to react to the deaths of Scrooge and Tiny Tim in the way we see them reacting?

What, then, has the Ghost shown Scrooge, if not what will, might, or must occur? Clearly (or so it seems to me) he has shown him what *would* occur were Scrooge not to amend his life. Not being a philosopher, the Ghost presents his message visually and aurally, not via propositions. But the message presented presumes that there is a fact of the matter about how things would go were Scrooge to continue living as before. In other words, it assumes that there are true counterfactuals of creaturely freedom here, ones to which Scrooge is miraculously given access. Scrooge himself finally seems aware that this is what has happened after he awakens to discover his room unpillaged:

> "They are not torn down," cried Scrooge, folding one of his bed-curtains in his arms, "they are not torn down, rings and all. They are here—I am here—the shadows of the things that would have been may be dispelled. They will be. I know they will!"[6]

This, Scrooge realizes, is what he has seen—"the shadows of the things that would have been."

In writing this story, then, Dickens is asking his readers to assume that there are truths of this sort which usually remain unknown but which might be revealed to us. In my experience, no one dismisses the story on the grounds that there simply are no such truths which ever could be revealed. The reason, I think, is that most people tacitly assume that there are such conditional truths. And Dickens, I suspect, was relying on this tendency in composing his story; in asking his readers to suppose that a man could be shown "the shadows of the things that would have been," he knew that he was not asking them to suppose anything which most of them would view as impossible.

Consider, by contrast, how different the story would seem were we to say that, there being no true counterfactuals of creaturely freedom, we must as-

---

[6] Ibid., Stave 5, p. 88.

sume the Ghost to be showing Scrooge only what *probably* would have happened had he not reformed. Would not various types of questions then arise
which weaken (if they do not kill) the force of the story? *How* probable, one
might wonder, is it that things would go exactly as Scrooge has been shown?
(As we shall see, the most plausible answer to such a question is surely, "Not
very probable.") Are there other outcomes that are at least nearly as probable
as the one the Ghost has revealed? How can we tell? If there are other near
contenders, might not the outcome for Scrooge be better than in the one
depicted, even if he doesn't change? These and similar questions inevitably
arise the moment we suppose that the Ghost could reveal nothing more than
probabilities. And these questions, it seems to me, inevitably dull the message
of the story. What Dickens is proposing is a story in which the incentive for
Scrooge to change is clear and unequivocal, not one in which the various
excuses for inaction opened by the probabilistic alternative can reasonably be
raised. What he is offering us, then, is a story built on the presumption of
Molinism.[7]

The same, I think, goes for the other Christmas classic mentioned above,
It's a Wonderful Life. George Bailey's despair at the scandal about to break out
at his financial institution leads him to wish that he had never been born.
Clarence, the angel on his wing-earning mission, grants George his wish—or
almost grants it. Like Scrooge's Ghost, Clarence allows George the rare privilege of seeing how things would have been—in this case, of how they would
have been had George never been born. And as George sees, his absence
would have had enormous (and horrendous) consequences for his family, his
friends, his community, and even his nation (George's brother Harry would
never have lived long enough to become a war hero had George not saved
his life when they were boys). Chastened by this vision, George retracts his
wish for nonexistence and is "restored" to life.

It seems evident to me that, in presenting this story in the way he does,
Capra is assuming that his audience will see nothing outlandish in there being
truths of the sort revealed to George (even if the way in which he comes to
see these facts is a tad extraordinary). And, as with Dickens's tale, the force
of the story here depends upon our thinking that what George has discerned
are full-blooded counterfactuals of creaturely freedom.[8] He has seen, not what

---

[7] Strictly speaking, all I have argued for is that Dickens is assuming that his readers will find
nothing odd in there being true counterfactuals of creaturely freedom. One might also reasonably contend, though, that the story supposes Scrooge to be free in the full libertarian sense.
Hence, I think one can make a strong case that Dickens is simply assuming his audience to
be tacit Molinists.

[8] Clearly, many of the truths George is coming to realize (e.g., "If I'd never been born,
Mary would have become a librarian") are counterfactuals of creaturely freedom. Others (e.g.,

did happen, or what could have happened, or what would probably have happened, but what would in fact have happened had he not been born. Dilute the revelation and you dilute the impact that it was intended to have on George and on us.

Let me be clear about what I am claiming here. My point is not that, since artists such as Dickens and Capra produce works presupposing the existence of true counterfactuals of creaturely freedom, we have strong evidence that there are or even could be such truths. Novelists and directors often assume certain things (e.g., time travel) to be actual or possible that we may have solid reason to doubt are either. The point, rather, is that the assumption in these two (and in many other) works of art that there are true counterfactuals of creaturely freedom supports the claim that this element of the Molinist picture is not one that, in the absence of telling objections, should cause the libertarian traditionalist concern, for it is an assumption that seems to be widely shared in everyday life.[9]

So, on the face of it, the libertarian traditionalist need not worry if Molinism is the only game in town. It seems to be a friendly enough game, one in which even nonresidents seem willing to participate.

3. Other Towns, Other Games

It is often (perhaps always) the case that the strengths and weaknesses of a philosophical position are most in evidence when the alternatives to that position are exhibited. So it is, I think, with Molinism. It is only by considering the positive proposals put forth by the opponents of Molinism that we can fully appreciate the advantages which the theory of middle knowledge offers to the orthodox Christian.

Three principal alternatives to the Molinist account of providence will be discussed in the sections that follow. In a sense, this is one more than I would

---

"If I'd never been born, no one would have saved Harry from drowning"), though not themselves counterfactuals of creaturely freedom, would evidently be based on such counterfactuals.

[9] Some of the members of a class on Greek drama I taught recently argued, with very little direction from me, that *Oedipus the King* makes sense only if we assume that there are truths of creaturely freedom (concerning, for example, how various characters would freely respond were they to receive certain prophecies) which the gods make use of in their interactions with humans. None of these college freshmen, I feel sure, had ever heard of Molinism (nor have they now, since I overcame the temptation to inform them), yet this way of dealing with the play seemed natural to them. Whether or not we are to count Sophocles as an incipient Molinist could be debated (as indeed it was in effect debated in this class). Still, an implicitly Molinist interpretation of the sort these students suggested surely does offer us one way of making coherent the puzzling elements of this difficult tragedy.

prefer to discuss. Molinism, as I have stated repeatedly, follows from the conjunction of traditionalism and libertarianism. To concoct an alternative to Molinism, then, one must weaken one or another of these twin pillars. Two of the positions to be considered—the Thomist alternative and the "open" alternative—do precisely this, the former abandoning libertarianism (though upholding traditionalism) while the latter retains libertarianism but jettisons traditionalism. Broadly speaking, *any* alternative to Molinism must be either more or less Thomist or more or less "open." But what I shall call the eternity alternative has generated so much comment and support throughout the history of Christendom that readers might suspect we were ignoring the Molinists' chief competitor were we not to pay it special attention. Hence, though I frankly don't view it as much of a rival to Molinism as a general account of providence, and though I feel confident that any advocates of the eternity alternative, when thoroughly dissected, would prove to be but members of species within either the Thomist or (more likely) the "open" genera, let us begin our canvassing of alternatives with a brief foray into eternity.

4. The Eternity Alternative

As I noted at the start of Chapter 2, one of the problems that has long perplexed orthodox Christians is how to reconcile divine foreknowledge with human freedom. Molinists, as we have seen, appeal to middle knowledge as the surest means of effecting such a reconciliation. But some Christians would view this appeal as unnecessary. What we need to solve our problems, they insist, is merely the recognition that God is eternal.

The notion of eternity involved here is one which has been commonly accepted by the vast majority of Christian philosophers and theologians until quite recently, one that has received considerable attention in recent years.[10] Divine eternity, in Boethius's classic formulation, is "the complete possession all at once of illimitable life."[11] To see God as eternal is to see him as com-

---

[10] Perhaps the most cogent defense of the doctrine in recent years is that offered by Eleonore Stump and Norman Kretzmann in "Eternity," *Journal of Philosophy* 79 (1981), 429–458. Among the many criticisms of the doctrine, the most discussed has been Nicholas Wolterstorff, "God Everlasting," in Steven M. Cahn and David Shatz, eds., *Contemporary Philosophy of Religion* (Oxford: Oxford University Press, 1982), pp. 77–98. For two other excellent discussions of the topic, see Hasker, *God, Time, and Knowledge*, pp. 144–185, and Edward Wierenga, *The Nature of God* (Ithaca: Cornell University Press, 1989), pp. 166–201.

[11] Or so, at least, Stump and Kretzmann translate Boethius's "Aeternitas igitur est interminabilis vitae tota simul et perfecta possessio." See "Eternity," in Thomas V. Morris, ed., *The Concept of God* (Oxford: Oxford University Press, 1987), pp. 219–252. The definition of eternity, which comes from *The Consolation of Philosophy*, book 5, prose 6, is discussed on pp. 220–224.

pletely unlimited by the temporal dimension which to us seems so inexorable
a part of life. As a simple and perfect being, it is argued, God must be totally
free of the kinds of complexity and limitation that time imposes on our lives.
Hence, most significantly in our current context, all that to us is future is to
God eternally present.

To advocate divine eternity is not by itself to challenge the Molinist account
of providence. Molina himself makes no secret of the fact that he views God
as eternal. Divine eternity offers an alternative to Molinism only if one claims
that eternity *by itself* offers us all we need to defend not only the compatibility
of foreknowledge and freedom but also the full traditional notion of providence—that is, only if one contends that, so long as eternity is affirmed,
middle knowledge can be denied by the libertarian traditionalist. It is this
claim that I am calling the eternity alternative.

According to the advocate of this alternative, it is easy to see how God can
know the future, and know it without introducing any such exotic creature
as middle knowledge. For from the perspective of eternity, things which (from
our temporal perspective) will come to exist are already in existence. Hence,
one such as God who has this eternal perspective can simply *see* what will
happen in the future. But to *see* that something will happen is hardly the same
as to *cause* that thing to happen. Hence, an eternal God's foreknowledge is
clearly compatible with the existence of human freedom even in the full-
blooded libertarian sense. And since this compatibility has been demonstrated
without any appeal to middle knowledge, we needn't be Molinists to be
libertarian traditionalists.

Molina and others have raised numerous objections to this alternative.
Many (though not, as noted above, Molina himself) have questioned the truth
and even the coherence of the thesis of divine eternity. Others have denied
that eternity by itself would provide God with the comprehensive foreknowledge his providence demands. For example, as Molina points out, if one is
convinced by Scripture (or, we might add, by the type of everyday intuitions
discussed in section 2 of this chapter) that there are true counterfactuals of
creaturely freedom with false antecedents and consequents, then eternity provides one with no means of accounting for God's knowledge of their truth;
even from his eternal perspective, God cannot see the Keilahites' surrendering
David to Saul if no such temporal event ever occurs.[12] Furthermore, Molina
argues that temporal events cannot be present in eternity before they come
to be in time, and hence that their presence in eternity cannot account for
divine foreknowledge.[13]

---

[12] See Molina, Disputation 49, section 9 (pp. 116–118).
[13] See Molina, Disputation 49, sections 15–20 (pp. 122–127). It seems to me that even

But the central problem with the eternity alternative, one that has been pressed both by friends and by foes of middle knowledge, lies elsewhere. The traditional notion of providence, as we saw, requires more than that God *know* our future; it also demands that he *control* our future. Indeed, as we have seen, the tradition insists that foreknowledge follows from and depends upon God's creative act of will, an act of will which is complete and particular; hence, nothing takes place unless God either specifically wills or specifically permits it to take place. The eternity alternative, though, with its observational metaphor of a passive God who knows our future *only* because his eternal stance permits him to perceive all of time, is clearly at odds with this active God of the tradition. For simply to *see* that something is so is essentially to be acted upon; it is to be influenced in a way that is independent of any free act of one's will. So, if foreknowledge is thought of as just a special kind of perception, it is hard to see how it could depend upon God's free will, or how God's providence could be complete and particular in the way the tradition demands.[14]

The eternity alternative, then, offers little to tempt the libertarian traditionalist. Whether or not she accepts the doctrine of divine eternity, the clear-thinking libertarian traditionalist is bound to concur with Molina that this doctrine "contributes nothing" toward an explication of providence.[15]

5. The Thomist Alternative

As we have just seen, the eternity alternative suffers from what Molinists would see as two fatal flaws. First, by appealing solely to eternity, it seems to leave no room for God to have knowledge of counterfactuals of creaturely freedom, especially those with false antecedents, and thus it unduly limits divine knowledge. Secondly (and consequently), by promoting a perceptual model of divine foreknowledge, it renders God passive and reactive, not the active, truly sovereign Lord which the traditional notion of providence requires.

Those who embrace what we shall call the Thomist alternative agree with

---

Molinists might well question the force of Molina's arguments here. For a discussion of this topic, see Freddoso, "Introduction," pp. 32–34.

[14] For Molinist presentations of this argument, see Molina, Disputation 49, sections 12–13 (pp. 120–122), and Freddoso, "Introduction," pp. 35–36. For an anti-Molinist presentation of much the same argument, see Hasker, *God, Time, and Knowledge*, pp. 53–63. The value of "simple foreknowledge" has been ingeniously (though not, I think, fully successfully) defended by David Hunt, "Divine Providence and Simple Foreknowledge," *Faith and Philosophy* 10 (1993), 394–414.

[15] Molina, Disputation 49, section 15 (p. 123).

Molinists on each of these points.[16] As Thomists see it, though, Molinists are as guilty as are "eternalists" of succumbing to the second of these temptations—that is, of rendering God passive. Insofar as Molinists think of counterfactuals of creaturely freedom as being contingent truths beyond God's control—so long as they think of them as being prevolitional—they fail to take seriously the central Christian tenet that God is in control of all contingent truths, and they thereby render God passive and dependent. As the eminent twentieth-century Thomist Reginald Garrigou-Lagrange put it:

> God's knowledge cannot be determined by anything which is extrinsic to Him, and which would not be caused by Him. But such is the *scientia media*, which depends on the determination of the free conditioned future; for this determination does not come from God but from the human liberty, granted that it is placed in such particular circumstances; so that "it was not in God's power to know any other thing . . . , but if the created free will were to do the opposite, He would have known this other thing," as Molina says in the passage just quoted. Thus God would be dependent on another, would be passive in His knowledge, and would be no longer pure Act. The dilemma is unsolvable: Either God is the first determining Being, or else He is determined by another; there is no other alternative. In other words, the *scientia media* involves an imperfection, which cannot exist in God. Hence there is a certain tinge of anthropomorphism in this theory.
>
> All the aforesaid arguments bring us to this conclusion: there is no determination without a determining cause, and the supreme determining cause is God, otherwise He would be determined by another. But this is nothing else than the principle of causality.[17]

Molinists, of course, would not be without a response here. God's middle knowledge is not determined by us, Molinists would insist, because the truths in question are already known by God logically prior to its being settled by him that we will even exist, and a fortiori prior to our performing any actions at all. Furthermore, there is no imperfection implied by God's knowing but having no control over truths which it is logically impossible that he have

[16] It should not be inferred that all followers of St. Thomas would endorse what we are calling the Thomist alternative; indeed, as will be evident in our discussion, Thomism is no more monolithic a stance than is Molinism. Because of this diversity, some (such as Freddoso) have taken to calling this alternative Bañezian rather than Thomist. In calling the view Thomist, though, I am following what I take to be still the more common practice.

[17] Reginald Garrigou-Lagrange, *The One God*, tr. Dom. Bede Rose (St. Louis: B. Herder, 1944), pp. 465–466. For a similar remark, see the comment to the Blackfriars translation of Aquinas's *Summa theologiae* (New York: McGraw-Hill, 1963), Pt. 1, Q. 22, A. 4, pp. 104–105.

control over, and counterfactuals of creaturely freedom (like necessary truths) are propositions of this sort.

This is not the place, though, to consider the strengths or weaknesses of either the Thomist objections to Molinism or the Molinist responses.[18] Our present concerns, rather, are to see just what the Thomist alternative is and to judge how attractive such an alternative would initially appear to the libertarian traditionalist.

Advocates of this Thomist alternative are as adamant as are Molinists in upholding the traditional notion of providence. Hence, they agree with Molinists that there must be true counterfactuals of creaturely freedom, and that God must be aware of these truths prior to his creative activity.[19] But, as we have seen, Thomists maintain that, if we intend to take seriously such notions as divine sovereignty, nondependence and nonpassivity, we cannot allow such contingent conditionals to be true independent of God's will. And this entails that we have to abandon the notion of middle knowledge, and with it the Molinist distinction between feasible and possible worlds. On the Thomist alternative, *every* possible world is feasible—*every* possible world is such that God could have created it had he chosen to do so.

Where, then, are the counterfactuals of creaturely freedom to be located on this Thomist alternative? Are they part of God's natural knowledge or part of his free knowledge? As I have indicated elsewhere, this is a question to which no straightforward reply can be given.[20] Still, so long as the antecedents of the counterfactuals are not thought of as including that very divine activity which brings about their truth, Thomists clearly are committed to thinking of them as contingent propositions made true by God, and thus as part of his free knowledge.

So, which counterfactuals of creaturely freedom, and consequently which nonconditional future contingents, are true is solely a function of God's will (or, as it is sometimes phrased, of God's decree). For genuine providence to be in place, of course, this decree needs to be prior (logically if not temporally)

---

[18] Thomist objections of the type noted here are evaluated in our consideration of the "grounding" objection in Chapter 5. For other Thomist objections to Molinism, see Chapter 4.

[19] See, for example, Franz Diekamp, *Theologiae dogmaticae manuale*, vol. 1 (Paris: Society of St. John the Evangelist, 1932), p. 204. Interestingly, when discussing his critics such as Bañez (in Disputation 50 of the *Concordia*) and Zumel (in Disputation 53), Molina seems to take it for granted that even his opponents will want to agree that there are true counterfactuals of creaturely freedom of which God is aware. For further discussion of this point, see Chapter 2, section 2.

[20] See my "Two Accounts of Providence," in Thomas V. Morris, ed., *Divine and Human Action* (Ithaca: Cornell University Press, 1988), pp. 147–181, especially pp. 163–168.

to the truths which it determines. Hence, these truths are properly said to be *predetermined* by God.

Now, with respect to an actual free action, one might think that, from the Thomist perspective, the effect of God's predetermining decree would be a deterministic causal chain involving other created agents and/or prior events which together lead via a necessity of nature to the action in question. For example, one might think that God brings about Cuthbert's buying the iguana by arranging for Cuthbert to be in circumstances which, given the laws of biology, psychology, and the like, render it naturally impossible that he not buy the iguana.

Most advocates of the Thomist alternative, though, would reject such a picture, for they deny that Cuthbert would be free if his actions were determined in the way delineated above.[21] Rather, they say, the effect of God's eternal determining decree is some *concurrent* divine activity which determines the creaturely action. Hence, in the case of Cuthbert, if he is genuinely free with respect to buying the iguana, then none of the circumstances obtaining temporally prior to his action, and none of the activities of other secondary causes at the time of Cuthbert's action, determine it. Rather, the action is determined by God's concurrent activity—his activity *at the time* when Cuthbert acts.[22] Given temporally prior circumstances, it was possible for Cuthbert to refrain from buying the iguana; given God's concurrent activity, though, such refraining isn't possible. For God's concurrence in such a case is *intrinsically* efficacious. That is, it is not up to Cuthbert to decide whether or not such concurrence is to be efficacious or not, for that would simply return us to the picture of a God who is not *really* in control, the picture which advocates of the Thomist alternative are trying to escape.

It is tempting here to simplify the Thomist alternative by reading it as claiming that contingent truths such as the one about Cuthbert are true because God, via his concurrent activity, directly causes them to be true. While this simplification works well enough with respect to virtuous actions (or morally neutral ones, if such there be), Thomists would reject it in the case of evil. If God is perfectly good, then we cannot have him directly causing

---

[21] See Theodore J. Kondoleon, "The Free Will Defense: New and Old," *The Thomist* 46 (1983), 19. For similar remarks, see Garrigou-Lagrange, *One God*, pp. 465 and 470; see also the remarks in the commentary to Aquinas's *Summa theologiae* cited above. For a Thomist whose position on freedom is much closer to that of contemporary compatibilists, see Thomas Loughran, "Theological Compatibilism" (Ph.D. diss., University of Notre Dame, 1986).

[22] It is worth emphasizing here that virtually all Thomists think of God's *action*, properly speaking, as one, simple, and eternal. What we are referring to as God's concurrent activity and viewing as the determinant of Cuthbert's action should really be thought of as the effect in time of this one timeless divine act.

evil, especially the morally evil actions which his free beings all too often perform. Evil is *permitted* but not *intended* by God; hence, we cannot have him predetermining it via intrinsically efficacious concurrent activity.

But then, how, on the Thomist alternative, *does* God exercise providential control over evil actions, and how does he have foreknowledge of them? The core of the Thomist answer seems to be: by not concurring efficaciously with the relevant *good* actions which the agent refrains from performing. Take Cuthbert once again, and consider the action of treating his newly-purchased iguana properly. Suppose we grant that such an action would be good, indeed even morally good. Suppose furthermore that God decides that he will not perform that concurrent activity that would lead necessarily to this action's being performed. What God knows, then, is that this good action will not take place. Instead, the evil action of Cuthbert's mistreating his iguana will cast its ugly shadow on the aggrieved earth. But it will not be an evil action which *God* has caused; Cuthbert is the sole malefactor in this baleful tale. Knowing that he would not concurrently effect any good action in this case, God of course knew from eternity that Cuthbert would mistreat the iguana; furthermore, since he could have efficaciously willed that Cuthbert treat the iguana well, Cuthbert's sin does not occur beyond God's providential reach. Still, since the causal impetus here is from Cuthbert, not from God, the sin and the blame rest solely on the creature, not on the creator.

What holds for Cuthbert holds, of course, for any other creature as well. Since whether or not to concur efficaciously with any particular good action is completely up to God, and since he knows that the good action will not take place if he doesn't so concur, God can have both control over and foreknowledge of both good and evil events, even though he causes only the former. It is in this way that, according to the Thomist alternative, the traditional notion of providence can be maintained in the absence of middle knowledge.[23]

It seems evident that this Thomist alternative offers the libertarian traditionalist all she could ever want as far as the notion of providence goes; a God of the Thomist description is clearly in a position to exercise the universal and loving sovereignty which the tradition views as nonnegotiable. However, it seems just as evident that the libertarian traditionalist will be repulsed by the conception of human freedom presupposed by the Thomist alternative. True, the Thomist does not try to suggest that actions can be free even when they are causally necessitated by temporally prior events; against this familiar type of compatibilism, Thomists and Molinists are united. But the picture of

---

[23] For a fuller explication of the Thomist alternative, see my "Two Accounts of Providence," pp. 162–170.

freedom embraced by the Thomist seems scarcely preferable from a libertarian perspective. For what is central to an action's being free, says the libertarian, is that the causal activity of *all* other agents up to *and at* the time of the action be compatible both with the agent's freely performing the act and with the agent's refraining from performing the act. As we saw in Chapter 1, there are powerful (though admittedly nondemonstrative) arguments in favor or such a conception of freedom. Since the Thomist alternative patently rejects this conception, it is an alternative which could have little appeal to the libertarian traditionalist.

Of course, advocates of the Thomist alternative might try to make it more appealing. For example, they might try to argue that, even on the Thomist account, we can say that a free agent has the ability to do otherwise. Let *EC* be God's intrinsically efficacious concurrence with my morally good action *A*. Then, the Thomist will say,

$$\Box(\text{If } EC, \text{ then } A)$$

is indeed true. But the necessity here is a necessity only of the *consequence* (i.e., only in the *composed* sense). It is not a necessity of the *consequent* (i.e., it is not a necessity in the *divided* sense). For

$$\text{If } EC, \text{ then } \Box A$$

is not true. But then, the Thomist would continue, the freedom of the agent is not compromised. Since *A* itself is not necessary, I could indeed have done other than *A*, for I would have done other than *A* if I had willed to do other than *A*; and I would have willed to do other than *A* had God not efficaciously concurred with my doing *A*. Hence, I could indeed have done otherwise.[24] And this freedom to do otherwise holds in the case of evil actions as well as in the case of virtuous ones. As Garrigou-Lagrange puts it:

> The sinner, to be sure, in the very moment of sinning, can avoid committing the sin, and God eternally willed that it be really possible for the sinner to avoid committing the sin, and this is known as God's antecedent will. But God did not efficaciously will that this sinner right at this moment should *de facto* avoid committing sin; and if God had efficaciously willed it, this sinner *de facto* not only really could avoid sin, but would avoid it.[25]

---

[24] Molina occasionally misrepresents the position of his Thomist opponents insofar as he implies that they see God's concurrence as eliminating an agent's *ability* to do otherwise. See, for example, Disputation 53, part 2, section 6, paragraph 2 (p. 215).

[25] Garrigou-Lagrange, *One God*, p. 469.

As the Molinist sees it, though, this Thomist defense is blatantly a failure, one redolent of the perplexities into which contemporary compatibilists have been led in their fruitless efforts to offer conditional analyses of "could have done otherwise."[26] Molina offers an expected libertarian response to the type of argument Garrigou-Lagrange presents, a response which ends with a particularly fitting metaphor:

> Now to say that it is *in the divided sense* that the faculty of choice retains the power not to elicit a nonevil act and not to sin, since (i) if God had not predetermined to confer efficacious concurrence, then the faculty of choice would not elicit a nonevil act, and since (ii) if He were to confer a concurrence that is efficacious for a nonevil act, then the faculty of choice would not sin—to say this is clearly not to establish that there is freedom in the *created* faculty of choice, but only to establish that there is freedom in *God* to move or not to move the faculty of choice toward a nonevil act, and to restrain it or not to restrain it from sinning, just as, when a beast of burden is being led in one direction or another by a halter, the freedom is not in the *beast*, but is instead in the *human being* who is leading the beast in the one direction or the other.[27]

While the evident renunciation of libertarianism is the element of the Thomist alternative that makes it least attractive from the perspective of the libertarian traditionalist, there are other problems with this alternative as well. A major one, as Molina recognized, is the attempt of his Thomist rivals to handle evil. As we saw, the Thomist suggestion seems to be that divine control over and foreknowledge of evil actions (such as Cuthbert's mistreating his iguana) can be retained, and retained without making God morally responsible for those actions, if we insist that God's deciding not to concur with the relevant good actions (such as Cuthbert's treating his iguana with kid gloves) entails the performance of the evil action. Molina sees at least four problems with such a suggestion.

First, argues Molina, the Thomist alternative is insufficient for God to have the detailed and complete foreknowledge and control that the traditional notion of providence proclaims. For, as Molina puts it,

> even if from the fact that God did not determine a created will to act well it followed with certainty that it would sin, God would still not be certain about whether it was going to sin by a sin of omission or of commission, or about whether it was going to use this means rather than that means in the act of

[26] For an excellent discussion of such attempts, see Peter van Inwagen, *An Essay on Free Will* (Oxford: Oxford University Press, 1983), pp. 114–126.

[27] Disputation 53, part 2, section 6 (p. 217).

sinning, or about whether it was going to sin with more or less intensity and effort, or about whether it was going to continue in the act of sinning for a longer or shorter time, and so on.[28]

There are avenues down which the Thomist might venture in attempting to meet this objection, but none of these routes makes for easy traveling. For example, as Molina notes, some Thomists suggest that every free creature, if not led by God to perform a good action, will naturally perform every evil action that it can, presumably with as much intensity as it can; in short, it will be as bad as it can be. Molina reasonably responds to this by saying that he doesn't see how creatures in such a situation could be free, whether what they did was good or evil. If the act is good, it is caused by God's concurrent activity; if it is evil, it results from a necessity of nature which God decides not to impede, a necessity which means that the act in question was not one the agent was truly able to avoid and hence was not clearly even sinful. Indeed, as Molina notes, the sin here seems in real danger of being transferred from the creature to the creator:

> In fact, I do not understand why our sins would not have to be attributed to God as the author of nature who has conferred upon the created faculty of choice a propensity toward those sins. For just as (i) the acts and effects of those agents that act by a necessity of nature are attributed to God because of the propensities and powers that He confers upon them, and just as (ii) for this reason the works of nature are called by philosophers the works of intelligence and hence of God, so too our sinful acts would have to be attributed to God as the author of nature who instills in the created faculty of choice this propensity toward committing sins.[29]

Though seeking a means of making God blameless for sin, then, the Thomists appear to have done just the opposite.[30]

Molina's second objection to the Thomists' account of evil focuses on the fact that some evil actions (for example, "advancing on the enemy and scaling the walls when the war is unjust and there is much danger and strong natural fear") are very difficult for the agent to perform, while some good actions ("for example, willing to go to sleep or to eat when one is able to do so without sinning and when both things are pleasurable; having sexual intercourse with one's wife; willing to go for a walk or to play for the sake of

---

[28] Disputation 50, section 13 (p. 139).

[29] Disputation 53, part 2, section 6 (pp. 216–217).

[30] For further discussion of this Molinist objection to the Thomist account of evil, see Freddoso, "Introduction," pp. 39–40.

reviving of one's spirits; and doing many other similar things") are "not difficult but rather delightful and pleasurable."[31] If the Thomist is going to say that the former "tough but evil" actions can be performed by the agent "on his own" (i.e., without the need for intrinsically efficacious divine concurrent activity), then isn't it a bit silly to say that the latter "easy and good" actions require such concurrence, and would be resisted by the agent in its absence?

A third Molinist objection is closely related to the second. One and the same act, Molina says, can be sinful or virtuous depending upon the occurrence or nonoccurrence of some prior event which plays no causal role at the time of the act itself. Molina uses an act of sexual intercourse as his example. If preceded by a wedding, the act can be virtuous; if not so preceded, the very same act can be vicious. Isn't it ridiculous, says Molina, to suggest that, in the absence of a marriage contract, the act can be performed on my own, whereas if the vows have been properly exchanged, I couldn't possibly go through with the act without God's concurrent nudge? Marriage is sometimes alleged eventually to have a dampening effect on sexual activity, but (implies Molina) no one can take seriously the implication of the Thomist position that it has so massive and immediate an effect on a couple's coital endeavors.[32]

Finally, Molina notes, sin is committed (on the Thomist account) if and only if God freely decides to withhold from the sinner that intrinsically efficacious concurrent activity which would have resulted in a good action's being performed. But then, asks Molina, how can the Thomist maintain that God intends that, say, Cuthbert not mistreat his iguana when he withholds from Cuthbert a *necessary condition* of his not sinning? How can God fault Cuthbert for sinning if God decides not to grant him that very assistance without which sinning is inevitable?

Molina uses the story of Jesus's words concerning the Tyronians and Sidonians to illustrate his point. Matthew 11:20–22 reads:

> Then he began to reproach the cities in which most of his deeds of power had been done, because they did not repent. "Woe to you, Chorazin! Woe to you, Bethsaida! For if the deeds of power done in you had been done in Tyre and Sidon, they would have repented long ago in sackcloth and ashes. But I tell you, on the day of judgment it will be more tolerable for Tyre and Sidon than for you.

As Molina notes, since the Tyronians and Sidonians *would* have repented had the wonders in question been performed there, whereas these wonders *didn't*

---

[31] Molina, Disputation 53, part 2, section 12 (p. 220).
[32] Molina, Disputation 53, part 2, section 13 (pp. 221–222).

lead to repentance in Chorazin and Bethsaida, it follows that the wonders themselves did not include intrinsically efficacious divine concurrent activity. But then, argues Molina, the Thomists can't take Jesus's words as straightforwardly true. Let M stand for the miracles worked in Chorazin and Bethsaida. The Thomist can accept

$$M \rightarrow \text{The Tyronians repent}$$

only if they think that there is some efficacious concurrence (call it EC) which God would have *in addition* conferred upon the Tyronians such that

$$(M \ \& \ EC) \Rightarrow \text{The Tyronians repent.}$$

But this, suggests Molina, is not only to "weaken and distort" the words of Christ, but also to make his clear criticism of the inhabitants of Chorazin and Bethsaida difficult to justify:

> For if, on the hypothesis that *those very wonders* should have been worked in Tyre and Sidon, the Tyronians and Sidonians would not have been converted unless God had, *in addition*, predetermined to confer on them some *other* assistance, intrinsically efficacious, which was not in fact conferred on them and with which the people of Chorozain and Bethsaida would have been converted had it likewise been predetermined for them—if this is so, then, I ask, what is it that Christ is reproaching the people of Chorozain and Bethsaida for, given that (i) the Tyronians and Sidonians need no less assistance than those people need in order to be converted, and given that (ii), according to the position of these doctors, both groups, taken in themselves, are equally likely to be converted or not to be converted, and given that (iii) their being converted or not being converted depends no more on the free choice of the one group than on that of the other?[33]

In other words, the Thomists have put themselves in the uncomfortable position of implying that, if anyone is to be upbraided for the absence of con-

[33] Disputation 53, part 1, section 7 (pp. 202–203).

version in Chorazin and Bethsaida, it isn't the inhabitants of those towns.[34] Hence, were God to punish those inhabitants, his act would manifest, not justice, but "cruelty and wickedness."[35]

There is, of course, more that could be said both in promoting these Molinist objections and in offering Thomist responses to them.[36] But it should be evident at this point that the advocate of the Thomist alternative will not have an easy job finding an acceptable means of dealing with evil. And it should be equally evident that most (though not all) of these problems are not ones which beset the Molinist approach. If the Thomist alternative seemed promising initially, one might be excused for trying to find some means of handling these objections concerning evil. But, as we saw, at least from the stance of the libertarian traditionalist, the Thomist alternative seemed bogus from the start. For such a Christian, then, there is ultimately little in this alternative to recommend it.

---

[34] Thomists might be tempted to employ a *tu quoque* argument against the Molinist at this point. For on the Molinist account, God allows certain evils to take place, and perhaps even allows some people to be damned. Is it at all plausible to think that there is never any way in which God could have prevented those evils, or saved those who are damned? Isn't it plausible for the Molinist to agree, for example, that there is something God could have done, some way in which he could have altered the circumstances in which Cuthbert was placed, such that, had God so acted, Cuthbert wouldn't have mistreated his iguana (assuming he did mistreat it)? If the Thomists' God is to be condemned for withholding his intrinsically efficacious concurrence from Cuthbert, why is not the Molinists' God equally blameworthy for not putting Cuthbert in these altered circumstances?

This objection is a powerful one and should serve to remind us that the presence and extent of evil in the world cannot easily (if at all) be explained by any Christian. Still, it does seem to me that the Molinist has a couple of cards up her sleeve which are not available to the advocate of the Thomist alternative. For example, she can point out that, on her construal of the case, *no* necessary condition of Cuthbert's treating his iguana properly was left absent by God; hence, Cuthbert can more appropriately be held accountable for his action. Furthermore, even if there *were* circumstances actualizable by God in which Cuthbert's free behavior toward his iguana would be impeccable (and, of course, there might *not* be any such circumstances), God might still have good reason not to bring about those circumstances. For example, he might see via his middle knowledge that the negative long-term consequences of his so acting (including the subsequent free actions of Cuthbert and of others) would outweigh the evils involved in Cuthbert's mistreating his iguana.

[35] Molina, Disputation 50, section 14 (p. 139).

[36] One of the more curious Thomist responses has been to suggest that their position *is* a bit perplexing, but that this is all but to be expected when one is dealing with a God so far beyond our abilities to fathom. Garrigou-Lagrange, in offering this response, penned such memorable lines as "There is, indeed, a mystery in this, but we now disclose the element of clarity in this light-transcending obscurity" and "Therefore, if in these conclusions there is obscurity, this is owing to God's incomprehensibility and His intimate action on our free will." See *One God*, pp. 469 and 470–471.

6. The "Open" Alternative

A number of contemporary philosophers and theologians would concur with our rejection of the eternity and Thomist alternatives, yet find the Molinist position unacceptable (for reasons we will discuss in Chapters 5 through 7). As these Christians see it, the Thomist alternative fails because libertarianism is true, while the Molinist account fails because middle knowledge is, given the truth of libertarianism, impossible. What we must do then, they say, is construct a picture of divine providence which sees God as creating beings who are free in the full libertarian sense, yet performing his creative activities without the guidance which the Molinists allege middle knowledge would provide him. Since this picture is part of a larger project of fashioning a picture of God which its advocates refer to as the open view of God, I shall call the account of providence they offer as an alternative to Molinism the "open" alternative.[37]

The overall picture of God which the devotees of openness (or, as we shall call them, the *openists*) offer is one which not only weakens the traditional notion of providence in the ways which will be discussed shortly, but also significantly alters the traditional concept of God by renouncing such divine attributes as simplicity, eternality, immutability, and impassibility. It is not, one would think, a picture which is likely to engender love at first sight among libertarian traditionalists. Furthermore, one can reasonably question

[37] The most extensive presentation and defense of the "open" view is offered in Clark Pinnock, Richard Rice, John Sanders, William Hasker, and David Basinger, eds., *The Openness of God* (Downers Grove, Ill.: InterVarsity Press, 1994); see also Hasker, *God, Time, and Knowledge*, pp. 186–205. One should also note that many other philosophers and theologians have embraced at least elements of the "open" view. For example, universal divine foreknowledge has been denied (implicitly if not explicitly) by such illustrious contemporaries as Peter Geach, *Providence and Evil* (Cambridge: Cambridge University Press, 1977), chap. 2, especially pp. 44–54, and Richard Swinburne, *The Coherence of Theism*, rev. ed. (Oxford: Clarendon Press, 1993), pp. 167–183, while Peter van Inwagen, "The Place of Chance in a World Sustained by God," in Morris, *Divine and Human Action*, pp. 211–235, rejects the type of specific sovereignty which the advocates of openness also find oppressive.

In calling this position the "open" alternative, I have resisted the temptation to give it other names that Molinists and Thomists might find more appropriate. Harry Boer, *An Ember Still Glowing: Humankind in the Image of God* (Grand Rapids, Mich.: Eerdmans, 1990), chap. 8, refers to a risk-taking God of the sort under discussion here as an ad hoc God; hence, one might have christened this position the *ad hoc* alternative. Another possibility, raised by Garrigou-Lagrange's note (*One God*, p. 450) that Cicero denied universal divine foreknowledge, would be to call this view the *Ciceronian*, or perhaps even the *Classical pagan*, alternative. Though the latter moniker would have been a tad ironic, charity and reason have prevailed.

both the reasoning behind and the precise shape of the radical transformations in the notion of divinity which the advocates of openness propose.[38] But our concern here is not with this picture as a whole, but rather with the alternative account of divine providence that it offers. What is this alternative, and how is the libertarian traditionalist likely to react to it?

As I see it, there are three major components to the picture of providence contained in the "open" alternative. First, because he lacks middle knowledge but has decided to create some beings who do not always behave deterministically, God lacks comprehensive knowledge of the future. Second, even in the absence of middle knowledge, God can know how his free creatures will probably act if placed in various situations, and God's providential activity is guided by his knowledge of these probabilities. And third, though God's knowledge and power give him a great deal of control over his world, this control is limited by his uncertainty as to how his creatures will freely react to his initiatives; hence, God needs to take risks in his governance of the world. Let us consider these three elements in turn.

According to the "open" alternative, God's knowledge of the future is

---

[38] For trenchant criticisms of the view, see Herbert McCabe, "The Involvement of God," *New Blackfriars* 66 (1985), 464–476, and especially Alfred J. Freddoso, "The 'Openness' of God: A Reply to Hasker," *Christian Scholar's Review*, forthcoming. Though I would slightly differ from McCabe and Freddoso in some of their criticisms, the main lines of their approaches seem right on target to me. Indeed, in one respect, they might not go far enough. As Freddoso notes, the openists, in their program of "dehellenization," put so much emphasis on their intuitions concerning divine perfection that it is unclear why their divergence from the tradition is not even more extreme. For example, asks Freddoso, why not dismiss immateriality as yet another of those Hellenic imports which modern Christians can and should turn away from their borders, especially given the advocacy within the openness camp for a God with a rich emotional life, for is it not more consonant with our experience to see such passions as at least requiring a physical base? But why, I wonder, should the proponents of openness stop there? Why not question the very concept of divine moral perfection itself? According to Hasker, it is "part of our conception of God that God is deserving of absolute, unreserved and unconditional worship and devotion" (*Openness of God*, p. 131), and such a conception, as he sees it, requires moral perfection of God. But couldn't it seem to some openists that we can never have this attitude of worship and devotion to a being whom we see as so very different from us as never to have sinned? Might it not seem that our allegiance could be greater to a God who, like us, sometimes succumbed to temptation, but who regularly repented and resumed the path of virtue? Might it not seem that our personal relationship could be stronger with a being of this sort than with one who was personally untouched by sinning? (Which of us mere humans do we normally think makes the better spiritual advisor—one who has been immersed in evildoing but overcome it, or one who has never been so tested at all?) Indeed, might it not seem that a God of this description fits in more easily with many biblical passages? It would seem that the advocates of openness have not taken sufficient note of the fact (suggested by McCabe; see pp. 467–468) that the road through Athens is not the only path to idolatry.

limited by the fact that he has created some beings whose behavior is not simply a function of prior states of the universe and natural laws. Of greatest interest here, of course, are free creatures. On the "open" alternative, God lacks knowledge (or at least lacks certainty) concerning what any of his free creatures will freely do in the future. Rather than foreseeing what a free being will do, God finds out at more or less the same time that the rest of us do.

Why do openists deny universal foreknowledge? William Hasker, perhaps the most prominent advocate of the "open" alternative, has presented a long and complicated argument attempting to show that creaturely freedom is incompatible with divine foreknowledge.[39] But despite the success or failure of this argument—and the Molinist can, I think, offer strong reasons for thinking it fails[40]—it should come as no surprise to see the openist arguing for this conclusion. For how, we might well ask, *could* God foresee what I will freely do if he doesn't predetermine my action (as the Thomist alternative suggests), doesn't know a counterfactual of creaturely freedom about me the antecedent of which he knows will be true (as Molinists insist), and doesn't simply look out from his aerie in eternity at the goings-on in the mundane temporal realm (as the eternity alternative proposes)? If one wishes to defend libertarianism yet deny middle knowledge, one can retain the picture of God as an active providential sovereign only if one is willing to concede that God lacks universal foreknowledge.

As many openists see it, though, this "concession" is a fairly minor one because of the second element noted above—God's knowledge of probabilities. Though openists reject middle knowledge, they see no reason to deny God knowledge of "would probably" conditionals. That is, for any situation in which one of God's free creatures might be placed, and for any action that creature might perform in that situation, God knows the probability of the creature's performing that action in that situation. Graced with this extensive knowledge concerning behavioral proclivities, God is hardly flying blind in interacting with his creatures. Knowing, for example, that Cuthbert would likely purchase the iguana if placed in situation C, and knowing full well the probable consequences of this purchase, God is well situated to influence events in ways that he sees will probably be beneficial for Cuthbert and the others involved.

But the "probably" is crucial here, and leads us to the third element of the

---

[39] See Hasker, *God, Time, and Knowledge*, pp. 64–143. For an earlier (and simpler) version of his argument, see his "Foreknowledge and Necessity," *Faith and Philosophy* 2 (1985), 121–157.

[40] See my "In Defense of Theological Compatibilism," *Faith and Philosophy* 8 (1991), 237–243.

"open" alternative. For, alas, improbable things do happen. God might place me in a situation in which he knows it is likely that I will act in a certain way, only to find me acting in a very different way instead, a way that does not fit in as well with his providential aims. Even with all the probabilistic evidence which is possible fully available to him, God is still taking risks, is still placing bets, with his actions, and there is no guarantee (as there is under the Thomist or Molinist accounts) that his wagering will succeed. As Hasker puts it: "God knows an immense amount about each one of us—far more, in fact, than we know about ourselves—but he does not, because he cannot, plan his actions toward us on the basis of a prior knowledge of how we will respond. And this means that God is a risk-taker; in expressing his love toward us, he opens himself up to the real possibility of failure and disappointment."[41]

Though all openists acknowledge this aspect of their picture of providence, some do it rather reluctantly, wishing that the image of God the gambler—or, as I once put it, of God as "the bookie than which none greater can be conceived"[42]—were not incumbent upon them.[43] Yet not all openists are hesitant in embracing this element of their picture of providence. William Hasker, for example, thinks the fact that God must take risks is actually an advantage to the "open" alternative. In other words, if we were given the choice as to whether our God was to be a risk-taker or one who needn't take risks, we should prefer the former. Hasker offers three reasons in defense of this preference:

> Those who admire risk taking and experimentalism in human life may feel that the richness of God's life is diminished if we deny these attributes to him. And, on the other hand, the significance and value of human creativity may seem diminished if our most ennobling achievements are just the expected printouts from the divine programming. But perhaps the most serious difficulty here is one that also plagues Calvinistic doctrines of predestination: If we accentuate God's absolute control over everything that happens, we are forced to attribute to him the same control over evil events and actions as over good. On the theory of middle knowledge we can *never* say that some act of God's failed of its intended purpose, no matter how disastrous the outcome may be. We cannot avoid saying, then, that God specifically chose for Hitler to become leader of the Third Reich and instigator of the Holocaust.[44]

[41] William Hasker, "A Philosophical Perspective," in *Openness of God*, p. 151.

[42] See my "Hasker's *God, Time, and Knowledge*," *Philosophical Studies* 60 (1990), 114.

[43] One proponent of this "reluctant openist" stance is David Hunt. As he once put it in conversation, though he is deeply skeptical of the Molinist account, he is rooting for it from the sidelines, for he prefers the risk-free God which Molinism endorses to the risk-taking deity to which the openists are committed.

[44] Hasker, *God, Time, and Knowledge*, pp. 199–200.

Hence, Hasker concludes, openists ought not blush when acknowledging their God to be a risk-taker, for such a conception of divinity is "not only *acceptable*" but "clearly *preferable*" to the Molinist or Thomist alternatives.[45]

How is the libertarian traditionalist likely to respond to the alternative the openists offer? As a libertarian, she will see nothing to question, since openists are openly and staunchly defenders of the picture of freedom she cherishes. But as a traditionalist, she is unlikely to be similarly pleased. For the "open" alternative clearly and unabashedly constitutes a rejection of the strong notion of providence she is endeavoring to defend. Her wish was to reconcile providence and freedom—real, red-blooded providence and genuine, true-blue freedom. As she will no doubt see it, openists are suggesting that she achieve a reconciliation (of sorts) by retaining a vibrant picture of freedom but diluting the notion of providence into a pale, washed-out imitation of the genuine article. Needless to say, this is not a proposal she is likely to find attractive.

Most openists concede that their position is in opposition to the tradition, yet insist that the advantages it offers us more than offset its lack of famous historical advocates.[46] But are the three major elements of the "open" alternative which we have identified really advantageous from the perspective of the orthodox Christian? Even were she open to a view that abandons so much of her intellectual heritage, would the three parts of this proposal in fact open the door to genuine enlightenment, or only to greater problems?

---

[45] Ibid., p. 205.

[46] Hasker, acknowledging that some find the openists' picture of providence "disturbingly unorthodox," concedes, "I have some sympathy with that reaction; the view is not one I have adopted easily or without prolonged reflection. . . . [In saying] that God has only limited knowledge of the future, I find myself in a minority position which runs counter to a great deal of the theological tradition. At that point, I must simply admit that the tradition, while invaluable as a guide, is not infallible and cannot always be followed in every detail" ("Response to Thomas Flint," *Philosophical Studies* 60 (1990), 123). It is interesting to note that the "open" alternative is so much a "minority position" in the overall history of the Church that Molina never even considers it as a rival to his own. When discussing Wisdom 4:11 ("They were caught up so that evil might not change their understanding or guile deceive their souls"), which appears to assume God's possession of middle knowledge, Molina considers the possibility of an opponent's reading such passages as including tacit "perhaps" clauses ("or guile *perhaps* deceive their souls"), but asks, "Is there anyone who would not recognize that such a reading of the text is forced, exotic and absurd?" (Disputation 49, section 10, p. 119). Later, he argues that, without middle knowledge, God would be unable to arrange things so that his plan would be fulfilled, but instead would "find out from their existence" how things had turned out; but to say this, Molina insists, "is plainly the height of absurdity and impiety, and should be so judged" (Disputation 49, section 13, p. 122). Obviously, the "open" alternative was so foreign to the intellectual climate of Molina's time that he thought we needn't take it seriously. Similar judgments, I suspect, would have been passed by most of those defenders of the tradition noted in Chapter 1.

Consider the first of the three elements of the "open" alternative—the denial of divine foreknowledge. The biggest problem the openist faces here is how to square this denial with the reality of prophecy. Scripture abounds with passages where God seems to reveal events (for example, Peter's denial of Christ) before they occur. How could such revelations be made if, as the openists insist, God is uncertain concerning his creatures' future free actions?

As Hasker sees it, "The difficulty is real but not insuperable."[47] He proposes three ways of dealing with apparent biblical prophecies. First, he says, some prophecies are implicitly conditional. Hasker's example of choice is Jeremiah 18:7–10:

> At one moment I may declare concerning a nation or a kingdom, that I will pluck up and break down and destroy it, but if that nation, concerning which I have spoken, turns from its evil, I will change my mind about the disaster that I intended to bring on it. And at another moment I may declare concerning a nation or a kingdom that I will build and plant it, but if it does evil in my sight, not listening to my voice, then I will change my mind about the good that I had intended to do to it.

As Hasker sees it, this passage implies that "prophecies are to be interpreted as conditional *even when this is not explicitly stated*."[48] Since issuing such a prophecy ("If you don't repent, I will bring disaster upon you") presupposes no detailed, nonconditional knowledge concerning how things will go in the future, prophecies of this sort are fully compatible with the openists' position on foreknowledge.

Second, suggests Hasker, some prophecies are based on existing trends and tendencies. Such prophecies, like those of the first category, are also implicitly conditional; they all assert that such-and-such will happen *if* present trends continue, where the "if" clause is generally left unstated.[49] So, for example, Jesus' prediction that Peter would deny him three times was based on God's knowledge of Peter's character, a character that made it likely that Peter would deny Christ in the circumstances which God saw were likely to occur.

Finally, as Hasker sees it, some prophecies are genuinely nonconditional, but of events that God can foresee because he intends to bring them about by himself. Perhaps, for example, God's decision to send his Son into the

---

[47] Hasker, *God, Time, and Knowledge*, p. 194.

[48] Ibid.

[49] For what it's worth, it seems to me that Hasker's second way of understanding prophecy is better thought of as simply a subcategory of his first way; some prophecies are implicitly conditional, and sometimes what they are conditional upon is the continuation of present trends and tendencies.

world was not conditional upon any of his creatures' actions. If so, he can make the prophecy because he knows of his own unswerving intention.

Though this three-pronged strategy of dealing with prophecy is ingenious and has much to offer us, whether or not we end up siding with the openists, few orthodox Christians will find it fully satisfactory. For example, in the case of Peter, how likely was it that Peter was going to end up in those circumstances in which he did in fact deny Jesus? It doesn't seem to me that the odds, even knowing the characters of Peter and of everyone else involved, would be particularly high. So one does have to wonder whether a God with only knowledge of tendencies (with only, as we might call it, *trendy* knowledge) would have ventured such a prediction. Furthermore, isn't it fairly clear that the evangelists included this story in the gospels because they saw it as a case of Jesus' making a prediction that conceivably could have been *wrong*, but in fact was confirmed by subsequent events, a confirmation that should have an impact on our faith as much as on Peter's? On Hasker's reading, there is no way in which later happenings could have either confirmed or disconfirmed the prophecy, for Jesus could have been right about the trends *at the time he was speaking* even if *later* tendencies were different. Yet if we do read the prophecy in the nonconditional way the writers of the gospel surely intended it, then doesn't Hasker have to say that Jesus' prediction might have been mistaken? And wouldn't such a claim be rather demeaning of the Word of God?[50]

There are also problems of internal consistency with Hasker's handling of prophecy. How, we might ask, can God make nonconditional predictions about what he *will* do based on his current intentions? After all, if one is an openist, why think that God cannot change his intentions? We surely change our minds in the light of new information; why think that God, who is (according to the openists) receiving new information all the time, wouldn't do the same? In fact, wouldn't an openist most naturally see the quotation from Jeremiah given above (not to mention the story of Jonah) as clear Scriptural evidence that God *does* change his mind, evidence we need no longer resist now that we have overcome the outdated Hellenic predilection for constancy over change?

Perhaps some openists would respond that, as they see it, *all* of God's

---

[50] Some might respond that it wouldn't be demeaning. After all, Jesus has two natures, human and divine; it is possible that some predictions are made solely by (so to speak) his human side, and hence are liable to error. A full examination of these issues would take us deeply into questions concerning Christology and biblical interpretation, questions which lie far beyond the scope of this book. For what it is worth, though, my hunch is that only a small minority of orthodox Christians would feel content with the suggestion that Jesus' prophecy concerning Peter might have been mistaken.

intentions are conditional—he intends to do this if that happens. If so, they might say, there would be no reason for him to change these intentions in the light of further information. But such a response seems inadequate. For if *all* of God's intentions are conditional, how could he ever make any predictions (as openists such as Hasker want to say he sometimes does) which are nonconditional? Furthermore, what exactly would preclude God's changing his conditional intentions? Don't we humans, to the extent that we form such intentions at all, often re-form them without incurring moral censure? Once we have been liberated from the Greeks' love of the static, why deny that God could similarly rethink things?

So it seems to me that prophecy remains a genuine embarrassment for the openists. Furthermore, it is worth noting that Scripture often seems to imply divine foreknowledge of free human actions even in cases where *no* prophecy is involved. For example, John 6:64, explaining Jesus' saying "The words that I have spoken to you are spirit and life. But among you there are some who do not believe," states: "For Jesus knew from the first who were the ones that did not believe, and who was the one that would betray him." Openists, it would seem, can grant only that Jesus, on the basis of his trendy knowledge, had a good guess as to who would hand him over.[51] Yet to say that this is all that John is affirming is surely to offer a strained reading of the passage.

The openists' rejection of foreknowledge, then, is a very problematic part of their position, one which makes dealing with biblical prophecy difficult if not impossible. Far from rejoicing in the denial of God's universal knowledge of the future, the orthodox Christian, it seems to me, could make such a denial (even if it were her sole live alternative) only with the greatest of reluctance.[52]

Similarly unappealing, I think, would be the second element of the "open" alternative, the suggestion that God's providential governance of the world is guided by his knowledge of probabilities. The major problem here is that it

[51] There is, to be sure, another alternative open to the openist: Maintain that Judas's betrayal of Jesus was already deterministically in the cards at the time of Jesus' statement. I leave it to the reader to determine just how unlikely a reading of the situation this alternative would present.

[52] It is worth reminding the reader of the point made in Chapter 1: the claim that God lacks knowledge of future free human actions was explicitly rejected by the First Vatican Council. For orthodox Roman Catholics at least, the unacceptability of the "open" alternative should on this count alone be manifest. As Hasker has noted, some Roman Catholic philosophers prominent in the discussion of these issues nevertheless do deny divine foreknowledge ("Response to Thomas Flint," p. 123). What Hasker says is surely true. The question for such Catholics, of course, is whether or not they think solemn pronouncements by ecumenical councils are binding on their faith, and, if not, what (if anything) they think is binding, and why.

does not seem likely that such probabilistic knowledge would afford God nearly so much guidance as openists sometimes imply.

First, one might ask, just how high are the probabilities God is supposed to know? If he lacks middle knowledge, God can't know that Cuthbert *would* buy an iguana if placed in circumstances C; the most he could know is that the probability of Cuthbert's buying the iguana in C is some number n, where $0 < n < 1$. But just how high is n supposed to be? Here, it seems to me, the openist faces a thorny dilemma.

Suppose he maintains that, in all such cases, n is very close to 1. That is, God is all but certain that Cuthbert would buy the iguana if placed in C. Were God's knowledge always of this nearly certain variety, then his governance of the world, though a tad more risky than on the Molinist or Thomist alternatives, would nonetheless be fairly sure; divine failures might occur, but they would be few and far between. Nevertheless, I feel confident that few openists would endorse this position.[53] For one reason, it simply seems extremely implausible (at least from a libertarian perspective) to think that, in every situation, the factors influencing a free agent in one direction vastly outweigh those inclining him toward some other action. In some cases, of course, the agent's reasons may all but determine his action in the way suggested here; but to think that this is always, or even usually, the case will not seem all that credible to many libertarians. Furthermore, for those openists who find the picture of a risk-taking God attractive, the advantages of the "open" picture will surely seem diminished the higher we make the probabilities God knows. If God is all but certain how we would respond in every situation in which we might be placed, then doesn't his life all but lack the element of risk-taking which (Hasker insists) we value in human beings? Doesn't God appear almost as great a manipulator of human beings as he does (according to openists) on the Molinist or Thomist pictures? Doesn't God's responsibility for evil—for Hitler and his ilk—become magnified to *nearly* the proportions which (openists say) beset Molinists and Thomists if his knowledge is *nearly* as certain as they maintain?

Suppose the openist, troubled by these consequences of viewing the probabilities God knows as universally extremely high, views the probabilities instead as a mixed bag—some being close to 1, others just above 0, and others in between. Such a position would surely have greater initial appeal to most libertarians than would its alternative, for our experience does seem to suggest just such a range: some free actions are performed in circumstances which appear to make them all but inevitable, others in situations such that none of

[53] Hasker, at any rate, has informed me (in conversation) that it is not a view he finds attractive.

us could reasonably have expected their performance, and still others under conditions which appear more equally weighted between factors favoring the action and those favoring some alternative. Still, the major problem with viewing the probabilities as mixed is both obvious and serious: God's control of his world, especially his long-range control, is drastically diminished. For long-range probabilities are a function of short-range ones, and when probabilities are multiplied, they swiftly decline. Hence, for example, the probabilities God knows (in 1997) concerning who will be elected President of the United States in 2004, being dependent upon so many specific probabilities concerning the likely free actions of so many people, are sure to be minuscule—indeed, not much better than our own. So the openists' myopic God might *try* to guide events, might *try* to work out his plan, but it is hard to see how knowledge of probabilities (if mixed) will give him much guidance. Indeed, any long-range plan, or even any short-range one that involves many free creaturely actions, will be such that God will have little idea as to whether or not he can really bring it off.[54] God will join mice and men in the category of those whose best laid schemes gang aft a-gley. Hence, the degree of providential control on this openist account seems remarkably weak.

The dilemma that arises from viewing God as having knowledge only of probabilities concerning free human action should now be apparent. Increase those probabilities and you increase the degree of God's providential control over his world; but by doing so, you emasculate the claim that God is a risk-taker and eviscerate the assertion that God *qua* risk-taker is more easily excused for the presence of evil. Lessen the probabilities God knows and you bring back all the (supposed) advantages of a deity who takes risks; but you also make a mockery of the thesis that a God with such knowledge would still be situated so as to govern his world efficiently and effectively. Hence, viewing God as cognizant only of "would-probably" conditionals simply cannot afford us all the "advantages" the openists allege.

Finally, what of the suggestion that viewing God as a risk-taker is at least acceptable (if not preferable) from the Christian perspective? No Thomist or Molinist, I would venture to say, would deny that there is often something admirable, noble, and virtuous (not to mention fun) about taking risks; most of us have little regard for those among us who are never willing to risk anything. Still, there are a couple of fairly obvious points that are worth reminding ourselves of in this context, points that have clear implications in the case of God.

First, the greater the stakes, the less we generally want to engage in risky

---

[54] It is worth noting that Hasker's views concerning the existence of genuine indeterminacy in nature would, if true, complicate things even more for God.

endeavors. Buying a lottery ticket engages me in a relatively risky enterprise, one where my odds of success are quite small. Provided that I am wagering only a dollar, though, most people would find nothing objectionable in such a gamble. But if the bet is substantially higher, so high that I risk losing my house, car, job, and the like, most of us would insist that we have gone beyond the realm of innocent amusement; indeed, the more others are depending upon me for financial support, the more reprehensible my action would surely seem. Of course, sometimes we have little choice but to engage in risky undertakings where much hangs on the outcome. (Think, for example, of an experimental operation which will either save or end my life.) But in such cases, we don't view the fact that the activity is risky as something desirable. If we could lessen or even eliminate the element of risk, we would be crazy not to do so.

The second point concerning risks is no more arcane than the first. Where others are involved, especially others to whom we have some special relationship, we are especially concerned to lessen or eliminate the risks our actions may pose to them. For example, it is arguably immoral for a father to drive without wearing his seat belt. But it seems clearly worse for him to drive and not provide a proper child-restraint seat for his two-year-old daughter. If he could completely eliminate the risks which driving poses for her, surely he would do it in an instant. Openist cries of "How dull!"; "Take a chance!"; "Live a little!" and the like would presumably have minimal effect.

These points are relevant, of course, because God's providential activities *do* affect others—others to whom he is intimately related as a loving Father— and because there *is* a lot at stake. Though we have used the image of playing games extensively in this chapter, it is worth reminding ourselves that, for the Christian at least, our relationship with God is not most properly thought of as a matter of fun and games; it is a matter of life and death, in the truest and fullest senses of those terms.[55]

Openists might (and do) accuse Molinists of turning God into an overprotective parent, "the manipulator than which none greater can be con-

---

[55] Some Christians might respond that things are not so grim as I have suggested here, for God will eventually save everyone. (For one powerful statement of this universalist position, see Thomas Talbott, "The Doctrine of Everlasting Punishment," *Faith and Philosophy* 7 [1990], 19–41.) But it is hard to see how universalism could turn out to be anything more than a happy accident if God lacks middle knowledge but creatures are genuinely free; God could "luck out" and save everyone, but things could just as easily have turned out less happily. So consistent libertarian universalists, it seems to me, are all but sure to be friends of middle knowledge, not foes. Furthermore, it would be somewhat surprising if those openists who are fans of risk-taking would find a God who *can't* really lose any of his *big* bets sufficiently romantic; universalism seems to fit uneasily with their picture of a dashing and daring deity.

ceived," as Hasker puts it.[56] But since both Molinists and openists see God, not as the hands-off observer of the deists, but as an active, providential Father, one who uses all the knowledge available to him concerning his free children before deciding which actions are most conducive to achieving his aims, it is hard to see much force to such a charge.

Indeed, the weakness of it comes to the fore if we place ourselves in a parental role and imagine ourselves being offered two options. Under Option One, you can place your child in circumstances in which you know with certainty that she will freely develop into a good and happy human being who leads a full and satisfying life. These circumstances may well produce certain difficulties in her life; she may have to struggle at many times and may have to face many challenges. Still, you know that, though to the uninformed outsider (and even to your daughter) she may at times seem to be treading the path to perdition, she will in fact overcome any obstacles, and all will ultimately be well with her.

Under Option Two, on the other hand, you don't have any knowledge of circumstances in which you could place your daughter in which things would turn out fine for her. All that you know are the likely outcomes for any such situations. Many of the probabilities of which you are aware aren't all that high, and you realize that they give you but the faintest glimmer of how things would turn out for any series of actions affecting her which you might perform. Still, you use your knowledge to take those actions you think will turn out for the best for her, and you keep your fingers crossed.

I can speak only for myself, but I must say that I wouldn't hesitate an instant to take Option One if I were given the choice, nor would I see myself as becoming more manipulative in doing so than I would have been had I chosen Option Two. The fact that we *don't* have a choice here, that we as parents are stuck with Option Two, is one of the things that is especially frustrating (and even terrifying) about being a parent. To view this situation as *preferable* to the one offered by Option One strikes me as just short of absurd.

Before concluding our discussion of the "open" alternative, a word or two concerning one of the alleged advantages of the openists' position is in order. Many openists (and even some Molinists) have suggested that viewing God as lacking middle knowledge makes the existence of evil at least somewhat easier for the Christian to explain; after all, if God cannot be sure how his free creatures will respond to his initiatives, he can hardly be blamed if (using his knowledge of probabilities) he does his best but occasionally finds them

---

[56] Hasker, "Response to Thomas Flint," p. 124.

responding poorly.[57] Though I can appreciate the attraction of this position, it seems to me that, all things considered, God's lacking middle knowledge would make the problem of evil even more difficult for the Christian to handle. For if God knows only probabilities, then he takes enormous risks in creating significantly free beings: he risks creating a world in which many, or most, or even all of his free creatures consistently reject him, a world in which they use their freedom to degrade others and themselves. It seems to me that one can reasonably argue that a good and loving God would not take such a risk. Rather than perform creative actions which might have such horrendous results, God would have created one of those innumerable good worlds open to him which do *not* contain significantly free creatures. By doing so, he would have sacrificed the great potential for goodness that creaturely freedom brings to a world. But that potential, in the absence of middle knowledge, is accompanied by dangers which, however unlikely, are of such a magnitude that a prudent creator would feel obligated to assure their nonoccurrence.

The case against the "open" alternative thus seems strong. Its being so at odds with the tradition, both in the overall concept of God that it defends and with the weakened account of providence that it offers, gives a libertarian traditionalist powerful prima facie reasons for rejecting it. Furthermore, when we examine carefully the three central elements of the view of providence the openists propose (i.e., the denial of universal divine foreknowledge, the replacement of middle knowledge by knowledge of probabilities, and the picture of God as a risk-taker), there seem to be significant problems with all three, while the advantages they are purported to offer us dissolve under closer scrutiny. For a traditionalist, then, the picture of providence crafted by the openists does not appear to be a genuinely open alternative.

7. The Burden of Proof

Let me attempt to summarize the main line of argument of these first three chapters. As we saw in Chapter 1, orthodox Christians are naturally drawn toward the position we have called libertarian traditionalism, a view that attempts to combine a libertarian concept of freedom with the strong traditional

[57] In addition to Hasker, see Adams, "Middle Knowledge and the Problem of Evil," p. 90. Plantinga (alas) has also implied that denying middle knowledge would be advantageous in addressing the problem of evil; see his "Reply," in *Alvin Plantinga*, p. 379. Freddoso, on the other hand, has argued effectively that openists are not in a significantly better position to deal with evil than are Molinists; see his review of Hasker's *God, Time, and Knowledge* in *Faith and Philosophy* 10 (1993), 99–107.

Christian notion of divine providence. The Molinist picture of providence, according to which God's governance of the world is guided by his knowledge of how his creatures would freely act in various situations, is thus one which would naturally seem quite appealing to the libertarian traditionalist. Indeed, as I argued at the start of this chapter, no coherent libertarian traditionalist could be anything but an advocate of Molinism; for her, it is indeed the only game in town. But as we have seen, her lack of options here ought not elicit feelings of philosophical claustrophobia, for the view that there are true counterfactuals of creaturely freedom is simply the common sense view of the proverbial man in the street—the view that virtually all of us come to philosophy with—and hence should be surrendered only if serious problems with it can be demonstrated. Nor ought the libertarian traditionalist be reluctant to embrace Molinism because some alternative picture of providence appears more attractive. For the three principal competitors to Molinism— the eternity alternative, the Thomist alternative, and the "open" alternative— not only jettison either traditionalism or libertarianism (and hence would initially prove distasteful to the libertarian traditionalist) but also enmesh us in problems (concerning, e.g., evil or prophecy) that can apparently be avoided by the Molinist.

The upshot of these considerations should now be evident. Since Molinism offers a picture of God's relation to the world that, from the perspective of the libertarian traditionalist, appears strikingly superior to the comparatively unattractive alternatives we have canvassed, the burden of proof lies squarely with those who would propose that she endorse something other than Molinism. It is a burden which conceivably can be met; indeed, some readers will no doubt conclude that it *is* met by one or another of the objections to the Molinist picture that we will examine in the next four chapters. But if Molinism falls, the libertarian traditionalist will have to abandon either the philosophical account of freedom or the theological notion of providence to which Christian orthodoxy seemed so naturally to lead, and she will need to replace the Molinist picture of providence with one of those three ungainly suitors whose advances she has seen reason to dismiss. No one could rationally expect the libertarian traditionalist to proceed down this rocky road unless major problems with Molinism are uncovered, problems of such a magnitude as to render the position utterly untenable.

If our argument to this point is on course, then, the Christian inclined toward libertarian traditionalism should consider divorcing herself from Molinism only if extremely powerful objections to the Molinist picture can be presented. Let us now proceed to see if objections of this sort are to be found.

[4]

Five Thomistic Objections to Molinism

Therefore it seems to follow that [for Molina] there is a dependence or passivity in God as regards futurables . . . for if God is not the first deter-mining Cause as regards free conditionate futures, He is determined by them, and there is no other alternative. If all things are not dependent on God, then God Himself is dependent on another. Here is the main difficulty of the question.

—Reginald Garrigou-Lagrange, *The One God*

1. Warming Up

To begin our examination of arguments that have been purported to offer the orthodox Christian compelling reason to reject the theory of middle knowledge, let us look at some of the allegations brought against Molinism by its Thomist critics.

In fairness to the opponents of Molinism, it must be admitted, I think, that the lines of reasoning to be examined in this chapter are not the strongest arguments that can be mustered against middle knowledge. Indeed, in the current discussion, they are objections that are rarely even voiced. In fact, even Thomists would not, I feel sure, view them as enunciating their central problem with the Molinist picture of providence. For that, we need to ex-amine what is commonly called the "grounding" objection, which will be our focus in the next chapter.

Why, then, discuss these five objections at all? Is my aim simply to give the defender of Molinism some easy victories before the more challenging battles of the following chapters? No, not *simply* that. Rather, the objections discussed here are all forwarded by the principal Thomist opponent of Mol-inism in this century, Reginald Garrigou-Lagrange, and are all presented by him as objections that have long been common among Molina's Thomist adversaries. To pretend that only the objections it is *currently* fashionable to discuss are worthy of our attention would be to cut ourselves off from a richer assessment of the types of anti-Molinist arguments that have in fact been offered.[1] Furthermore, as we shall see, at least some of these objections are of genuine interest, and probably should attract more discussion than they are typically afforded.

Five objections will be considered. The first two can, I think, be handled rather easily by the Molinist, while the remaining three pose more serious questions.

2. Objection One: The Power of Prayer

As we have seen, Molinism has as one of its twin foundations the libertarian picture of freedom. Given libertarianism, no one distinct from a particular free agent can causally determine that agent's freely performing a certain action, for such external determination is incompatible with the act's being free. But this entails, say some Thomist critics, that the scope and value of prayer become seriously diminished for the consistent Molinist. For God can no more cause us freely to act in particular ways than can other external agents. And this entails that the Molinist "could not ask God for the efficacious grace that makes him will, that takes away from him the stony heart, that compels the rebellious will to turn to God," as Garrigou-Lagrange puts it.[2] Hence, prayer on the Molinist picture becomes less important than it should be for the sincere Christian.

To handle this objection, it seems to me, all that the Molinist need do is call our attention to two distinctions. First, some of the elements in conversion of the sort under discussion (for example, the removal of a stony heart) are at least arguably things that happen to the sinner—things that are done to and for him—as opposed to things he freely does; others (for example, willing to sin no more) seem clearly to be at least partially products of the creature's free will. Second, "bring about" can be given (at least) two rather different meanings. On the one hand, we can be said to bring about that which we directly cause; on the other hand, we can be also be said to bring about those states of affairs which result, albeit not with causal necessity, from situations which we directly cause. It was, for example, in the first of these senses that Henry

---

[1] In a sense, this chapter can be seen as a compromise between, on the one hand, completely ignoring objections to Molinism which were common before the resurrection of the Molinist debate (among English-speaking philosophers of religion) occasioned by Plantinga's work, and, on the other hand, engaging in the kind of thorough survey of the history of Molinism which would take us far beyond the confines of this book (and which, to be honest, I am ill-equipped to pursue).

[2] Reginald Garrigou-Lagrange, *The One God*, tr. Dom. Bede Rose (St. Louis: B. Herder, 1944), p. 467.

II brought it about that he uttered the words, "Will no one rid me of this turbulent priest?"; it was presumably only in the second of these senses that Henry could be said to have brought about the death of Thomas Becket.[3] To use the terminology introduced by Plantinga, Henry may have *strongly actualized* his pronouncing those words, but he only *weakly actualized* Becket's death.[4]

Given these two distinctions, an answer to this first objection is readily apparent. For any element of conversion or sanctification that does *not* involve his own free action, the agent in question can pray that God bring about, even in the sense of strongly actualizing, that element. For any element that *does* involve his own free action, he can still pray that God bring it about. Not, to be sure, by strongly actualizing it, for that would be to do the impossible (because free actions cannot be strongly actualized by anyone other than the agent in question); rather, he can pray that God bring it about by weakly actualizing it.

So the scope and importance of prayers of this sort would seem to remain undiminished on the Molinist account. Hence, this first objection has little force.

3. Objection Two: The Scent of Semi-Pelagianism

Semi-Pelagians have been condemned for holding (among other things) that salvation begins with our own efforts rather than with God's. But, the charge goes, isn't this precisely what the Molinists are maintaining? For they hold that two people can be in identical situations with respect to the grace they receive, yet one respond negatively to this grace while the other responds positively. Thus, as Garrigou-Lagrange puts it, "the true beginning of salvation appears to be only in the one who is converted" rather than, as orthodox Christians must maintain, in the One who is doing the converting.[5] Instead of serving as a bulwark to orthodoxy, then, Molinism seems to offer encouragement to heresy.[6]

---

[3] The presumption being made here, of course, is that the four knights who reacted to Henry's words by slaying Becket were acting freely; i.e., Henry's utterance did not causally determine their riding to Canterbury Cathedral and doing their deadly deed.

[4] See Alvin Plantinga, *The Nature of Necessity* (Oxford: Clarendon Press, 1974), pp. 172–173.

[5] Garrigou-Lagrange, *One God*, p. 467. It is interesting to note that, though the view we now call Semi-Pelagianism flourished primarily in the fifth and sixth centuries, the term itself was coined as part of the Thomist attack upon Molinism. See S. J. McKenna, "Semi-Pelagianism," *New Catholic Encyclopedia*, vol. 13 (New York: McGraw-Hill, 1967), p. 75.

[6] For another, more recent Thomist attempt to link Molinism to Semi-Pelagianism, see

Little reflection is needed to see that this charge is bogus. Molinists can insist just as heartily as do Thomists upon the necessity of prevenient grace—that gratuitous activity on God's part which precedes and prepares the way for any salutary act we may perform. Hence, Molinists can concur with the orthodox contention that salvation begins with God's action, not with our own.

An analogy may be of assistance here. Consider the woman who throws a rope to a drowning man. Suppose that no further activity on her part determines either that he grasp or that he reject the rope. Should he grasp it, we might well say that his doing so was a free action. But it would be preposterous to say that the process of his being saved from drowning began with his grasping the rope. Clearly, it began with her offering him the rope in the first place.

As the Molinist sees it, of course, God is like the woman in our story; he is the one who takes the initiative in the process of salvation. The fact that his activity is nondeterminative of our response is simply and utterly irrelevant to the issue of priority here; for the Molinist as for the Thomist, salvation begins with God. And so this second Thomistic objection can be dismissed.[7]

4. Objection Three: The Naughtiness of Novelty

One of the objections leveled against Molina which is most likely to strike modern readers as curious was the charge that his view must be wrong because it had not been presented previously. Garrigou-Lagrange is aware of this criticism ("the *scientia media* has been frequently condemned because of the novelty of this theory"[8]), but it is not one of which he is particularly fond, given his inclination to paint the Molinist with Semi-Pelagian colors. Molina himself seems to have encountered the novelty objection in his own time as well, in the following form: the theory of middle knowledge cannot be right, because

---

David Burrell, *Freedom and Creation in Three Traditions* (Notre Dame: University of Notre Dame Press, 1993), p. 127.

[7] Garrigou-Lagrange (in *One God*, p. 467) and others sometimes hint that other, less central elements of Semi-Pelagianism, such as that God rewards baptized infants for the good works they would have performed, and punishes unbaptized infants for the evil they would have done, presuppose and thereby taint Molinism. It may well be that, in these areas, Semi-Pelagianism does presuppose Molinism. But the interesting question, of course, is whether the inference runs in the other direction as well. (After all, Semi-Pelagianism presupposes theism as well; presumably even the Thomist would concur that the later ought not be anathematized with the former!) It seems clear to me (as, it seems, it was clear to Paul V, the pope who refused to declare Molina's views heretical) that none of the condemned elements of Semi-Pelagianism are entailed by Molinism.

[8] Ibid., p. 467.

it so easily solves problems that were (at best) difficult to solve before the theory was presented. Speaking of Zumel and other opponents, Molina says:

> it matters little to them that on the basis of the certitude of middle knowledge we have so plainly reconciled this same freedom with foreknowledge, providence, predestination, and reprobation. In fact, they insist that middle knowledge should be rejected precisely because all these things come into harmony so plainly and easily on the basis of it, whereas the holy Fathers labored greatly in reconciling them with one another and always thought of the exact reconciliation of freedom of choice with these four things and with divine grace as one of the most difficult of tasks.[9]

Two questions seem most relevant in evaluating this objection. First, is the theory of middle knowledge as novel as these critics allege? And second, would novelty properly be taken as a sign of falsity?

The first of these questions is by no means easy to answer. Molina himself denies the charge of concocting something new; all he has done, he maintains, is to "have laid out just a little more clearly the foundation on which all these things [providence, freedom, and the like] cohere with one another." He does concede that his language is novel, but he insists that the Fathers of the Church "affirm middle knowledge—at least in fact, if not in our very words."[10]

Despite his protestations of unoriginality, though, I think that even a Molinist can reasonably question Molina's claim here. It would be one thing (and a distinctively Molinist thing at that!) to claim that the Fathers *would have* embraced the theory of middle knowledge had they encountered Molina's work. To claim that they actually *did* endorse it seems to me to be stretching things a bit.[11]

But, of course, what makes for novelty in a theory or in a statement? The mere fact that it has never been stated before? The claim that God is more powerful than an iguana is one which may well never have been considered before my making it here. Does that make the claim a novel one in any interesting sense? Probably not. No one inclined explicitly to endorse that statement upon my making it would be likely to experience that flash of illumination which we normally think of as accompanying the genuinely original insight; "Of course!", not "Oh my!", would be our likely response. True novelty, I take it, involves seeing things in a new way more than it does

---

[9] Molina, Disputation 53, part 2, section 22 (p. 228).

[10] Ibid., p. 229.

[11] At least Molina's attempt to defend his claim (in the following section of part 2 of Disputation 53, pp. 229–232) strikes me as unconvincing.

making ourselves more conscious of the way we have always seen them. And as we noted in the last chapter, most people seem to start off as tacit Molinists; they feel no difficulty in granting that there are truths about what free people would have done had they been in different situations. What Molina does, then, can reasonably be seen as merely applying to theology what the man in the street already implicitly believes.

How is the theory of middle knowledge, then, to be ranked in terms of novelty? No easy answer seems available. Molina's claim that his illustrious predecessors consciously held to the substance (if not the name) of his theory seems a bit extreme. Yet if the point made in the preceding chapter concerning the widespread prephilosophical inclination toward Molinism is conceded, then the charge that the theory of middle knowledge represented a radical innovation also seems exaggerated.

But, moving to our second question, one might well wonder whether the presence of novelty should be seen as a negative factor in our evaluation of a theory. Indeed, in our own time, originality is popularly seen as a virtue, unoriginality a vice.[12] If Molina's theory were completely novel, many of us moderns would be inclined to say, so much the better, for him and for the theory. Even those of us who are not so enamored with the new are apt to see originality as irrelevant to the question of truth. If the theory gets things right, we might say, it simply doesn't matter how novel it is; truth, whether old-fashioned or newfangled, is what we should be after.

Are these attitudes toward originality, attitudes either of approval or of indifference, the ones which those of us engaged in philosophical theology should adopt? Quite the contrary, I think. Significant novelty should serve as a red flag warning us that something has probably gone awry. The justification for approaching novel theories with this prejudice should be obvious. Some of the sharpest minds in Western history have wrestled with the philosophical questions raised by Christianity for nearly two thousand years. To assume that an approach that is genuinely new, that has never been endorsed by any of our predecessors, is likely to augment our understanding is surely to engage in an act of intellectual arrogance. To the extent that Garrigou-Lagrange and his allies are warning us that radical inventiveness in theology is more likely to signal a dead end than a highway to enlightenment, they are offering us a reminder that many of us surely and sorely need.[13]

---

[12] In saying that novelty is *popularly* seen as a virtue, my intention is not to imply that we academics are immune to this predilection. Think, for example, of a letter of recommendation stating that a particular graduate student had produced work notable for its lack of originality; we all know what effect such a reference would have on that individual's job prospects.

[13] It is perhaps worth mentioning (even in our well-Kuhnianized times) that the conser-

On the other hand, conservatism ought not be confused with intellectual stagnation; suspicion of novelty need not degrade into a mindless, automatic rejection of the new. Genuine progress is indeed possible. To be conservative is not to deny this possibility, but only to view breathtakingly innovative approaches as more likely to asphyxiate than to resuscitate. Even one who sees radically novel theories as guilty until proven innocent must remain open to being swayed if the evidence for innocence is compelling.

So even if Molinism's pedigree could be traced back no farther than the sixteenth century (and as we have seen, this is far from clearly the case), our assessment of it need not be negative. Indeed, given the remarkable degree to which the theory of middle knowledge is able to render coherent beliefs concerning freedom and providence which are dear to the hearts of many orthodox Christians; given the absence of any other theory that allows these beliefs, without being diluted or distorted, to be brought into harmony; and given the perplexities that (as we saw in the last chapter) appear to beset the alternatives to the theory—given all these facts, even the most conservative of investigators, I think, could be forgiven for inclining toward the theory no matter how truly novel she were to judge it.

The novelty objection, then, though more worthy of serious consideration than some of us might be inclined to acknowledge, is clearly insufficient to lead a reflective libertarian traditionalist to abandon Molinism. Not only is it unclear what degree of novelty should be accorded the theory, but the evidence in favor of middle knowledge seems clearly to outweigh whatever negative presumption the theory's originality might have warranted.

5. Objection Four: The Sin of Symmetry

As we have already seen, orthodox Christians are reluctant to have God related to our good actions in precisely the same way that he is related to our evil actions. What we want instead is a clear and definite asymmetry. We want to see God as the ultimate source of the good that we do, but not of the evil that we do.

Some Thomists have argued, though, that Molinists are unable to endorse this thesis of asymmetry. For as we have noted, Molinists insist that the concurrent grace by which God endeavors to promote our free virtuous actions is intrinsically neutral, not (as the Thomists contend) intrinsically efficacious. That is, Molinists believe that the very same assistance on God's part can result either in a good action or in an evil action. And this means that, in whatever

---

vative approach advocated for philosophical theology here seems little different from the approach actually taken in most developed fields of study, including many areas of science.

sense Molinists say God is the author of good actions, they are committed to viewing him as, in that very sense, the author of evil actions as well.[14]

Surrendering asymmetry would indeed be a major defect in the Molinist approach, one that could reasonably lead the orthodox Christian seriously to consider renouncing the theory. Fortunately, though, as Freddoso has pointed out, the Molinist need not abandon the thesis of asymmetry. For the Molinist is committed to saying that, in cases of free action, God's assistance (prior and concurrent, natural and supernatural) is *neutral* only in the sense that it doesn't *determine* the agent to perform a good action. But assistance that is nondetermining can nevertheless *incline* an agent toward the good. And this is precisely what God's assistance does. It is not a gift certificate which can be used just as easily for ill as for good. Rather, it is a push (or, perhaps better, a pull) in one definite direction—toward the good—albeit a pull that can be resisted.

Hence, in cases where we do not resist God's influence, it is appropriate to see him as truly the ultimate source of the good that we do, and to see ourselves as cooperating with God in its realization. On the other hand, in cases where we resist his influence, it is appropriate to see ourselves as acting in opposition to God, and hence mistaken to ascribe authorship of the act to him. Therefore, the Molinist can indeed uphold the asymmetry thesis.[15]

It seems to me that the only plausible response open to the Thomist at this point would be to question one of Freddoso's major assumptions—namely, that we as libertarians can meaningfully speak of God's assistance inclining us toward an action which it does not necessitate. What, the Thomist might ask, does it mean to say that something inclines but doesn't determine an agent's free action? What analysis or criterion of inclination can the libertarian offer? In the absence of such an analysis, can we really be sure Freddoso's approach succeeds?

These are difficult and important questions. Indeed, as I indicated in Chapter 1, I believe that they are also questions to which no easy answers are evident, for it is not at all clear just what analysis of inclination the libertarian ought to endorse.[16] On the other hand, it seems to me that they point to the fact that the Thomists' objection concerning asymmetry are not really crucial to an evaluation of Molinism. For libertarianism is essential to Molinism, and the notion of inclination is one which would seem to be central to any plausible libertarian position. Therefore, if no sense can be made of the notion of inclination, Molinism has a far more serious and a far more fundamental

---

[14] See Garrigou-Lagrange, *One God*, p. 466.

[15] See Freddoso, "Introduction," pp. 64–65.

[16] See Chapter 1, section 5. Of course, one option for the libertarian here would be to deny that any analysis is needed—i.e., to view the notion of inclination as primitive.

problem on its hands than any difficulties it may have with the asymmetry thesis.

So the asymmetry thesis itself seems unlikely to offer the Molinist serious trouble. While it may remind us of a bit of unfinished business to which the Molinist would need to attend should she wish to make her picture of freedom complete, it offers us no reason to think that such attention will prove unfruitful. Hence, by itself, it provides the orthodox Christian scant motivation to abandon Molinism.

6. Objection Five: The Principle of Predilection

According to Garrigou-Lagrange, it is part of orthodox Christian belief that God is the one who is ultimately responsible for some people's being saved and for other's not being saved. The acceptance of God's offer of salvation on the part of the elect may well be necessary for their salvation to occur, but we should not allow that fact about our cooperation to obscure the more important fact that it is God who decides both the number and the identity of the saved. As Garrigou-Lagrange puts it, "the singling out of one from another must finally be sought not in the human will, but in God who singles out one from another by His Grace."[17] Garrigou-Lagrange contends that this traditional teaching is incompatible with the picture of providence enunciated by Molina, for as we have seen, on that picture, God's grace is not intrinsically efficacious. He illustrates his point in the following way:

> Let us suppose that Peter and Judas situated in equal circumstances receive equal prevenient grace; then God sees Peter consenting to accept that grace, and hence singling himself out from Judas who does not consent, not on account of the grace, for an equal grace is indifferently offered to each. Therefore it is because the will decides to accept the grace. Thus do all Thomists argue against Molina, and they thus affirm as revealed the principle that can be called "the principle of predilection," namely, that no one would be better than another unless he were loved more and helped more by God.[18]

By defending an extreme picture of human freedom, then, Molinism ends up contradicting a central Christian claim.

In responding to this charge, some Molinists might be tempted to reject the principle of predilection. Indeed, such a rejection is sure to appeal to those

---

[17] Garrigou-Lagrange, *One God*, p. 462. Garrigou-Lagrange cites several passages from St. Paul in support of the principle he is here expounding; see especially 1 Cor. 4:7, Rom. 9:15, and Phil. 2:13.

[18] Ibid., p. 463.

many Christians, Molinist or not, whose sense of fairness recoils at talk of God's loving or helping one of us more than another. As Freddoso rightly notes, though, such a course would be a perilous one indeed, given the grounding which the thesis Garrigou-Lagrange identifies clearly has in Scripture and tradition. Whether we like it or not, the principle of predilection does seem to be part of the Christian message Molinism sees itself as defending.[19]

So the Molinist has little choice but to endeavor to reconcile this principle with the theory of middle knowledge. Fortunately, such a reconciliation seems readily attainable. For on the Molinist account, it is totally up to God what grace Peter receives and what grace Judas receives. Furthermore, God's middle knowledge informs him, for any bestowal of grace the two might receive and any situation in which they might be placed, how the two would respond in that set of circumstances (i.e., receiving that grace in that situation). So if Peter acts virtuously, it is because God knowingly put him in a set of circumstances in which he would freely act well, and knowingly refrained from putting him in a set of circumstances in which he would sin. Similarly, if Judas sins, it is because God knowingly put him in a set of circumstances in which he would sin, and knowingly refrained from putting him in a set of circumstances in which he would act virtuously. Even if the graces and situations of Peter and Judas are identical, then, it remains true that Peter is loved more and helped more by God, for given God's middle knowledge, his bestowal of identical graces in identical situations simply manifests his intentions to save Peter and to allow Judas to sin. And so the principle of predilection seems fully compatible with Molinism.

Or *almost* fully compatible; there is one remaining complication. One might plausibly propose, as a tacit corollary to (or perhaps merely as an explication of) the principle of predilection the claim that

(a)   For any free creature, there are circumstances in which God could place it in which it would freely attain salvation, and others in which it would freely reject the offer of salvation and thereby merit damnation.

One might also suggest that this corollary ought not be limited only to those free beings whom God in fact created, but should be seen as extending to all creaturely essences. That is, one might propose that the principle of predilection should be seen as implicitly incorporating the claim that

[19] See Freddoso, "Introduction," pp. 65–66.

    (b)   For every creaturely essence, God saw prior to his creative act that there
             were circumstances in which he could instantiate the essence such that
             the instantiation of that essence would freely attain salvation, and other
             situations in which he could instantiate it such that the instantiation
             would reject the offer of salvation and freely merit damnation.

Finally, one might contend that the principle of predilection commits us to
thinking of the kind of power which (b) ascribes to God as one which he
could not possibly have lacked. In other words, it might be proposed that

    (c)   It is necessarily the case that (b)

is also implied by the principle of predilection.

    It should be evident that the Molinist could endorse (a) and (b). For it
could well be that the creaturely world-type with which God is presented is
such that he has the kind of power over the ultimate fate of all actual and
"merely possible" beings which (a) and (b) ascribe to him. With (c), though,
the Molinist cannot be so accommodating. For (c) seems clearly false from
the Molinist standpoint. Since God has absolutely no control over which
counterfactuals of creaturely freedom are true and which are false, it surely is
possible (however unlikely we might think it) that there be a creaturely essence which is such that there is simply no set of circumstances in which God
could instantiate it such that its instantiation would freely reject God's offer
of salvation. Similarly, it also is surely possible (even if unlikely) that there be
a creaturely essence which is such that there is simply no set of circumstances
in which God could instantiate it such that its instantiation would freely accept
God's offer of salvation. Essences of the first sort, we might say, are blessed
with *transworld salvation*, while those of the second variety suffer from *transworld
damnation*.[20] Since it is clearly possible that there be essences exhibiting these
properties, there are worlds in which God lacks the kind of power (b) ascribes
to him. Thus, from the Molinist perspective, (c) must be rejected.

    Does her inability to embrace (c) mean that the Molinist does after all need
to reject the principle of predilection? I think not. For (c) seems to me to be
a claim much stronger than can be justified by either Scripture or tradition.
The Molinist, as we have seen, can easily go as far as (b); and that, I think,
is going quite far enough to capture both the letter and the spirit of the

---

[20] The second of these terms is taken from William Lane Craig, " 'No Other Name': A
Middle Knowledge Perspective on the Exclusivity of Salvation Through Christ," *Faith and
Philosophy* 6 (1989), 184. Both names, of course, are patterned on Plantinga's celebrated notion
of transworld depravity. See *Nature of Necessity*, pp. 186–188.

principle of predilection. Hence, the anti-Molinist argument grounded in this principle must ultimately be judged a failure.

7. Conclusion

It seems clear to me that none of the objections canvassed in this chapter are of sufficient potency to derail Molinism. Still, it is worth noting that four of these five objections (not including the argument based on novelty) share a common theme, a theme suggested by the passage from Garrigou-Lagrange with which we began this chapter. In each of these objections, the Thomist is in effect charging the Molinist with giving us a God who is too passive, who is not sufficiently in charge of things. As we shall see in the next chapter, the same basic theme can be used both to support and to give a particular twist to what is commonly called the "grounding" objection to middle knowledge. Hence, though the objections we have examined here can indeed be dismissed, the root from which they spring remains a potential threat to the viability of the Molinist project. It is to that threat that we now turn.

The "Grounding" Objection to Middle Knowledge

The objector to the truth of counterfactuals seems to be presupposing the
same wooden understanding of truth as correspondence as does the opponent
of the truth of future contingent propositions.
—William Lane Craig, *Divine Foreknowledge and Human Freedom*

1. Preview of Coming Attractions

As we have seen, the Molinist picture of providence arises from an attempt
to combine a strong libertarian account of freedom with a robust traditional
stance concerning God's governance of the world. In the last chapter, we
examined several objections offered by those Thomists who are intent on
maintaining that traditional picture of providence, but skeptical concerning
libertarian freedom. This chapter and the following two focus on criticisms
that emanate primarily from those embracing the other approach one might
take in countering Molinism—that of endorsing libertarianism, but weakening
the orthodox view of providence. To the best of my knowledge, this "openist" approach was all but unknown in Molina's day; in our own, it seems to
have become much more common than the other, more characteristically
Thomistic type of alternative.[1] Some might view this shift as a sign of greater
philosophical sophistication in our understanding of freedom; others might
deem it a sad indication of the alacrity with which heterodox positions are
embraced by contemporary philosophers of religion unanchored by significant
dogmatic commitments. Of course, it may be that both assessments are on target,
or that neither is. In any case, the types of objections to be discussed in these
three chapters are much more commonly encountered in the current discussion of Molinism than in the debates of earlier eras; hence, these criticisms,

---

[1] For a discussion of the Thomist and "open" alternative to Molinism, see Chapter 3,
sections 5 and 6.

though logically no less significant than those discussed in the previous chapter, do follow them chronologically.

Many libertarian objections to the Molinist picture have been proposed in recent years, and many contemporary Molinists have attempted to answer them.[2] Nothing would be gained by my attempting to summarize all of these objections and responses; in many cases, I have little significant to add to what I and other defenders of Molinism have previously said, and a simple litany of such rejoinders, along with suitably situated Amens and Alleluias, might prove tedious. Thus, I will limit myself in these chapters to looking at three major objections to the Molinist picture.

First, in this chapter, the "grounding" objection will be examined. Putting this objection first makes sense for a number of reasons. As we will see, such an objection, though now usually offered by libertarians, can rather easily be transformed into a nonlibertarian one, an objection which was indeed often leveled against Molina in earlier generations. Hence, this objection, unlike many of the criticisms brought forth by opponents of Molinism, bridges the gap between the nonlibertarian opposition highlighted in the last chapter and the libertarian opposition that provides our focus in these three. Since the "grounding" objection is also the one that non-Molinists today seem to find most telling, it seems eminently reasonable to begin with it.

---

[2] Robert Adams and William Hasker have emerged as among the most insightful critics of the Molinist account. See Adams, "Middle Knowledge and the Problem of Evil," *American Philosophical Quarterly* 14 (1977), 109–117, reprinted with additional notes in Adams, *The Virtue of Faith and Other Essays in Philosophical Theology* (New York: Oxford University Press, 1987), pp. 77–93; "Plantinga on the Problem of Evil," in James E. Tomberlin and Peter van Inwagen, eds., *Alvin Plantinga* (Dordrecht: D. Reidel, 1985), pp. 225–255; and "An Anti-Molinist Argument," *Philosophical Perspectives* 5 (1991), 343–353. For Hasker, see his *God, Time, and Knowledge* (Ithaca: Cornell University Press, 1989), chap. 2, and "Response to Thomas Flint," *Philosophical Studies* 60 (1991), 117–126. Other interesting criticisms of the Molinist picture are found in Anthony Kenny, *The God of the Philosophers* (Oxford: Oxford University Press, 1973), pp. 68–71; Linda Zagzebski, *The Dilemma of Freedom and Foreknowledge* (New York: Oxford University Press, 1991), pp. 125–152; and Nelson Pike, "A Latter-Day Look at the Foreknowledge Problem," *International Journal for Philosophy of Religion* 33 (1993), 129–164. Among the more prominent contemporary defenses of middle knowledge are Alvin Plantinga, "Replies," in Tomberlin and van Inwagen, *Alvin Plantinga*, pp. 372–382; Freddoso, "Introduction," pp. 1–81; Richard Otte, "A Defense of Middle Knowledge," *International Journal for Philosophy of Religion* 21 (1987), 161–169; David Basinger, "Middle Knowledge and Human Freedom: Some Clarifications," *Faith and Philosophy* 4 (1987), 330–336; Edward Wierenga, *The Nature of God* (Ithaca: Cornell University Press, 1989), chap. 5; William Lane Craig, *Divine Foreknowledge and Human Freedom* (Leiden: E. J. Brill, 1991), pp. 237–278; Rod Bertolet, "Hasker on Middle Knowledge," *Faith and Philosophy* 10 (1993), 3–17; and my "Two Accounts of Providence," in Thomas V. Morris, ed., *Divine and Human Action* (Ithaca: Cornell University Press, 1988), pp. 147–181, and "Hasker's *God, Time, and Knowledge*," *Philosophical Studies* 60 (1991), 103–115.

In the next chapter, William Hasker's distinctive objections to middle knowledge are examined. In a sense, these objections can properly be seen as clever variations on the "grounding" objection, variations which call for a deeper Molinist response.

Finally, in Chapter 7, I examine a more recent argument against Molinism offered by Robert Adams. Though he presents this argument as a variation on Hasker's anti-Molinist argument, I suggest that it is perhaps more properly seen as a variation on a type of vicious circle argument that a libertarian critic of Molinism might propose.

2. Does Groundlessness Ground the Molinist Stance?

The "grounding" objection, which has been proposed in one form or another by many eminent critics of the theory of middle knowledge, is as easy to state as it is difficult fully to resolve.[3] According to Molinists, God uses his knowledge of counterfactuals of creaturely freedom which are *contingent* and *prevolitional* in deciding which persons to create in which situations. But if such conditionals are contingent, they might not have been true. Who, then, *makes* them true? Or, to phrase this question more carefully: Who or what actually *causes* the ones that are true to be true, and the ones that are false to be false? In whose actual activity are we to find adequate metaphysical grounds for such truths?

Could *God* be the one who by himself causes their truth? Clearly not. The truths in question are supposed to be true prior to, and hence independent of, God's will. To suggest that God can decide which such counterfactuals are to be true is to abandon the libertarian standpoint essential to Molinism. Thomistic opponents of middle knowledge, as we have seen, might advocate such a surrender, but the opponents we are considering here would not.

Could it be, then, that *we free creatures* are the ones who, by the actions we perform in the actual world, make the relevant counterfactuals true—that is, I cause the ones about me to be true, you cause yours to be true, and so on? Here, too, a negative answer seems to be required, and that for (at least) four reasons.

[3] Perhaps the best-known source for this objection is Adams, "Middle Knowledge and the Problem of Evil." See also his "Plantinga on the Problem of Evil." Other public proponents of the "grounding" objection include: William Hasker, *God, Time, and Knowledge*, pp. 29–52; David Paul Hunt, "Middle Knowledge: The 'Foreknowledge Defense'," *International Journal for Philosophy of Religion* 28 (1990), 1–24; and Timothy O'Connor, "The Impossibility of Middle Knowledge," *Philosophical Studies* 66 (1992), 139–166. Many other philosophers have suggested to me in conversation that they see the "grounding" objection as the principal obstacle to endorsing the Molinist picture.

First, counterfactuals of creaturely freedom are supposed to be true well *before* we are around, for they are supposed to be of guidance to God in deciding whether or not we are going to be at all. So our current activity could cause them to *be* true only if that activity caused them to *have been* true in the past, and thus caused God to *have known* them. And this would be to have the cause come later in time than its effect. If, like most philosophers, we reject the notion of backward causation, it seems we must resist the suggestion that we cause counterfactuals of creaturely freedom to be true.

A second reason to resist this suggestion is independent of the claim that backward causation is impossible. According to Molinists, counterfactuals of creaturely freedom are true independent of God's will. Regardless of which creative action within his power God were to perform, those counterfactuals of creaturely freedom that are true would remain true. But our existence *isn't* independent of God's will—it is not true that we are around to cause things *regardless* of what God does. So how could the counterfactuals be caused to be true by us?

Furthermore, some of the counterfactuals in question refer to "people" who never get created—more precisely, to *uninstantiated creaturely essences*. As we saw in Chapter 2, it seems that the counterfactuals of which God is aware when deciding upon his creative activity would refer to creaturely essences rather than to individual creatures; in the wake of his creative decisions, some of these essences will be instantiated, but others will not be. If the consequents of those conditionals involving uninstantiated essences refer to genuine free actions, it is not up to God or any of us whose essences were instantiated to decide which such counterfactuals are to be true and which false. Clearly, then, the Molinist has to say that at least these counterfactuals are such that no one who actually exists ever causes them to be true. But if one grants this about some counterfactuals of creaturely freedom, why not grant it about all?

Finally, one might be tempted to ground the truth of counterfactuals of creaturely freedom in our *character* as opposed to our *actions*. That is, one might suggest that I don't *do* anything to make such conditionals true; rather, their truth flows from certain traits or tendencies that I possess. But such a proposal seems untenable. In the first place, character is (in part, at least) a result of my actions. Hence, if the previous three arguments against seeing our actions as grounding our counterfactuals of freedom are sound, they seem to discredit any attempt at character-based grounding as well. Furthermore, formed character provides an insufficient base for the truths at issue. My having developed the habit of honesty, for example, may justify your belief that I would freely resist a bribe if it were offered to me. But, if my action truly is free in the full libertarian sense, my possession of the virtue cannot entail that I resist; action out of character is always open where freedom is present.

We have seen, then, that neither God nor his free creatures cause true counterfactuals of creaturely freedom to be true. But between God and us free creatures, we have exhausted our list of the usual suspects. There are, perhaps, other causal agents in the world—amoebae, earwigs, perhaps even iguanas—who never act freely, but to view their activity as grounding these conditionals is clearly preposterous. The conclusion that seems forced upon us, then, is that *nobody* actually causes the counterfactuals in question to be true.

Once this conclusion is granted, the proponent of the "grounding" objection feels that the collapse of Molinism is imminent.[4] For how can there be *contingent* truths that *no one* causes to be true? Mustn't a contingent truth be *grounded* in the actual causal activity of some being or other? "Counterfactuals of freedom," says Adams, "are supposed to be contingent truths that are not caused to be true by God. Who or what does cause them to be true?" Saying that *nobody* causes them to be true, according to Adams, "would be very unpalatable, not only to determinists, but also to those indeterminists who believe that facts that are not completely determined causally must be due to the activity of beings endowed with spontaneity."[5] Indeed, even if one doubted that such causal grounding is required for *every* contingent fact, isn't it clearly needed at least in the case of contingent conditionals? As Hasker puts it: "In order for a (contingent) conditional state of affairs to obtain, its obtaining must be grounded in some categorical state of affairs. More colloquially, truths about 'what *would be the case* . . . *if*' must be grounded in truths about what *is in fact* the case."[6] Since there are no such grounds for the truth of counterfactuals of creaturely freedom, we must conclude that there are no such truths.[7] The Molinist picture, then, is untenable.

---

[4] The remainder of this paragraph describes the manner in which the "grounding" objection typically proceeds. However, not all proponents of the objection would pursue the issue in exactly the way described here. For a prime example, see Hunt, "Middle Knowledge."

[5] Adams, "Plantinga on the Problem of Evil," p. 232. For Freddoso's statement of this step in the "grounding" objection, see his "Introduction," p. 70.

[6] Hasker, *God, Time, and Knowledge*, p. 30. Hasker refers to this thesis as an intuition, one which, as he sees it, "underlies Adams's objection even though Adams does not explicitly formulate it." I think Hasker is right to see this intuition as implicit in Adams's, and in most, versions of the "grounding" objection.

[7] See ibid., p. 52; see also n. 4, p. 91, added by Adams to the version of "Middle Knowledge and the Problem of Evil" in his *Virtue of Faith*. Adams's more recent position is slightly different. On p. 345 of "An Anti-Molinist Argument," he says: "More precisely, I believe that all counterfactuals of freedom about possible but non-actual creatures, and all that have false consequents, are false, and that if counterfactuals of freedom with true consequents about actual creatures are true at all, their truth arises too late in the order of explanation to play the part in divine providence that it is supposed to play according to Molina's theory."

Or so, at least, the contemporary proponents of the "grounding" argument reason. The older Thomistic turn on this argument proceeds somewhat differently. As we have seen, Thomists are just as insistent as Molinists that there are true counterfactuals of creaturely freedom. Indeed, they will even grant to the Molinist that there are some such truths which are not necessary truths, that there are some true conditionals in which the antecedent entails no particular action on the agent's part. For the reasons given above, Thomists contend that we are not causally responsible for such truths. But, given their contingency, *someone* has to be responsible for them. Hence, what we need to conclude is that God causes the truth of those contingent counterfactuals of creaturely freedom which are true. If traditional libertarianism is incompatible with this conclusion, so much the worse for libertarianism.[8]

Though the alternatives toward which the contemporary and the Thomistic proponents of the "grounding" objection drive are diverse, the core of their objections is the same: Contingent truths must be grounded in some being's causal activity, and counterfactuals of creaturely freedom are not grounded in our activity. It is this core that the Molinist must address if this objection is to be met.

3. Grounding the "Grounding" Objection: Plantingean Hints

There are a number of ways in which one might try to defuse the problems raised by the "grounding" objection. Some of these approaches, I think, would be rather feeble signs of desperation. For instance, to counter the first argument purporting to show that we don't cause counterfactuals of creaturely freedom to be true, one might say that backward causation poses no problem to the Molinist. Or, to counter the second argument, one might argue that my counterfactuals of creaturely freedom are as a matter of fact caused by me to be true, but would still have been true (though not caused by me) had I not existed. Such responses, I think, should be resisted by the Molinist—the first because of the implausibility of the notion of backward causation, the second because (among other reasons) it simply highlights problems concerning backward causation and uninstantiated essences. The arguments of the previous section, in my opinion, provide a compelling case for the claim that we don't cause counterfactuals of creaturely freedom to be true. Any Molinist response predicated upon the denial of this claim is unworthy of our allegiance.

A somewhat more promising approach is to call into question the notion

---

[8] See, for example, Reginald Garrigou-Lagrange, *The One God*, tr. Dom. Bede Rose (St. Louis: B. Herder, 1944), especially pp. 464–466.

of grounding presupposed by this objection. This strategy is suggested by Alvin Plantinga:

> To investigate this question properly, we should have to investigate the implied suggestion that if a proposition is true, then something *grounds* its truth, or *causes* it to be true, or *makes* it true. Is this supposed to hold for all propositions? What sorts of things are to be thought of as grounding a proposition, and what is it for a proposition to be grounded by such a thing? What grounds the truth of such a proposition as *this piece of chalk is three inches long*? I don't have the space to enter this topic; let me just record that the answers to these questions aren't at all clear. It seems to me much clearer that some counterfactuals of freedom are at least possibly true than that the truth of propositions must, in general, be grounded in this way.[9]

Plantinga is surely right that there are many unanswered questions concerning the notion of grounding. Still, I think that few Molinists would feel comfortable responding to the "grounding" objection with nothing more than a plea of Socratic ignorance. The suggestions that counterfactuals of creaturely freedom are true for reasons, and that those reasons ultimately have something to do with the causal activities of free creatures, seem both clear enough and plausible enough for Molinists to feel uneasy about straightforwardly denying them.

Indeed, Plantinga himself seems to agree that the Molinist ought to and can go beyond this kind of response. Even if we do concede, at least for purposes of argument, that contingent truths require grounds, he says, counterfactuals of creaturely freedom seem no worse off than other truths involving free agents:

> Suppose . . . that yesterday I freely performed some action *A*. What was or is it that grounded or founded my doing so? I wasn't *caused* to do [so] by anything else; nothing relevant *entails* that I did so. So what grounds the truth of the proposition in question? Perhaps you will say that what grounds its truth is just that in fact I did *A*. But this isn't much of an answer; and at any rate the same kind of answer is available in the case of Curley. For what grounds the truth of the counterfactual [that if Curley had been offered a bribe of $35,000, he would have freely accepted it], we may say, is just that in fact Curley is such that if he had been offered a $35,000 bribe, he would have freely taken it.[10]

[9] Alvin Plantinga, "Replies," in Tomberlin and van Inwagen, *Alvin Plantinga*, p. 378.
[10] Ibid.

As it stands, Plantinga's argument is open to several responses. For example, the proponent of the "grounding" objection might point out that, though the claim that Plantinga did *A* is grounded in Plantinga's actual activity yesterday, *no* such activity on Curley's part sufficiently grounds the truth of that counterfactual about him. But it seems to me that the type of response Plantinga adumbrates here can be developed into one that adequately meets the challenge of the "grounding" objector. And the way in which this development might proceed, I think, has been ingeniously suggested by Freddoso.[11]

4. A Freddosoan Response

Freddoso's response to the "grounding" objection has two essential stages. First, he points out that the "grounding" argument against counterfactuals of creaturely freedom (which he calls *conditional* future contingents) parallels arguments against *absolute* future contingents, so that the former argument is only as plausible as are the latter.[12] Second, he contends that we have reason to reject the argument against absolute future contingents, and that these reasons can be extended to the "grounding" argument against counterfactuals of creaturely freedom. Let us examine these two stages in turn.

Consider first the assertion that there is a parallel between the "grounding" objection and the objection to non-conditional future contingents—that is, between (as Freddoso calls it) antirealism regarding conditional future contingents and antirealism regarding absolute future contingents. According to the "grounding" objection, if contingent counterfactuals of creaturely freedom are to be true at all, they need to be grounded in some actual causal activity; truths about what *would be* the case need to be grounded in truths about what *is in fact* the case. Thus, a proposition such as

(1)   If I were to offer Albert Gore a one million dollar bribe not to run for president in 2000, he would freely accept my offer

cannot be true here and now (so to speak) because Gore is doing nothing here and now (in 1996) which grounds the truth of (1). Perhaps there are truths about Gore which entail that he *probably* would freely accept were I to

---

[11] See also William Lane Craig's impressive presentation in *Divine Foreknowledge and Human Freedom*, pp. 247–263. For a dissenting Molinist opinion on the wisdom of advancing Plantinga's point in the way Craig and Freddoso do, see Richard Gaskin, "Conditionals of Freedom and Middle Knowledge," *Philosophical Quarterly* 43 (1993), pp. 412–430; esp. n. 39, pp. 425–426.

[12] This stage of Freddoso's argument had been independently proposed by Richard Otte, "Defense of Middle Knowledge."

offer him the bribe, but these facts are insufficient to ground a nonprobabilistic claim such as (1). Such claims, then, are false.

Such an argument, when put in this way, seems very reminiscent of—indeed, all but inseparable from—the type of argument characteristically forwarded by antirealists concerning absolute future contingent truths. Consider a proposition such as

(2)   Albert Gore will freely decide to run for president in 2000.

Those who deny that propositions such as (2) can be true generally defend their antirealism by pointing out that such propositions lack sufficient metaphysical grounds. Nothing that Gore is doing here and now, and nothing about his present character, entail that (2) is true. Perhaps there are truths about Gore which entail that he *probably* will freely decide to run, but these facts are insufficient to ground a nonprobabilistic claim such as (2). Such claims, then, are false.

According to Freddoso,

> Sophisticated Molinists will not only welcome but insist on this parallel between antirealism regarding conditional future contingents and antirealism regarding absolute future contingents. Indeed, they will go so far as to claim that the former entails the latter. For on the Molinist view the absolute future is conceptually posterior to, and emerges by divine decree from, the many conditional futures that define the creation situation God finds Himself in.[13]

Freddoso, I think, is clearly right here; from the Molinist perspective, the two antirealisms go hand in hand. Indeed, even from a non-Molinist perspective, it is at least difficult to see how the two could be separated. If (1) is false because ungrounded, isn't the same true for (2)? In any event, it is, perhaps, worth noting that, to the best of my knowledge, neither Robert Adams nor William Hasker, two of the foremost contemporary proponents of the "grounding" objection, affirm in their published writings on this topic that there are any truths such as (2) about the contingent future.[14]

---

[13] Freddoso, "Introduction," p. 70.

[14] Adams says at one point that he doesn't mean to commit himself one way or the other on the question of divine foreknowledge of free human actions. (See "Plantinga on the Problem of Evil," n. 5, p. 254.) Still, the crucial *assumption* ("that what a person's character and dispositions do not causally determine, they do not render absolutely certain") which he mentions in his earlier "Middle Knowledge and the Problem of Evil" would seem to lead inevitably toward the denial of absolute future contingent truths. (The quotation comes from p. 88 of the article as reprinted in *Virtue of Faith*.) Hasker is a bit more forthcoming here; he

It seems to me, then, that at least a strong prima facie case can be made that the two antirealisms stand or fall together, and thus that the first stage of Freddoso's response to the "grounding" objection succeeds. What, then, about the second stage? Why reject antirealism about absolute future contingents?

Freddoso contends that our common attitude toward predictions provides strong evidence in favor of realism here. Were I to assert (2) and Gore subsequently to run for president in 2000, I would be inclined in 2000 to claim that what I had asserted in 1996 was true, and few of us (or, at least, few of us without certain philosophical axes to grind) would be inclined to challenge such an assertion. We might be inclined to question the declaration that I *knew*, or was *certain of*, (2) in 1996; we might suggest that the evidence available at the time justified only a conjecture as to what *probably* would happen. But even if we grant this, contends Freddoso, the probability here is epistemic, not metaphysical. Perhaps I should have had only limited confidence in the truth of (2) in 1996. But this should not blind us to the facts that it was (2) that I believed, and it was (2) that was true.[15] After all, I probably should have had only limited confidence in 1996 in the claim that Oswald shot Kennedy; my lack of certainty hardly entails that this proposition was not true in 1996.

The mention of past tense propositions such as that about Oswald leads us into a further defense of non-conditional future contingents, a defense propounded by Freddoso and at least adumbrated in the second passage from Plantinga quoted above. While the status of absolute *future* contingents is controversial, antirealists about the *past* are in short supply; just about everyone agrees that there are many absolute past contingents which are true. The claim that Oswald shot Kennedy may be debated, but hardly anyone would deny that

(3)   Bill Clinton decided to run for president

is now true. But, asks Freddoso, what is it that grounds the truth of such propositions? Is it causal activity that is going on *here and now*? Of course not. If we wish to ground this truth in someone's (i.e., in Clinton's) actions, we need to look, not at actions that are going on here and now, but at actions

---

straightforwardly *denies* that God has foreknowledge of the sort at issue, and at one point at least implied that there are no truths about what a free creature *will* do. (See pp. 122–125 and the final chapter of *God, Time, and Knowledge.*) Hasker has informed me (in correspondence), however, that he does believe that there are truths about the contingent future, but he maintains that it is impossible for anyone to know them.

[15] See Freddoso, "Introduction," pp. 71–72.

that took place at some point in the past—say, in 1991. Of course, in 1991, what Clinton's activity immediately grounded was not a past-tense proposition such as (3), but the present-tense counterpart of it—namely,

(4)   Bill Clinton decides to run for President.

It would appear, then, that (3) is *now* grounded just in case (4) *was* grounded—that is, just in case "(4) is now grounded" was the case.

Of course, our claims here regarding the grounds of (3), if valid, should be generalizable. So, letting z stand for any nonconditional present-tense contingent proposition, it seems reasonable to assert the following general truth:

> "It *was* the case that z" is now grounded iff "z is now grounded" *was* the case.[16]

Note that this formula can also work for more specific past-tense propositions. At times, past contingents specify precisely when in the past something occurred. For example, we might wish to say, not just that Clinton decided to run for President, but that he decided *two years ago* to run for President. For such a past-tense assertion to be true, it seems clear, the grounding activity needs to take place, not just *somewhere* in the past, but *precisely where* the additional temporal indicator points. So, letting Y stand for any such indicator ("two years ago," "last Thursday," "sometime last month," and the like) which may or may not appear in a past-tense assertion, we seem to be justified in endorsing the following general schema:

> "It *was* the case (Y) that z" is now grounded iff "z is now grounded" *was* the case (Y).

---

[16] There are some cases which, at first glance, might appear to be counterexamples. Take, for example, the proposition, "This white house was red." This surely looks like a past-tense proposition, and one might reasonably think that its present-tense counterpart is "This white house is red." But, of course, this latter proposition clearly isn't such that, at some time in the past, one could truly say that it was then grounded. Do such cases present genuine problems? I think not. What they illustrate, rather, is that apparently simple propositions may in fact have a somewhat more complex form. "This white house was red," for example, is not in fact a simple past-tense proposition; rather, it is most properly understood as a conjunction—i.e., as "This house is white and this house was red." Here, of course, only the second conjunct is past, and it presents no problem for the general schema we have endorsed. Similar purported counterexamples to the schemata I present in the next few pages might also be forwarded, and similar responses seem to be in order.

Freddoso suggests that we model our understanding of the grounding of future contingents on this understanding of past contingents. Just as a past contingent requires grounding activity, not in the present, but only in the past, so a future contingent, he suggests, requires grounding activity only in the future, not in the present. In other words, once we have accepted the formulae noted above concerning past contingents, we have a solid reason for endorsing parallel formulae dealing with future contingents—both the general

> "It *will be* the case that z" is now grounded iff "z is now grounded"
> *will be* the case

and the more specific

> "It *will be* the case (Y) that z" is now grounded iff "z is now grounded"
> *will be* the case (Y).[17]

In commenting favorably upon these claims, Linda Zagzebski notes that a similar biconditional seems to hold with respect to claims concerning possibility.[18] Most of us, for instance, would agree that it is possible that Jack Kemp will freely decide to run for president in 2000; hence, we would agree that

(5)   It might be the case that Jack Kemp freely decides to run for president in 2000

[17] In "The Impossibility of Middle Knowledge," Timothy O'Connor charges that such principles lead to a vicious infinite regress. Suppose we let Fz stand for "It will be the case that z" and Gz stand for "z is now grounded." Our schema can then be interpreted as asserting that $G(Fz)$ iff $F(Gz)$. But $F(Gz)$ is itself a future contingent which (we are assuming) needs to be grounded. So, we seem to be committed to $G[F(Gz)]$. Applying our principle again, we see that $G[F(Gz)]$ iff $F[G(Gz)]$. The latter of these, in turn, commits us to $G\{F[G(Gz)]\}$. And then, of course, we can simply keep going.

As O'Connor sees it, such a sequence is vicious because "At no point in the process is some element independently grounded by the state of the world. Obviously, if a ground is to be a ground, then all conditions for its being so must be satisfied. But this will not be the case where any condition c of the putative ground is such that every condition on [*sic*] *it* must satisfy some further condition" (p. 156). But O'Connor's reasoning here seems less than compelling. So long as z itself is at some point independently grounded by the state of the world, the fact that the various biconditionals to which O'Connor calls attention are all true seems to me to be an innocuous fact. In any event, it is worth pointing out that a similar principle which O'Connor endorses (note 32, pp. 164–165)—namely, Fz is true iff $F(Gz)$—seems to lead to much the same regress. If the regress is innocuous when O'Connor's principle leads to it, why think it suddenly turns vicious when engendered by Freddoso's?

[18] Zagzebski, *Dilemma of Freedom and Foreknowledge*, p. 142.

is true. But what, we might ask, grounds the truth of such a proposition? Is it grounded by anything Kemp does here and now? Again, Zagzebski suggests, the answer is clearly no. Our belief that (5) is true is linked to our belief that there is a possible world in which Kemp decides to run. If we wish to look for some causal activity to ground the truth of (5), we need to look for it *there*, not *here*. So it looks as though we can assert, as yet another general truth about grounding, the following:

> "It *might be* the case that z" is now grounded iff "z is now grounded" *might be* the case.

But, if the grounding activity for a proposition true in our world can take place in another, then the claim that counterfactuals of creaturely freedom are ungrounded seems itself ungrounded. Just as the grounding activity for (5) is to be found in Kemp's free actions in another world, so the grounding activity for (1) is to be found in Gore's free actions in another world. Of course, we can't locate the appropriate grounding action for (1) in quite so general a way as we did for (5). We can't, for instance, say that (1) is true just in case there is *some* world in which Gore accepts the bribe. Nor can we assert the more general:

> "It *would be* the case that z" is now grounded iff "z is now grounded" *would be* the case.

For "would" counterfactuals, unlike simple "might" assertions, require a specifier—a condition under which such-and-such would be the case. Proposition (1), like any counterfactual of creaturely freedom, contains such a specifier: the entire antecedent specifies the condition under which the consequent is asserted to hold. What (1) tells us, we might say, is that it would be the case (if I were to offer the bribe) that Gore would accept. What activity can plausibly be seen as grounding such a proposition? Gore's activity of accepting the bribe, an activity which takes place not in our world (presumably), but in those nearby worlds where the bribe is offered. The more general formula that would apply to counterfactuals of creaturely freedom of the form $(c \rightarrow z)$, then, would seem to be

> "It *would be* the case (if c were true) that z" is now grounded iff "z is grounded" *would be* the case (if c were true).

By extending what seems to be an intuitively very plausible model for grounding general absolute (i.e., nonconditional) past contingent truths, then, we seem to able to formulate plausible analogous principles concerning the grounding of specific absolute past contingents, general absolute future contingents, specific absolute future contingents, possibility claims, and conditional future contingents. In each of these cases, the general form of the biconditionals we have proposed is identical, namely,

> "It X the case (Y) that z" is now grounded iff "z is grounded" X the case (Y).

Rephrasing the right hand side, we see that this general form can also be presented, perhaps more illuminatingly, as

> "It X the case (Y) that z" is now grounded iff
> it X the case (Y) that "z is now grounded."

Whichever of these versions we prefer, we can see now that the general formulae we have endorsed give us, in essence, the same advice in terms of locating the grounding of a proposition. If we want to know whether a temporally or modally qualified proposition of the form

> It X the case (Y) that z

is grounded *here and now*, we need to look where the temporal or modal operator X tells us to look (into the past of our world, the future of our world, some other world), look precisely where the specifier Y tells us to look (three years ago, two months from now, the nearest world in which I offer Gore the bribe[19]), and see if the present-tense proposition z is grounded *there* by the causal activity of some agent. If it is, the proposition in question is grounded; if it isn't, the proposition is ungrounded.

The Freddosoan response to the "grounding" objection seems to me to be a strong one. Is it conclusive? Of course not. The adamant proponent of the objection has a number of places where he might call this response into question. One might attack the first stage of Freddoso's argument by denying that antirealism regarding conditional future contingents entails antirealism regarding absolute future contingents, and by pointing out that no non-Molinist argument for the alleged entailment has thus far been presented. One might

---

[19] The last example here, and the subsequent discussion in this chapter, assumes (for purposes of expository simplicity) Robert Stalnaker's view concerning counterfactuals. Were one to side with David Lewis, the statement of where the antecedent of (1) tells us to look, along with subsequent statements, would be considerably more complex, but not substantially altered.

resist the second stage by arguing that Freddoso's reliance upon our common reaction to predictive claims is unconvincing, and by denying that only epistemic probability is relevant to such claims. Or one might attempt to break the alleged analogies between the ways in which past, future, and counterfactual propositions can be grounded by actions occurring at times and in worlds other than our own. One might, for example, insist that all contingent propositions need to be grounded solely in current activities; past contingents can satisfy this condition insofar as their causal traces are present here and now, but neither future nor counterfactual contingents could be similarly grounded.

While some of these responses strike me as more believable (or at least less incredible) than others, I must confess that none of them seems to me particularly attractive; each, I think, exudes a clear scent of artificiality and implausibility. One final objection to the Freddosoan response, however, seems more powerful, and deserves a more extended examination.

The objection I have in mind grants that past and future activities can ground past and future absolute contingents, but denies that such activity is available for counterfactual conditionals. Actual world exercises of causal power, one might say, can provide grounds for actual world truths; what goes on solely in other possible worlds, though, cannot provide analogous grounds for the truth of counterfactuals of creaturely freedom. Why not? Because, according to the formula we have adopted, a counterfactual such as $(c \rightarrow z)$ is grounded only if z would be grounded if c were true—in other words, only if, in the nearest world in which the agent in question is in c, she grounds z—say, by performing action Z. But if the agent is truly free, then aren't there worlds in which she is in c and *refrains* from performing Z that are just as close to our world as any world in which she is in c and *performs* Z? If a Z-less world *is* just as close to the actual world as is a Z-ful one, then the claim that z would be grounded if she were in c is false; and if it is false, then our biconditional entails that $(c \rightarrow z)$ is ungrounded.

In response to such an objection, Molinists can probably do no better than repeat the point made years ago by Plantinga that, in comparing worlds, one point of similarity is similarity regarding counterfactuals.[20] A Z-less world may be no less similar to the actual world than is a Z-ful one if only fundamentally non-conditional propositions are considered. But if, as Plantinga contends, "one feature determining the similarity of worlds is whether they share their counterfactuals,"[21] then the Z-ful world may well be more similar to the actual

[20] See Plantinga, *The Nature of Necessity*, p. 178. See also Wierenga, *The Nature of God*, pp. 145–148, and Plantinga, "Replies," pp. 377–378.
[21] Plantinga, *The Nature of Necessity*, p. 178.

world due to the fact that, both in it and in the actual world, $(c \rightarrow z)$ is true, whereas the same counterfactual is false in the relevant Z-less worlds.

Experience has taught me that many find this Plantingean response to be unsatisfying, question-begging, even a bit amusing (or, as one discussant put it to me, Pickwickian).[22] Others see it as nothing less than a surrender of the claim that counterfactuals of creaturely freedom are grounded and a tacit endorsement of the claim that their truth is a brute or primitive fact about the world.[23] Such reactions are not entirely unwarranted; after all, as even Freddoso has conceded, the Plantingean response surely "cuts against the spirit, if not the letter, of the standard possible-world semantics for subjunctive conditionals,"[24] for, as usually interpreted, such semantics imply that similarity among worlds is independent of or prior to the truth of counterfactuals. Nevertheless, the fact that Plantinga's line exudes a hint of heterodoxy in this respect seems to me poor grounds for rejecting it, since it is a kind of heterodoxy which seems but a natural extension for a realist about the future. Once again, comparing antirealist arguments against Plantinga's line with antirealist arguments against absolute future contingents proves to be illuminating.

Suppose the antirealist were to point out that (2), the claim that Gore will freely run for president, cannot now be grounded because there are possible futures (call them Goreful ones) in which "Gore freely runs" is true and other possible futures (call them Goreless ones) in which "Gore freely runs" is false, and there is no reason to view either type of future as privileged with respect to (or, as we might be tempted to say, as more similar to) the world as it is here and now. The natural realist response, I take it, would be to say that the two types of possible futures are *not* equal, for only one is part of the actual world. But won't such a response be rejected by the antirealist, whose whole point is that there is no such thing as *the* actual, fully determinate world? Won't he ask what it is about the world *here and now* which grounds the claim that the Goreful future will come to be? In reply, the realist, I think, would have to grant that the Goreful future may not have any privileged status over the Goreless ones if only fundamentally nonfuture propositions are allowed into consideration. However, if fundamentally future propositions

---

[22] Even some *friends* of Molinism view Plantinga's move here with disdain. Gaskin, for example, dismisses it as a "desperate tactic" and prefers a more radical break with the Stalnaker-Lewis approach: as Molinists, he argues, "we cannot find a role for the relation of comparative similarity of possible worlds in our semantics for conditionals of freedom." See Gaskin, "Conditionals of Freedom and Middle Knowledge," p. 429.

[23] See n. 22, p. 93, added by Adams to the version of "Middle Knowledge and the Problem of Evil" in *Virtue of Faith*.

[24] Freddoso, "Introduction," p. 74.

(such as the temporally indexed "Gore runs for president in 2000," or the simpler "Gore will run for president") are acknowledged as truths about the way things are here and now, it follows that the privileged status of the Goreful futures can indeed be defended. But, of course, to the antirealist, assuming there to *be* such truths here and now is sure to seem unsatisfying, question-begging, perhaps even amusing in a Pickwickian sense.

The upshot of our discussion should be clear. Perhaps there is a sense in which those who embrace the Plantingean response outlined above are viewing counterfactuals of creaturely freedom as basic, primitive, ungrounded facts about the way things are. But if so, it would seem that, in much the same sense, realists about the future are viewing absolute future contingents as equally basic, primitive, ungrounded facts about the way things are. To reject the antirealist demand for non-Pickwickian "here and now" grounding for absolute future contingents, but insist upon such grounding for conditional future contingents, would hardly be a consistent or reasonable stance.

5. Conclusion

The Freddosoan type of response to the "grounding" objection which we have examined in this chapter admittedly falls short of the status of a demonstrative rejoinder. Still, it seems to me to provide us with powerful reasons to reject that objection. At the very least, I think, it shows us that the "grounding" objection is far from the conclusive refutation of Molinism it is sometimes made out to be. Given that the cost for the libertarian of rejecting Molinism is the demolition of the traditional notion of providence, the "grounding" objection gives the orthodox Christian insufficient incentive to pay so high a price.

[6]

Hasker's Attack on Middle Knowledge

Facts are stubborn things; and whatever may be our wishes, our inclinations, or the dictates of our passions, they cannot alter the state of facts and evidence.

—John Adams, arguing in defense of the British soldiers during the Boston Massacre trials

1. Hasker's Argument

In his remarkable book *God, Time, and Knowledge,* William Hasker offers a tantalizing and intricate twist on the standard sort of "grounding" objection, a variation distinct enough and sophisticated enough to warrant individual attention.[1] Hasker's concern is with whether or not Molinists are committed to the claim that we *bring about* the truth of those counterfactuals of creaturely freedom which are about us. He attempts to show that, if we tentatively grant that there are such truths, the Molinist must say that we do not bring about their truth. But if we don't bring about their truth, it follows that we lack the power to do anything other than what we do. Since no libertarian can countenance such powerlessness, Hasker concludes that the tentative concession mentioned above needs to be withdrawn: there are no true counterfactuals of creaturely freedom.

As anyone who has examined Hasker's argument knows, offering so meager a summary of it is rather like offering a five-second sketch of a rococo altarpiece. The argument against middle knowledge contained in Hasker's text comprises a lengthy, fascinating, and complicated chain of reasoning. Still, I don't think it would be an improper simplification for us to view it as depending crucially upon the following four premises, premises which he suggests the Molinist should accept:[2]

---

[1] William Hasker, *God, Time, and Knowledge* (Ithaca: Cornell University Press, 1989).
[2] Hasker, at any rate, has agreed that a very slightly simpler predecessor of what follows is

(1)   If E brings it about that "Q" is true, then E is a token of an event-
        type T such that [(some token of T occurs) $\rightarrow$ Q] and [$\sim$ (some token
        of T occurs) $\rightarrow$ $\sim Q$], and E is the first token of T which occurs.[3]

(2)   Counterfactuals of creaturely freedom are more fundamental features of
        the world than are particular facts. (Hence, worlds that differ from the
        actual world with regard to factual content are closer than those that
        differ from it with regard to counterfactuals of creaturely freedom.)[4]

(3)   If it is in A's power to bring it about that P, and "P" entails "Q" and
        "Q" is false, then it is in A's power to bring it about that Q.[5]

(4)   If S freely does B in situation A, then it was in S's power to bring it
        about that ($\sim B$ & A).[6]

Let me briefly summarize Hasker's argument.[7] Suppose that there is a true
counterfactual of creaturely freedom about me (symbolized by $A \rightarrow B$) with
a true antecedent. Suppose furthermore that we say that I can bring about
the truth of this counterfactual, and that I do so by performing the action
specified by B. If (1) is true, then I can bring about the truth of this counterfactual only if it is true that, had I *not* performed the action specified in
the consequent B, the counterfactual would not have been true. But, argues
Hasker, if (2) is true, then this necessary condition will never be satisfied, for
there will always be a world in which some of the circumstances specified in
the antecedent A are false that is closer to the actual world than is any world
in which the counterfactual of creaturely freedom $A \rightarrow B$ is false. Therefore,
there is no counterfactual of creaturely freedom the truth of which I can bring
about. But if (3) is true, then for me to have the power to bring it about that
$\sim B$ even though A is true, I must have the power to bring it about that
$A \rightarrow \sim B$, for the Molinist is committed to saying that [(A & $\sim B$) $\Rightarrow$
($A \rightarrow \sim B$)]. Since, as we saw, it follows from (1) and (2) that I don't have
the power to bring about the truth of a counterfactual of creaturely freedom,
it follows from (1), (2), and (3), along with our initial assumption that there
is a true counterfactual of creaturely freedom, that I don't have the power to

---

an "accurate paraphrase and simplification of an argument which, in its original version, is
both lengthy and formidably complex." See his "Response to Thomas Flint," *Philosophical
Studies* 60 (1990), 118.

[3] My (1) is identical to Hasker's (16) on p. 42 of *God, Time, and Knowledge.*

[4] See *God, Time, and Knowledge,* pp. 45–47.

[5] My (3) is identical to what Hasker calls (PEP); ibid., p. 49.

[6] This premise is never stated explicitly by Hasker but is, I think, assumed in the discussion
of (3), ibid., pp. 49–52. It should also be noted that we are assuming here that situation A is
not one of those unusual ones which give rise to Frankfurt-type concerns about whether
freedom in this case requires the ability to do otherwise.

[7] The argument as presented ibid. extends from p. 39 to p. 52.

bring it about that $\sim B$ given A. But of course, as a libertarian, the Molinist
is committed to (4)—that is, to the claim that, as a free agent, I *do* have the
power to bring it about that $\sim B$ given A. If our four crucial premises (1)
through (4) are beyond reproach, it follows that we have no choice but to
surrender our initial assumption. In other words, it follows that there are no
true counterfactuals of creaturely freedom.

Now, it seems to me that Hasker's argument is surely valid; if (1) through
(4) were all undeniable from the Molinist perspective, Molinists would have
no choice but to abandon that perspective. But are (1) through (4) all clearly
true, or all theses that no self-respecting Molinist could reject? It seems to me
that the answer is clearly no.

2. Is the Molinist Committed to (2)?

Hasker's Two Arguments for (2)

Let us take (2) to begin with. Why should we think Molinists are committed to it? Hasker gives us two reasons. First, he says, that great guru of
modern Molinists, Alvin Plantinga, "is pretty clearly committed to the view
that, in deciding the comparative similarity of possible worlds, counterfactuals
outweigh differences in matters of fact *whether or not* they are backed by laws
of nature."[8] Now, if one looks at the passage from Plantinga's *Nature of Necessity* to which Hasker refers us here, one will search in vain for anything
equivalent to (2). Plantinga's conclusion, which he states twice, is that "one
feature determining the similarity of worlds is whether they share their counterfactuals," and it is far from evident how one could derive (2) from this
conclusion.[9] It seems to me that, given the context of Plantinga's discussion,
he might be committed to the claim that, in deciding the comparative similarities of possible worlds, counterfactuals outweigh differences in matters of
fact that obtain *after* the time specified by the antecedent of the counterfactual.[10] But this modified version of (2) will do Hasker no good, for his ar-

---

[8] Ibid, p. 45.
[9] Alvin Plantinga, *The Nature of Necessity* (Oxford: Clarendon Press, 1974), p. 178.
[10] Plantinga's discussion centers on the following counterfactual:

(α)   If Robbins had slipped and fallen at Thanksgiving Ledge [at *t*], he would have
        been killed.

Suppose that Robbins in fact *didn't* slip and fall at *t* and hence is still alive. One might be
tempted, says Plantinga, to argue for the falsity of (α) by contending that a world (call it Float)
in which Robbins does slip and fall, but immediately thereafter reappears unharmed where he
was in the actual world (call it *W*), is closer to the actual world than is a world (call it Squash)
in which Robbins is killed after slipping and falling. Plantinga rejects this argument because,

gument requires that the Molinist think that counterfactuals outweigh differences in matters of fact which occur *before* the time specified by the antecedent. So far as I can see, then, Plantinga's discussion in *The Nature of Necessity* gives us no reason to think that the Molinist needs to embrace (2).

Hasker's second argument for (2) is more complex than a mere appeal to a Molinist holy book. He suggests that (2) is derivable from two other statements to which the Molinist is committed, namely,

(a)   Counterfactuals of creaturely freedom are more fundamental features of the world than are counterfactuals backed by laws of nature.

and

(b)   Counterfactuals backed by laws of nature are more fundamental features of the world than are particular facts.

Indeed, he suggests that we don't even need anything quite so strong as (a). His argument, he says, can get by with the weaker

(a*)   Counterfactuals of freedom are *just as* fundamental features of the world as are counterfactuals backed by laws of nature.

Hasker claims that the Molinist is committed to (a), and argues for this claim. (a*) is offered more as a fallback position; even if the Molinist were to escape from (a), (a*) would be harder to deny.[11] Hence, in examining Hasker's argument, we will look primarily at (a), but consider also whether the reasons offered for (a) would support the weaker (a*).

First, though, a word about (b) seems in order. Hasker seems to think that (b) is beyond dispute, but it seems to me that we might have reason to question whether or not it expresses anything like a general truth. Surely the Molinist will want to say that some facts (e.g., that God exists) are more fundamental features of the world than are *any* natural law counterfactuals. Even if we limit ourselves to contingent facts, might not the Molinist—indeed, might not just about anybody—think that some such facts are more funda-

---

though Float is more like *W* after *t* than is Squash, this similarity concerning matters of fact after the time of the antecedent of (α) is outweighed by the fact that the causal laws (and, presumably, the counterfactuals grounded in them) that obtain in Float are very different from those that obtain in *W* and Squash.

[11]   See Hasker, *God, Time, and Knowledge*, pp. 45–48, and "Response to Thomas Flint," pp. 118–120.

mental than are some natural law counterfactuals? For example, might one not argue that *God became man* is more fundamental to our world than is, say, some counterfactual about potential causal interaction between two specific hydrogen molecules? Surely, many natural law counterfactuals *are* more fundamental than are many particular facts. But I don't think it is nearly as neat a situation as (b) suggests.

So there are reasons, I think, for doubting (b). But suppose we bracket such doubts for the moment and concentrate on (a) instead. Why should we think that (a) is true? Hasker offers three reasons.

Hasker's First Argument for (a): Who's in Control Here?

First, he notes, Molinists think that God has no control over which counterfactuals of creaturely freedom are true. But God clearly does have control over which laws of nature are true, and thus does have control over which counterfactuals based on such laws are true. Hence, the counterfactuals of creaturely freedom are more fundamental than the counterfactuals based on natural laws.[12]

In responding to this argument as presented in a prior paper by Hasker,[13] both Edward Wierenga and I separately noted that it comes perilously close to simply begging the question.[14] The point under discussion is whether or not I as a Molinist can plausibly claim that I have a kind of control over my counterfactuals of creaturely freedom that no one else has, not even God. For Hasker to imply that, because God has no control over counterfactuals of creaturely freedom, neither do the agents involved, doesn't seem to amount to much more than assuming what was to be shown.

Though denying that his argument was question-begging, Hasker concedes in *God, Time, and Knowledge* that it is not a particularly powerful one for him to employ in defense of (a) or (a*). Instead, he offers us two new reasons for thinking that (a) is true.

Hasker's Second Argument for (a): Necessitation Conditionals

According to Hasker, the Molinist is committed to viewing counterfactuals of creaturely freedom as what John Pollock refers to as *necessitation* conditionals. But counterfactuals based on laws of nature, he says, are not asserting

---

[12] Hasker, *God, Time, and Knowledge*, p. 45.
[13] William Hasker, "A Refutation of Middle Knowledge," *Noûs* 20 (1986), pp. 545–557.
[14] See Edward Wierenga, *The Nature of God* (Ithaca: Cornell University Press, 1989), p. 155, n. 73, and my "Hasker's 'Refutation' of Middle Knowledge" (unpublished).

necessary connections; for since "we now know with virtual certainty that the fundamental laws of nature are probabilistic rather than strictly deterministic," counterfactuals grounded in natural laws must rate as *would-probably* conditionals. Hence, he concludes, counterfactuals of creaturely freedom must be weighed more heavily than counterfactuals based on natural laws in determining the relative closeness of possible worlds.[15]

It seems to me that Hasker has been misled by a name here. It is true that the counterfactuals endorsed by the Molinist must be what Pollock calls necessitation conditionals, but this fact hardly has the mammoth ramifications that Hasker ascribes to it. For note Pollock's definition of a necessitation conditional:

$$P > > Q \text{ iff } \{(P \to Q) \, \& \, [(\sim P \, \& \, \sim Q) \to (P \to Q)]\}[16]$$

(Note that "> >" here stands for the necessitation conditional, while "→" stands for what Pollock calls the simple subjunctive.) Now, if this is all that is meant by calling a conditional a necessitation conditional, then the Molinists need have no fear in granting that counterfactuals of creaturely freedom are necessitation conditionals. For, despite the name, there simply is no necessitation required in order for the definiens to be true. Even Pollock seems to realize that these conditionals are more innocuous than their name might suggest; as he puts it, "one should realize that necessitations are not 'necessary connections,' except perhaps in a very weak sense."[17] Indeed, Pollockian necessitations are so weak that I see no reason to doubt that even the counterfactuals based on natural laws would rank as necessitation conditionals in his sense.[18] Be that as it may, I suspect that, had Pollock chosen a different name

[15] Hasker, *God, Time, and Knowledge*, p. 47.

[16] John Pollock, *Subjunctive Reasoning* (Dordrecht: D. Reidel, 1976), p. 41. Pollock calls this definition theorem 6.14.

[17] Ibid., p. 36.

[18] Hasker's assumption that the fundamental laws of nature are nondeterministic is itself quite controversial. But even granting that assumption, why should he expect the Molinist (of all people) to agree that, in the absence of determining conditions, the most we can have is a would-probably conditional? If one agreed to such a restriction, one wouldn't be a Molinist in the first place. For Hasker's most recent attempt to defend his position, see "Middle Knowledge: A Refutation Revisited," *Faith and Philosophy* 12 (1995), 225. As I see it, this piece fails to give us good reason to think that the Molinist, or anyone else for that matter, should view all natural law counterfactuals as would-probably conditionals.

Furthermore, even if we *did* so view them, it is far from clear that these would-probably conditionals would be less fundamental truths about our world than are counterfactuals of creaturely freedom. Suppose that natural laws could support nothing stronger than conditionals of the form "*Y* would *probably* occur if conditions *X* obtained." Given that we think of natural laws as fundamental features of our world, shouldn't we think of these conditionals as equally

for his necessitation conditionals—say, had he called them "very weak conditionals"—Hasker would not so much as thought of presenting this second argument, for there wouldn't be much rhetorical force in suggesting that *very weak* conditionals are more fundamental than *would-probably* conditionals! In any event, it seems evident that this second argument offers us little reason to endorse either (a) or (a*).

Hasker's Third Argument for (a): Miracles

Hasker's third argument for (a) is based on the fact that God can and does perform miracles. "If this is so," he says, "then some counterfactuals backed by laws of nature have counterexamples *in the actual world itself,* and therefore also in possible worlds as close to the actual world as you please." Therefore, counterfactuals of creaturely freedom count for more in determining similarity of worlds than do counterfactuals based on natural laws.[19]

It seems to me that Hasker shows here only that counterfactuals based on natural laws are not *always* more important in determining similarity than are counterfactuals of creaturely freedom. In those (presumably) rare instances when a miracle occurs, when a specific law of nature is violated, then at least one counterfactual based on that law will be false in the actual world, and hence its falsity in some other world needn't count against that world's similarity to our own. But it seems to me that this (rather obvious) fact about what is true in rather extraordinary circumstances gives us no reason to think that the same holds in ordinary, non-miraculous circumstances. If there is no miraculous activity on God's part and hence no violation of a certain law of nature, is it clear that a world in which such a violation does occur, and hence in which counterfactuals based on that law are false, is closer than a world in which a counterfactual of freedom true in our world is false? I see no reason to think so.

Perhaps an example borrowed from Hasker will help here. Suppose I am making a poster and using an open bottle of ink. Suppose that I have done this often in the past and, thanks to my noticeable lack of physical dexterity, have generally ended up knocking over the bottle and spilling the ink, much to the dismay of my wife, who, despite her distress at the fact that our floor

---

fundamental—as false only in rather distant worlds? Compare with the case of a million-sided die, the sides numbered with the integers from 1 through 1,000,000. Suppose the existence of this die warranted nothing stronger than the conditional "If I were to roll this die, I would probably not roll a 54." Wouldn't we still think of this would-probably conditional as one that is false only in rather distant worlds?

[19] Hasker, *God, Time, and Knowledge,* p. 47.

is starting to look like a product of Pollock (Jackson, not John), has always agreed to buy me more ink. Suppose my clumsiness strikes again; I jostle the bottle, it falls, and the ink spills. This time, however, my wife reacts differently; she freely decides not to buy me any more ink.

Suppose we let C stand for the circumstances in which I knock over the ink. C, then, will include facts about my past adventures in ink-spilling, the present state and position of the bottle of ink, and much information about my wife and the various reasons she has had for and against buying me more ink. According to the Molinist, in the world we have imagined—a world, note, in which God doesn't intervene miraculously to save me from the natural effects of my clumsiness—the following two counterfactuals would be true:

(5)   I am in circumstances C and I knock my ink bottle in such-and-such a way → the bottle of ink falls and the ink spills

(6)   I am in circumstances C and I knock my ink bottle in such-and-such a way → my wife (freely) refuses to buy me more ink

The first of these is clearly a counterfactual based on a law of nature, while the second is a counterfactual of creaturely freedom. Now ask yourself: Which of these two is the less fundamental truth about our world? Which has counterexamples in worlds closer to the actual world? According to Hasker, the answer is (5). But this response seems clearly wrong to me. Assuming (5) to be grounded by natural laws, the easiest way for it to turn out false might well be for God to perform a miracle. But, as we know, miracles are few and far between, especially miracles regarding my clumsiness with ink bottles. With (6), on the other hand, it is fairly clear that it could easily have been false. For my wife has been in very similar situations in the past and has agreed to buy me more ink. All that we need for (6) to be false is for her to act on the same reasons she has repeatedly acted on in the past. Thus, in nonmiraculous cases such as this, it seems evident that Hasker is mistaken. Hence, the possibility of miracles offers precious little support to (a).

Given a lengthy response he formulates in a footnote to a point raised by Alvin Plantinga, I suspect that Hasker would question my suggestion that my wife could easily have rendered (6) false.[20] Adapting this footnote to the present example, I can imagine Hasker arguing:

[20] The note in question is 46 on p. 48 of God, Time, and Knowledge.

Starting with the assumption that (6) is true, and that Flint's wife in fact refuses to buy him more ink, we ask ourselves this question: What is the minimal change that would be needed in the actual world, such that if things were different in that way, his wife would freely buy him more ink? It may not be obvious what the answer is, but surely there must *be* an answer, an answer specifying some change in the circumstances in which his wife found herself. Suppose we let 'D^*' stand for the proposition saying that she is in these modified circumstances. We then ask: If Flint's wife were to buy him more ink, would it be because D^* was true rather than D (where D is to be thought of as C expanded to include Flint's knocking the ink bottle), or because (6) was false? And for the reasons already discussed, the correct answer will be that if she were to freely buy the ink this would be because the circumstances were different than they are in the actual world (in which she refuses), and not because (6) would be false.[21]

If we let I stand for my wife's freely buying more ink, the suggestion being made by our imaginary Haskerian is that, not only is it that case that (6)—($D \to \sim I$)—is true, but furthermore (6) *would still have been* true even had my wife bought more ink; that is,

$$(7) \quad I \to (D \to \sim I).$$

But (7) could be true only if

$$(8) \quad I \to \sim D$$

were also true.[22] So our Haskerian is suggesting that the Molinist is committed to thinking that (8) is true.

But is she? Why couldn't the Molinist just as coherently insist that (8) is false—that, had my wife bought me more ink, she would have done so in D? Indeed, isn't this position the far more plausible one for the Molinist—indeed, for any libertarian—to take? Were it already demonstrated that (2) was true, the case for (7) and (8) would undoubtedly be much stronger. But, of course, (2) is precisely the premise of Hasker's argument which we are currently investigating. Hence, we can hardly appeal *to* it in defense of our Haskerian attempt to build a case *for* it.

---

[21] Hasker has indicated in correspondence that he would be inclined to endorse the argument I have constructed for him here.

[22] Since *modus tollens* holds for counterfactuals, we know that

$(7^*) \quad [I \,\&\, (D \to \sim I)] \to \sim D.$

(8) then follows from (7) and (7^*) by means of the valid inferential principle *If $(X \to Y)$ and $[(X \,\&\, Y) \to Z]$, then $X \to Z$.*

It is worth highlighting the rather extraordinary power that (8) would be ascribing to my wife. To affirm (8) is to claim that my wife has the power to do something such that, were she to do it, certain truths about past events would have been false, even though her so acting is not logically tied to those truths. In other words, it is to ascribe to my wife merely counterfactual power over the hard past. (By merely counterfactual power, I mean counterfactual power where no stronger connection such as logical or causal implication is being asserted.) As we shall see in our discussion of petitionary prayer in Chapter 11, I think the Molinist ought to leave open the possibility of merely counterfactual power over the past. But I doubt that such power should be multiplied beyond necessity. And our Haskerian would be asking the Molinist to embrace a rather mind-boggling multiplication of such power. For *any* true counterfactual of creaturely freedom $C \rightarrow A$ with a true antecedent, the Haskerian would have the Molinist endorse the claim that the agent in question had the power to do something ($\sim A$) such that, were he to do it, the past (C) would have been different. In other words, whenever I freely act, I could have acted in such a way that the past *would* have been, though it wouldn't *have* to have been, other than it was. Soft determinists might find such a thesis attractive, but so far as I can see, there is no reason whatsoever for the Molinist, or for any libertarian, to embrace so outlandish a claim.

The reasonable Molinist, I think, will grant that, on rare occasions, we may have counterfactual power over the past of the sort our Haskerian proposes, and thus, on rare occasions, may *lack* counterfactual power over a counterfactual such as (6). Similarly, it is at least conceivable that, on rare occasions, we may *have* counterfactual power over a natural-law counterfactual such as (5). Perhaps there is something I or someone else could do such that, were we to do it, God would suspend the normal course of nature and bring it about that the ink not spill as a result of my knocking the ink bottle. But I think any reasonable Molinist will see these as clear exceptions to the rule. In general, such a Molinist will insist, we *do* have counterfactual control over our own counterfactuals of creaturely freedom, and *don't* have such control over counterfactuals backed by laws of nature; facts of the latter sort are for us simply much more stubborn things than are facts of the former variety. So the possibility of miracles gives us no reason to think that the former counterfactuals are even *as*, let alone *more*, fundamental features of the world than are the latter. Miracles, then, lend no support either to (a) or to (a★).

Indeed, even Hasker has been led to concede—for reasons other than those offered above—that his appeal to miracles fails to demonstrate (a). As he notes,

Many theists are inclined to say that natural laws, when correctly understood, contain an implicit "boundary condition" to the effect that the law prescribes what will occur *absent interference by a supernatural being*. When a miracle does occur, one could then say that the counterfactual which has been violated was *not* in fact backed by the corresponding law of nature; since the boundary conditions have been breached, the law in question no longer applies. If this way of understanding laws of nature can be upheld, my argument would be neutralized.[23]

Since Hasker nowhere suggests that this way of understanding laws of nature *can't* be upheld, it seems that even he is willing to concede that his miracle-based argument for (a) and (a★) fails.

Summary of the Case for (2)

Let me sum up the situation we have thus far reached concerning Hasker's argument against middle knowledge. That argument, recall, is based on the four premises (1) through (4). But as we have seen, neither of Hasker's arguments for the claim that the Molinist is committed to (2) seems to stand up. The first argument, based on the allegation that (2) is endorsed by Plantinga, seems clearly mistaken in its interpretation of Plantinga. The second argument relies upon either (a) or (a★) as a premise, but Hasker tries three times and fails three times to show that the Molinist (or anyone else, for that matter) should endorse either (a) or (a★). So Hasker has given us no solid argument for the Molinist to accept (2). And since just about any Molinist, I think, would initially be strongly inclined to *reject* (2)—since it is not the sort of premise one would expect the Molinist to accept *without* argument—Hasker's argument simply dissolves. Regardless of what we say about premises (1), (3), and (4) of the argument, it seems clear that his attempt to refute the doctrine of middle knowledge is a failure.

3. Is the Molinist Committed to (1), (3), and (4)?

"Bringing About": A Causal Analysis?

Well, now, what *are* we to say about (1), (3), and (4)? Given Hasker's failure to support (2), Molinists might be free to endorse any or all of them without fear of undermining their position. But should they, indeed should anyone, endorse any or all of them? That depends, I think, upon what concept of *bringing about* Hasker is employing. That he has to be using the same notion

[23] See Hasker, "Response to Thomas Flint," p. 125, n. 2.

in (1), (3), and (4) seems clear, for otherwise the argument would be a simple case of equivocation. But what *does* Hasker mean by "bring about"?

Initially, one might suspect that a straightforwardly causal analysis is the appropriate one: a person brings about the truth of a proposition just in case the person *causes* the proposition to be true. Putting this schematically, we have:

(BA$_1$) S brings it about that Y is true =df. S causes it to be the case that Y.

Though such an analysis suffers from a degree of vagueness (containing as it does what Peter van Inwagen has called that "horrible little word 'cause' "),[24] I think it is fairly clear that there is a respectable notion of bringing about which is at least approximated by (BA$_1$). However, it also seems clear that (BA$_1$) will be of little help to Hasker in refuting the doctrine of middle knowledge, for few if any Molinists will see any reason to accept (3) if "bring about" is understood in this causal sense. For if (as Molinists believe) a creator God has foreknowledge essentially and necessarily, then my wife's agreeing to buy me ink would entail that God foreknew that she would agree. But then, according to (3), my wife has the power to agree to buy me ink only if she has the power to *cause* it to be that case that God foreknew that she would so agree—that is, only if my wife has causal power over the past. Since, as we have seen, most Molinists would follow Molina in rejecting the suggestion that we have causal power over the past, few of Hasker's opponents would see any reason to accept (3) read in the causal way suggested.

What is more, it is evident that Hasker himself would reject (3) if read along the lines of (BA$_1$). When explaining that he means "bring about" to stand for a relation weaker than causation, he notes: "By reading this paper I bring it about that 'Hasker will read a paper tomorrow' was true yesterday, but I don't think I *cause* that proposition to have been true yesterday."[25] Let us call the paper in question X and suppose, as seems reasonable, that Hasker's reading of X is done freely. In that case, he presumably had the power to cause it to be the case that he not read X today. But his not reading X would have entailed that "Hasker will *not* read X tomorrow" was true yesterday, when in fact, of course, it wasn't true yesterday. If *bring about* were read as *cause*, then, (3) would leave Hasker no choice but to conclude that he did have the power to cause it to be the case that "Hasker will not read X

---

[24] Peter van Inwagen, *An Essay on Free Will* (New York: Oxford University Press, 1983), p. 65.

[25] Hasker, "Response to Thomas Flint," p. 121.

tomorrow" was true yesterday. Therefore, Hasker clearly would insist that (3) is false if interpreted via (BA_1).

So the version of (3) engendered by (BA_1) is a principle that hardly anyone would endorse. Definition (BA_1) would seem to suit Hasker's purposes only against those relatively few opponents who believe in backward causation. It hardly offers the resources for a genuine refutation of Molinism.

"Bringing About": A Counterfactual Analysis?

Recalling Plantinga's distinction between what he calls strong and weak actualization, one might suspect that the problem just noted with reading "bring about" in the former sense suggests that we should instead read it in the latter sense.[26] That is, one might think that what Hasker needs is a concept of bringing about such that what one brings about is not [à la (BA_1)] *causally* dependent upon what one does, but only *counterfactually* dependent. Perhaps the notion of bringing about which Hasker requires for his argument to succeed, then, is:

> (BA_2) S brings it about that Y is true =df. For some X, S causes it to be the case that X, and $(X \rightarrow Y)$.

(BA_2) has an obvious advantage over (BA_1): the reading of (3) which (BA_2) engenders is uncontroversially true. Unfortunately for Hasker, the reading of (1) to which (BA_2) gives rise is just as clearly false. By raising my arm today, I bring it about, in the sense delineated by (BA_2), that the sun rises tomorrow morning, for I cause it to be the case that my arm rises, and—assuming that the sun *does* rise tomorrow morning, and assuming that the inference from $(X \& Y)$ to $(X \rightarrow Y)$ is legitimate—*my arm rises today* implies *the sun rises tomorrow morning*. If (1) were true, then my raising my arm would have to be the first token of some event-type such that, had no such event occurred, the sun would not have risen tomorrow. Needless to say, it is exceedingly implausible to think that there *is* any such event-type of which my arm-raising is the first token. And from this it follows that the (1) we get by employing (BA_2) is an extremely implausible principle. So (BA_2) is, from Hasker's point of view, no improvement upon (BA_1).

"Bringing About": Other Possibilities

Since neither the initially most plausible causal nor the initially most plausible counterfactual understanding of bringing about seems at all amenable to

[26] Plantinga, *Nature of Necessity*, pp. 172–173.

Hasker's argument, one might wonder if some alternative account of bringing about is what he has in mind. And when we turn to Hasker's discussion of bringing about in both *God, Time, and Knowledge* and "Response to Thomas Flint," we discover that this is indeed the case. Definition (BA₁), he suggests, is far too strong for the notion he has in mind, for there are many cases of bringing about that are not cases of causing that which is brought about; (BA₂), on the other hand, is much too weak, for there are many cases of the kind of counterfactual dependence stipulated by (BA₂) which are not cases of bringing about. So *bring about* lies somewhere in the territory between causal power and counterfactual power.[27]

But the territory between causal and counterfactual power is a vast and largely uncharted land, one which harbors a plethora of distinct accounts of bringing about. Failure to recognize the variety of concepts inhabiting this land has, I think, led to confusion on a number of philosophical issues, a prime example being alleged libertarian refutations of soft determinism.[28] Failure to tell us exactly what is meant by "bring about" would lead to similar perplexities in this case as well. In the absence of such an analysis, there is simply no way to tell whether (1), (3), and (4) are plausible from a Molinist (or, for that matter, any other) perspective. Indeed, the whole motivation for employing power entailment principles such as (3) against the Molinist collapses if we don't know precisely what those principles are affirming; for all we know, the principles may be perfectly compatible with the Molinist position! (The fact that the Molinist thinks we can't *cause* God to have believed certain things gives us scant reason to suppose that the Molinist thinks we can't *bring it about* that God believed certain things so long as "bring about" is left undefined.) I believe that Hasker was right to view (BA₁) and (BA₂) as inadequate analyses of the concept he has in mind here. But unless he replaces them with another equally specific account of what is meant by "bring about," I think he guarantees the failure of his argument.[29]

[27] See Hasker, *God, Time, and Knowledge*, pp. 104–108, and "Response to Thomas Flint," pp. 121–122.

[28] See my "Compatibilism and the Argument from Unavoidability," *Journal of Philosophy* 84 (1987), 423–440.

[29] Hasker initially responded to this point by suggesting that I was subject to a kind of blindness here. "Bringing about" is *the* notion between causal and counterfactual power, he implied, rather in the way 3 is *the* integer between 2 and 4. Nothing more really needs to be said about it, for just about anybody (other than the unfortunately defective Flint) can just see exactly what the concept is. As he put it, "If Flint has in mind some specific ambiguity involving this notion, then I would ask him to tell us what the ambiguity is so that it can be addressed. His general remarks about a 'vast and largely uncharted land' between causal and counterfactual power do not strike me as particularly helpful" ("Response to Thomas Flint," p. 122). In a more recent work, though, Hasker (having seen an earlier version of this chapter) has softened his stance a bit. In "Middle Knowledge: A Refutation Revisited," he concedes

Since some might question the need for greater specificity here, it seems prudent for me to offer a word or two in defense of my assertion concerning the plethora of distinct accounts of bringing about. An earlier paper of mine provides us the material to construct numerous definitions of "bring about," all distinct from one another and all between (BA₁) and (BA₂).[30] This earlier paper, in the course of examining purported libertarian disproofs of soft determinism, had looked at various ways in which the notion of *unavoidability* might be understood. Now, to say that I can *bring about* the truth of a certain proposition seems very close to saying that the falsity of the proposition is *not unavoidable* for me. Hence, any analysis of unavoidability offers us the resources easily to construct a parallel analysis of bringing about. Given my discussion of unavoidability in the earlier paper, a minimum of eight possible interpretations of "bringing about" are easy to formulate.

A couple of preliminaries are necessary in order to present these eight candidates. First, since we normally don't think of ourselves as having the power to bring about necessary truths, our definiens henceforth will make clear that only contingent truths are eligible to be brought about. Also, I will be using H to stand for the history of the world prior to the time in question, and L to represent the laws of nature. The fact that H and L might be variously interpreted, of course, suggests that our eight suggestions are themselves open to different interpretations and thus actually represent more than simply eight new understandings of "bring about."

As before, in each of these cases, the definiendum is:

> S brings it about that Y.

Our eight definiens can then be presented as follows:

(BA₃) $\Diamond \sim Y$, and for some X, S causes it to be the case that X, and $X \Rightarrow Y$

(BA₄) $\Diamond \sim Y$, and for some X, S causes it to be the case that X, and $(X \,\&\, H) \Rightarrow Y$

(BA₅) $\Diamond \sim Y$, and for some X, S causes it to be the case that X, and $(X \,\&\, H \,\&\, L) \Rightarrow Y$

(BA₆) $\Diamond \sim Y$, and for some X, S causes it to be the case that X, and $(X \,\&\, H) \rightarrow Y$

---

that, by pointing to the variety of ways in which "bring about" might be analyzed, "Flint has presented a challenge that must be taken seriously" (p. 230). Hasker may not quite have come around to my view that there *is* no such thing as *the* notion between causal and counterfactual power (just as there is no such thing as *the* integer between 2 and 200), but he clearly realizes that this view is one he cannot so cavalierly dismiss.

[30] "Compatibilism and the Argument from Unavoidability."

(BA$_7$) $\Diamond \sim Y$, and for some X, S causes it to be the case that X, and
$(X \& H \& L) \rightarrow Y$

(BA$_8$) $\Diamond \sim Y$, and for some X, S causes it to be the case that X, and
$X \Leftrightarrow Y$

(BA$_9$) $\Diamond \sim Y$, and for some X, S causes it to be the case that X, and
$(X \& H) \Leftrightarrow (Y \& H)$

(BA$_{10}$) $\Diamond \sim Y$, and for some X, S causes it to be the case that X, and
$(X \& H \& L) \Leftrightarrow (Y \& H \& L)$

Should we desire, we could easily add to this list still further by adding clauses to our various definiens. For example, we might well want to insist that our account of bringing about not be one according to which, whenever we act, we bring about any and all past events. If so, we might want to add a clause to (BA$_4$) stating that H by itself *doesn't* entail Y. Similar amendments, of course, would lead to further variations on these eight accounts.

Of course, not all of these definitions are equally plausible; some, in fact, seem to delineate concepts that we would hardly ever use the words "bring about" to express. Still, that we *have* a number of distinct concepts here, and that several of them are plausible candidates for what in different contexts is meant by "bring about," seem to me undeniable. Only a fear of committing oneself to one or another of the many possibilities here could blind one to the fact that there *are* so many possibilities here—that we confront, as I said, a vast and largely uncharted land.

"Bringing About": More Failures

For one forwarding Hasker's argument, though, leaving things unsettled has an obvious advantage. So long as our understanding of bringing about is left comfortably vague, one can point to each of (1), (3), and (4) and ask if the premise in question doesn't have a plausible ring to it. And, of course, for each one, there is a reading of "bring about" given which no one could reasonably deny the premise in question. Once we commit to a single, specific, precise account of that locution, though, one or more of those premises quickly become all too dubitable. As we have seen, (3) becomes exceedingly questionable if (BA$_1$) is endorsed, while (BA$_2$) renders (1) untenable. A similar sorry fate awaits Hasker's argument should we attempt to employ any of the other eight accounts we have displayed. For (BA$_3$) through (BA$_7$), (1) is demonstrably false, while for (BA$_8$) through (BA$_{10}$) the same fate confronts (3). Finding a plausible account of "bring about" that will render *each* of (1), (3), and (4) undeniable from the Molinist perspective is no mean feat.[31]

---

[31] It is, perhaps, worth noting that the problem of finding a suitable account of bringing

There are, to be sure, some rather *implausible* accounts which will do the trick. Proposition (1), for example, asserts only a necessary condition of bringing about. Suppose one were to claim that what it offers us is actually a necessary *and sufficient* condition for bringing about. One might then use (1) to build the following definiens of "*S* brings it about that *Y*":

(BA_{11}) *S*'s performance of some action *X* is a token of an event-type *T* such that [(some token of *T* occurs) → *Y*] and [~(some token of *T* occurs) → ~*Y*], and *S*'s performance of *X* is the first token of *T* that occurs.

Such an account of bringing about would render (1) true by definition; and, so far as I can see, there would be no reason for the Molinist to dispute the truth of (3) read along the lines of (BA_{11}). But such an account would not further Hasker's cause significantly, and that for at least two reasons.

First, as intimated at the start of the last paragraph, this understanding of bringing about, taken by itself, seems fairly implausible, for it rather drastically inflates the category of things we bring about. For example, it seems to follow from (BA_{11}) that I bring about all of my descendants' actions, even their free ones, by the very act of conceiving them. Furthermore, (BA_{11}) leads to counterintuitive claims in those cases where one's actions are caused by someone or something else. Suppose, for example, that *Z* causes me to wiggle my right foot. (BA_{11}) would then lead us to say that, by wiggling my right foot, I bring it about that *Z* causes me to wiggle my right foot. And this surely sounds amiss.

The real problem with (BA_{11}), though, lies elsewhere. Suppose we were willing to live with the implausibilities noted in the last paragraph. Suppose, furthermore, we were to dismiss the problems with (2) already examined. (BA_{11}) would then provide us with an account of bringing about that would permit us to endorse each of (1), (2), and (3). Would it thereby turn Hasker's argument into a genuine refutation of Molinism? That depends. For that argument, recall, had *four* major premises, not just the three we have thus far been examining. In order for the argument to succeed, we need an account of bringing about that justifies our acceptance not only of (1) through (3), but also of

---

about has obvious repercussions on the argument for (3) which Hasker offers on pp. 122–123 of "Response to Thomas Flint." There surely are many understandings of "bring about" that will make this argument sound. But the argument *won't* succeed given just *any* understanding; recall (BA_1), which even Hasker agrees makes (3) false.

(4)   If S freely does B in situation A, then it was in S's power to bring it
        about that ($\sim B$ & A).

But, woe and alas, (4) turns out to be a premise which no Molinist employing
(BA_{11}) could be expected to accept if she had already endorsed (1) and (2).
Suppose S freely does B in A. According to (4), this would entail that S had
the power to bring it about that ($\sim B$ & A). Presumably, S would do this by
bringing about $\sim B$. If (BA_{11}) is being used, though, S's doing $\sim B$ would
bring it about that ($\sim B$ & A) only if [(S's doing $\sim B$) $\rightarrow$ ($\sim B$ & A)]. But S's
doing $\sim B$ *doesn't* imply ($\sim B$ & A) if (2) is true. For, as we saw earlier, (2)
commits us to the claim that a free agent would have acted other than she
did only if the situation in which she was placed had been different. In other
words, (2) commits us to saying that, since S freely did B in A, S's doing $\sim B$
would imply $\sim A$. And, of course, if S's doing $\sim B$ implies $\sim A$, it clearly
doesn't imply ($\sim B$ & A). It follows, then, that no one could reasonably be
expected to endorse (4) had they utilized (BA_{11}) to underwrite (1) and (2).
So (BA_{11}) is, from the Haskerian perspective, yet another failure.

Hasker's Best Hope?

There is, however, at least one account of bringing about that comes close
to doing what Hasker wants, an account which he himself has (somewhat
tentatively) proposed:

(BA_{12}) For some X, S causes it to be the case that X, and [(X & H) $\Rightarrow Y$],
        and $\sim(H \Rightarrow Y)$, and $\sim(\sim X \rightarrow Y)$.[32]

(BA_{12}) has many attractive features for Hasker. As he notes, (1) and (3) are
demonstrable given (BA_{12}). Premise (4) would seem to be hard to deny as
well. Furthermore, (BA_{12}) doesn't seem to warrant the rather disturbing "bring
about" ascriptions which other candidates such as (BA_{11}) support.

To be sure, (BA_{12}) does have its drawbacks. As Hasker himself notes, it
entails that, for example, by chopping down a tree, I *don't* bring it about that
the tree dies.[33] Furthermore, as Hasker doesn't note, a more serious problem
with (BA_{12}) is that it may not guarantee some of the formal features which
Hasker wishes "bring about" to have. Hasker has argued that " 'bringing

---

[32] This analysis, which Hasker develops from my (BA_4), is labeled ($BA_4^\star$) in his "Middle
Knowledge: A Refutation Revisited," p. 231.

[33] Ibid., p. 235, n. 22.

about' is a relation which is transitive, asymmetrical, and irreflexive."[34] But does (BA$_{12}$) give us such a relation?

Note first that (BA$_{12}$) isn't really of the right form for us to speak of transitivity, since it presents bringing about as a relation between an agent and a proposition, not between one event and another. Given Hasker's reasonable remarks about the connection between the relation understood in the former sense and the relation understood in the latter sense,[35] it seems that one committed to (BA$_{12}$) would embrace something along the lines of the following account of "bring about" construed as a relation between events:

(BA$_{12}$*) X brings about Y iff for some event Z:
        (i) X causes Z;
        (ii) $[(Z$ occurs and $H) \Rightarrow Y$ occurs$]$;
        (iii) $\sim(H \Rightarrow Y$ occurs$)$; and
        (iv) $\sim(\sim X$ occurs $\rightarrow Y$ occurs$)$.

On the surface, it is hard to see how such an account could guarantee transitivity. The problem comes with condition (iv) in the analysans. Take a case where a brings about b and b brings about c. Given (BA$_{12}$*), this will imply (to put it simply) that $\sim(\sim a \rightarrow b)$ and $\sim(\sim b \rightarrow c)$.[36] To conclude that therefore a brings about c, we would have to be able to deduce that $\sim(\sim a \rightarrow c)$. But, given the failure of transitivity for counterfactuals, it is hard to see how such a deduction could be effected. Thus, (BA$_{12}$*), and derivatively (BA$_{12}$), seem to be delineating relations which are not transitive.

I must admit that I am not convinced that these objections to (BA$_{12}$) and (BA$_{12}$*) are lethal. Perhaps transitivity can be demonstrated in some way; or perhaps the drawbacks to (BA$_{12}$*), though genuine, don't infect (BA$_{12}$) itself. Suppose, then, that we agree to ignore these apparent problems with this account of bringing about and stick with (BA$_{12}$). If we do so, what are we to say about Hasker's argument? Hasker's assessment is that our arrival at (BA$_{12}$) "represents real philosophical progress" because it renders (3) demonstrable. My assessment is somewhat different; though I agree with the ascription of progress, I see progress of a much different sort. What (BA$_{12}$) helps us to see, I think, is that (3) is actually *irrelevant* to the wrangle between Molinists and their Haskerian opponents. It is (2), not (3), which lies at the center of the dispute.

To see this, suppose we have found some account of bringing about— (BA$_{12}$) or some replacement for it—which makes both (1) and (4) clearly undeniable for the Molinist. And suppose again that S freely does B in A.

[34] Ibid., p. 230.
[35] Ibid., p. 235, n. 19.
[36] The representations here are simplified in that the "occurs" are being omitted.

According to (4), this entails that S had the power to bring it about that ($\sim B$ & A), presumably by bringing about $\sim B$. Now, according to (1), S's doing $\sim B$ would bring it about that ($\sim B$ & A) only if [(S's doing $\sim B$) $\rightarrow$ ($\sim B$ & A)]. But, as we have seen, S's doing $\sim B$ *doesn't* imply ($\sim B$ & A) if (2) is true, for (2) commits us to the claim that a free agent would have acted other than she did only if the situation in which she was placed had been different. So (2) commits us to saying that, since S freely did B in A, S's doing $\sim B$ would imply $\sim A$. And, of course, if S's doing $\sim B$ implies $\sim A$, it clearly *doesn't* imply ($\sim B$ & A).

It follows, then, that *any* analysis of bringing about which renders (1) and (4) plausible to the Molinist will simply provide her with yet another reason for questioning (2). For what we have just seen is that the conjunction of (1) and (4) *by itself* entails $\sim$(2).[37] There may well be analyses such as (BA_{12}) which render (1) and (4) plausible; to the extent that they do, though, they render (2) implausible. Of course, things would be different had we seen that (2) was a principle that no self-respecting Molinist could deny; in that case, recognizing that (2) could not be true if (1) and (4) were both true would no doubt be a tad disturbing to the Molinist. As the reader will recall, though, our assessment of (2) was that no Molinist would be predisposed to accept it nor moved by any of Hasker's arguments to embrace it, and this assessment of (2) would presumably remain unchanged whatever analysis of bringing about we might endorse, for (2) itself does not employ any notion of bringing about.

The lessons we should take from this discussion, I think, are twofold. First, we will make little progress in considering Haskerian arguments against Molinism if we focus upon (3), for (3) is utterly superfluous to Hasker's purposes. And second, the real issue is (2). For future reference, let us refer to the claim that the Molinist should embrace (2) as *Hasker's Hypothesis*, or (HH). More formally:

> (HH)   If there are true counterfactuals of creaturely freedom, they are more fundamental features of the world than are particular facts.

If Hasker can make a strong case that Hasker's Hypothesis is true, then the Molinist is finished; but if (as, I think, we have seen) he cannot, then Hasker's purported refutation is demonstrably and irretrievably a failure.

---

[37] I am assuming here a reading of (2) according to which it implies that there are true counterfactuals of freedom. Were one not so to read it, then we would need to add

(5)   There are true counterfactuals of creaturely freedom

to (1), (2), and (4) to get our inconsistent set of propositions.

4. Conclusion

Let me conclude by summarizing our discussion in this chapter. Hasker's argument against Molinism relies upon premises (1) through (4). But Hasker tries repeatedly and fails repeatedly to give us any solid reason to think that Hasker's Hypothesis is true—that is, to think that the Molinist (or anyone else) ought to endorse (2). Furthermore, finding a plausible account of "bring about" which will (so to speak) bring it about that the Molinist is committed to (1), (3), and (4) is quite a challenge. Definition (BA_{12}) or a near relative may be able to meet this challenge, but to the extent that they do, they actually point to the superfluity of (3) and the centrality of Hasker's Hypothesis to his alleged refutation. Far from refuting Molinism, then, Hasker's argument fails even to call it seriously into question.

Adams and Vicious
Circle Arguments

"I don't know what you mean by 'glory,' " Alice said.

Humpty Dumpty smiled contemptuously. "Of course you don't—till I tell you. I meant 'there's a nice knock-down argument for you!' "

"But 'glory' doesn't mean 'a nice knock-down argument,' " Alice objected.

"When I use a word," Humpty Dumpty said, in a rather scornful tone, "it means just what I choose it to mean—neither more nor less."

"The question is," said Alice, "whether you can make words mean so many different things."

"The question is," said Humpty Dumpty, "which is to be master—that's all."

—Lewis Carroll, *Through the Looking-Glass*

1. Adams and the Loop

Let me now turn to another type of argument that has been offered against the Molinist picture, this one by Robert Adams in an article aptly named "An Anti-Molinist Argument."[1] Though Adams presents his argument as a revision of the one offered by Hasker, I am doubtful that this is the right way to view it, for it is really more akin to an argument suggesting that a nasty explanatory circle threatens the Molinist.[2] To see this, let me first present an informal version of this type of vicious-circle argument which is at least closely related to Adams's argument—which is, we might say, a member of the Adams family. I will then turn to a more precise presentation of the argument that Adams actually offers.

According to the Molinist, as we have seen, certain truths are prior—if not

---

[1] Robert Merrihew Adams, "An Anti-Molinist Argument," in James E. Tomberlin, ed., *Philosophical Perspectives*, vol. 5 (Atascadero, Calif.: Ridgeview, 1991), pp. 343–353.

[2] Adams refers to his project as a "recasting of Hasker's anti-Molinist argument." See ibid., p. 346.

temporally, then at least logically or (to use Adams's preferred locution) explanatorily—to others. True counterfactuals of creaturely freedom, for example, are explanatorily prior both to God's knowledge of those counterfactuals and to any creative decision he makes. Thus, his decision to create our friend Cuthbert and put him in situation C is based in part on his (middle) knowledge of what Cuthbert would freely do in that situation. But God's decision to put Cuthbert in situation C is in turn prior to Cuthbert's freely deciding to buy an iguana in that situation. If we were to give a full account of Cuthbert's free decision, we could hardly fail to include in that explanation the fact that he decided in situation C, and that God had arranged things so that Cuthbert was in C. So, thus far we have seen that the true counterfactuals of creaturely freedom are prior to God's knowledge of those counterfactuals, which in turn is prior to God's creative decision, which in turn is prior to Cuthbert's action (which we will call A). But, as libertarians, don't we also want to say that his action is in turn prior to the truth of the relevant counterfactual of creaturely freedom—that is, prior to $C \rightarrow A$?[3] If we ask ourselves why $C \rightarrow A$ is true, don't we want to say that, since Cuthbert actually is in C, the counterfactual is true because he does A—that is, that his doing A in C explains the truth of $C \rightarrow A$? But if we do grant this, then we have woven for ourselves a nasty explanatory loop. That it is a loop can be easily seen in Diagram 5.

Diagram 5

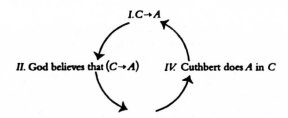

I. $C \rightarrow A$

II. **God believes that** $(C \rightarrow A)$ *IV.* **Cuthbert does A in C**

III. **God decides to put Cuthbert in C**

That it is nasty also seems evident, for it suggests that any element in this loop is ultimately explained by itself, and that is usually seen as a simple impossibility; Cuthbert can't *explain why* he did A in C by noting that he did A in

---

[3] Technically, since C stands for a situation and A stands for an action, the relevant counterfactual should be presented as *Cuthbert is in situation C → Cuthbert performs action A*. For obvious reasons, $C \rightarrow A$ will be used as a convenient shorthand for this counterfactual.

C. What we have here, then, is a loop, and a nasty one. In fact, those given to more colorful imagery might even say that what we have here is a noose, one which presages the last gasp of Molinism.

As a Molinist who feels that neckties are torture enough, I feel some sense of urgency about finding a way to sever this noose.[4] But before I try to indicate how I think the Molinist can get some breathing room, let us look more carefully at the argument Adams actually offers, for it is a bit different from the one I have just sketched.

How is it different? In one important respect: Adams doesn't make the final, noose-completing step mentioned. The Molinist, he says, is committed to thinking of true counterfactuals of creaturely freedom as explanatorily prior to God's creative decision; to thinking of those decisions as prior to our existence, choices and actions; and hence, given that explanatory priority is a transitive relation, to thinking of the counterfactuals of creaturely freedom as explanatorily prior to our choices and actions. So, to apply this to our Cuthbert example, *I* is explanatorily prior to *IV*. But the final step needed to fashion the noose—the claim that, for the Molinist, our actions are explanatorily prior to the truth of counterfactuals of creaturely freedom (in Cuthbert's case, that *IV* is prior to *I*)—isn't taken by Adams. Instead, he endorses the following premise:

(1)   If I freely do *A* in *C*, no truth that is strictly inconsistent with my refraining from *A* in *C* is explanatorily prior to my choosing and acting as I do in *C*.[5]

Since *C* → *A* is (according to the Molinist) true, inconsistent with Cuthbert's being in *C* but not buying the iguana, and (given that *I* is explanatorily prior to *IV*) explanatorily prior to Cuthbert's choices and actions, it follows from (1) that Cuthbert doesn't freely buy the iguana. But, of course, Cuthbert was introduced simply as our exemplar of a free agent; if the Molinist can't say that his iguana-buying was free, how can she say that any action is free?

---

[4] As Trenton Merricks has pointed out to me, one way to try to effect a bit of noose-loosening would be to focus on the tenses of *I* through *IV*. On the surface, each appears to be in the present tense. But, if read as present, *IV* is true only at the moment Cuthbert acts, and so affords us (at most) only a momentary noose. To provide a noose with more staying power, we need to read *IV* in some other way. But how? As a tenseless proposition? (What if the Molinist denies that there are any such things?) As an implicitly future-tense assertion? (But then, isn't the claim that *IV* is prior to *I* weakened?) Focusing upon tense does, I think, show that the circle is less simple than it appears. Still, since I believe there are more serious objections the Molinist can lodge against the vicious circle argument, I shall not pursue this line of response.

[5] Our (1) is given the number (12) in Adams, "Anti-Molinist Argument," p. 350.

Adams's conclusion, then, is that Molinists, though purporting to defend the libertarian picture, are in fact committed to principles incompatible with the existence of free human action.

2. Adams's Argument and Explanatory Priority

What are we to say about Adams's argument, or about the nasty noosy argument to which it bears a family resemblance? The first thing to note, I think, is the central role that the notion of explanatory priority plays in these arguments. Take Adams's argument. For it to hold up, each of the following has to be true in addition to (1):

(2)   Counterfactuals of creaturely freedom are explanatorily prior to God's creative decisions.

(3)   God's creative decisions are explanatorily prior to our free decisions and actions.

(4)   The relationship of explanatory priority is transitive.

Clearly, an argument relying upon these premises will not work if there is any equivocation on the term "explanatory priority"—if we take it to mean one thing in one of these premises, and something else in another, then the argument will be less than impressive. So explanatory priority has to have a single meaning that renders all of these propositions true.

Well, does it have such a meaning? What explication of explanatory priority does Adams offer us? None. He tells us (quite correctly) that the notion of priority is one that Molinists implicitly employ, and hence he feels it is appropriate for him to employ it in an anti-Molinist argument, and to do so without giving it any explicit definition.

Now, of course, some things do have to be taken as undefined; the challenge "define your terms" at some point has to be met with the polite but firm response, "No." But in complex arguments of this sort, I don't think it is inappropriate to ask that a term such as "explanatory priority"—a term which is hardly part of our everyday lives or one whose meaning is prephilosophically pellucid—be explained by one who is employing it. As I noted in Chapter 6, Hasker's argument against Molinism would be crippled were he not to explain just what he means by "bring about"; since most relatively simple explications of the term render one or another of the premises of his argument unacceptable from a Molinist perspective, one would naturally begin to suspect that the argument itself hinges upon using the term in an equivocal way. Might not this suspicion be justified in the case of Adams' argument? Might it not be that, for any plausible explication of explanatory priority that we might propose, one or another of the premises of his argument turns out to be one that no Molinist could be expected to accept? I suspect that this is indeed the case, and that Adams's argument gains whatever plausibility it has from equivocating on the notion of explanatory priority.

Note first of all that the concept that is needed for Adams's argument isn't explanatory priority in general, but a specific kind of explanatory priority—something's being explanatorily prior to someone's choosing and acting. It is this kind of explanatory priority, I think, that we need most to examine. And I say this not only because it is the kind of explanatory priority that is employed in Adams' argument, and thus the only kind of explanatory priority that Adams really needs, but also because it is the principal kind of priority that the Molinist needs to discriminate between middle knowledge and free knowledge. In saying that middle knowledge is distinct from and prior to free knowledge, the Molinist means to say that the former is independent of God's will, while the latter is not. For any element of his free knowledge, there were actions within God's power which would have led to that proposition's being false. No element of his middle knowledge is thus dependent upon his action; what he knows by middle knowledge are facts about which he can do nothing.

In considering Adams's argument, it is vital that we not be misled by the terminology involved. It is fairly clear that, in talking about what he calls explanatory priority, Adams means to be referring to the kind of priority Molinists have in mind. For instance, when describing the Molinist position, Adams says: "Alone among contingent facts, however, true counterfactuals of freedom are prior to the will of God, in the order of explanation, according to the Molinist view. For they are data that God takes into account in deciding what to do."[6] Explanatory priority for Adams, then, is supposed to be priority in the order of explanation, and priority in this sense has to do with what is and isn't "data that God takes into account"—that is, with facts of which he is aware but over which he has no control.

Now, there are surely notions of explanatory priority other than the one being discussed here. The vicious circle argument we introduced previously, for example, may well be using the term "explanatory priority" in a somewhat different sense. Indeed, one might even argue that "explanatory priority" is somewhat of a misnomer for the kind of priority the Molinist has in mind,

---

[6] Ibid., p. 344. It is perhaps worth reminding ourselves that the Molinist is surely *not* committed, as Adams here implies that she is, to the claim that counterfactuals of creaturely freedom are the *only* contingent truths that are prevolitional.

since, for example, all necessary truths will for the Molinist be seen as prior to contingent truths even though few if any necessary truths would seem to offer much assistance in explaining why particular contingent propositions are true. Still, for purposes of discussion, let us agree to retain Adams' rather unfortunate terminology. Since, as we have seen, what is crucial to that notion of priority is one's inability to bring about the falsity of the proposition in question, what we need to do, I think, is try to make this notion of inability more specific.

In thinking about this issue, one might suppose that a natural place to start would again be with the distinction pointed out by Plantinga between strong actualization and weak actualization—that is, between causal power and counterfactual power. Loosely speaking, to say that a certain true proposition is explanatorily prior to my choices and actions might be to say that the proposition is true and I have no causal power to make it false; alternatively, it might be to say that the proposition is true and I have no counterfactual power to make it false. Putting this a bit less loosely, it could be that

> (A) x is explanatorily prior to my choices and actions ≡ x is true, and there is no choice or action within my power that would cause it to be the case that x is false.

This account would explicate explanatory priority in terms of causal power. Using counterfactual power instead, we might try

> (B) x is explanatorily prior to my choices and actions ≡ x is true, and there is no choice or action within my power such that, were I so to choose or so to act, x would be false.

Let us see how well Adams's argument would hold up if we were to employ one of these accounts of explanatory priority.

3. Can Adams Use a Causal Account?

First, let us try (A), where explanatory priority is understood as causal powerlessness. Would the crucial premises of the argument—the ones we have called (1) through (4)—be such that no reasonable Molinist could deny them? Well, I think that (2) would be very hard to deny. To ascribe to God causal power over counterfactuals of creaturely freedom would be to endorse an extreme version of what we have called Maverick Molinism, a position which we showed to be untenable in Chapter 2. Nor would (3) be easy for the Molinist to reject. For God's creative decisions concerning Cuthbert are made long before there even is a Cuthbert on the scene. But then, for any such divine decision, Cuthbert could have causal power over it only if he could do something that would cause the past to have been different than it was. Now, the notion of causation is a deep and mysterious one, and there is little consensus about most matters connected with it. But one matter on which there is at least wide agreement is that effects don't occur earlier in time than their causes. One can argue this point—several eminent philosophers have—but I am strongly inclined to side with what I take to be the majority here. So I, and I think most Molinists, would concede that (3) is true if we are using (A) as our explication of explanatory priority. And the same, I suspect, would go for (4).

How about (1)? Would it too be above reproach? Not if we retain the orthodox picture of God as a being who has foreknowledge of our actions. Suppose that Cuthbert freely buys that iguana in situation C. For orthodox Christians, this entails that God foreknew, long before Cuthbert's birth, that Cuthbert would freely buy the iguana in C. But then, there is a truth, namely,

(5)   God foreknew, long before Cuthbert's birth, that Cuthbert would freely buy an iguana in C,

which is strictly inconsistent with Cuthbert's refraining from buying the iguana in C and which is, in the sense offered by (A), explanatorily prior to anything Cuthbert might choose or do in C, for (again assuming retrocausation to be impossible) there is nothing Cuthbert can do that can *cause* a proposition that was true to be false. So anyone, Molinist or non-Molinist, who is orthodox with regard to divine foreknowledge will reject (1) if (A) is our account of explanatory priority. And so (A) is of no use to Adams.[7]

4. Can Adams Use a Counterfactual Account?

Will (B) do any better? Well, I think it does do better with respect to (1)—or, to be precise, with respect to a proposition very close to (1) which could easily replace it in Adams's argument. For reasons suggested by Harry Frankfurt's famous attack upon what he calls the Principle of Alternate Possibilities, (1) itself may be indefensible if explanatory priority is understood in the sense

[7] Indeed, so long as one believes that there are true future contingent propositions, one will reject (1) interpreted via (A) *whether or not* one believes in divine foreknowledge. One can see this by simply replacing "God foreknew" in (5) with "It was true."

of (B).[8] Suppose God has put in place a mechanism that would cause Cuthbert to do *A* if and only if Cuthbert didn't decide to do it on his own, and suppose that God intends to keep this mechanism in operation. Suppose that Cuthbert then does *A* freely, thereby precluding the mechanism's moving him to act. Would it not be true in this situation that there is a truth (about God's establishing the mechanism and intending to keep it in operation) that is both strictly inconsistent with Cuthbert's refraining from *A* and explanatorily prior to his choices and actions, in the sense of explanatory priority offered by (B), where priority amounts to counterfactual powerlessness?[9]

Proposition (1), then, seems shaky. But even if it is, there is another very similar proposition which would seem immune to Frankfurtian objections— namely,

(1*)   If I freely do *A* in *C*, no truth that is strictly inconsistent with my refraining from freely doing *A* in *C* is explanatorily prior to my choosing and acting as I do in *C*.

God's creation of and intentions regarding the mechanism postulated above might be inconsistent with Cuthbert's not doing A, but they are clearly consistent with his not *freely* doing A. Since (1*) would thus be resilient in the face of the kind of counterexample that troubles (1), and since (1*) could equally well play the role played by (1) in Adams's argument, I will henceforth focus on (1*) rather than (1).

If (B) is our notion of explanatory priority, (1*) seems hard to deny. Frankfurtian examples show that freedom may be compatible with the inability to do otherwise, but they leave intact the characteristic libertarian claim that, if

[8] Actually, (1) is also in trouble for the same Frankfurtian reasons if explanatory priority is understood in the sense of (A). Since (1) à la (A) faced more serious problems, I delayed bringing up Frankfurt-style objections until now. For the source of such objections, see Harry Frankfurt, "Alternate Possibilities and Moral Responsibility," *Journal of Philosophy* 66 (1969), 829–839. The relevance of Frankfurtian considerations to our evaluation of (1) was brought home to me by my reading of William Lane Craig, "Robert Adams's New Anti-Molinist Argument," *Philosophy and Phenomenological Research* 54 (1994), 857–861. I am grateful to Craig for having sent me an earlier version of this essay, which proved of great assistance in my thinking about Adams's argument.

[9] If, as I suggest in Chapter 11, it is possible for a person to have counterfactual power over the past, then it is possible that there is some action I have the power to perform such that, were I to perform it, God wouldn't have created the mechanism in question, or wouldn't have maintained it in operation. Even if this is so, though, it would not be enough to save (1). For the possibility of counterfactual power over the past shows only that *some* substitution instances of (1) are defensible. Since (1) is making a universal claim, its defense would require us to say that, in *every* case of this sort, the agent has the relevant sort of counterfactual power over the past. No one, I take it, would be willing to make so implausible a claim.

I do something freely, I could have refrained from freely doing that thing. But if I could have refrained from freely doing a certain thing, and some true proposition entails that I don't refrain from freely doing it, then surely I must have at least counterfactual power over that truth. And if I have counterfactual power over it, then it is not explanatorily prior, in the sense given by (B), to my choosing and acting. Hence, if I freely do something, there is no truth which entails that I freely do it which is also explanatorily prior to my choices and actions. Premise (1*), then, seems unimpeachable if we are employing (B) as our account of explanatory priority.

What about the other premises? Premise (2) would still be unassailable, given our refutation of Maverick Molinism in Chapter 2. Premise (3), though, seems on somewhat shakier ground. Might it not be that some of God's creative decisions are linked to our actions in such a way that, were we not so to act, God would not so have decided? Since an affirmative answer seems quite reasonable from a Molinist perspective, (3) seems far from obviously true when read as (B) requires. Still, I think there is a close relative of (3) that the Molinist could not plausibly reject. For surely there are *some* divine decisions (the decision to create Alpha Centauri might be a good candidate) which *are* counterfactually independent of our decisions and actions. If (2) and (3) were read as referring only to such divine decisions, there would remain little ground for the Molinist to question them. So let us henceforth read them in such a manner, and grant that, given such a reading, the first three premises of Adams's argument seem solid if (B) is employed.

This leaves only (4), the claim that explanatory priority is transitive. Does (B) render this premise undeniable for the Molinist? I think not. For (B), recall, offers us a counterfactual analysis of explanatory priority, and the counterfactual relation is not one for which transitivity holds.

Perhaps a fuller discussion of this point is in order. Given (B), (2) tells us (roughly) that the true counterfactuals of creaturely freedom would have been true no matter what God had decided to do. Letting T stand for the true counterfactuals of creaturely freedom and D stand for a proposition describing God's actual creative decisions, what (2) tells us is basically that T would have been true whether or not D had been true—that is, that

$$(2^\star) \quad (D \to T) \ \& \ (\sim D \to T).$$

Premise (3), on the other hand, tells us that what God decided to do he would have done no matter what we were to decide to do. Letting A stand for a proposition describing our actual decisions, (3) says basically that D would have been true whether or not A had been true—that is, that

(3*) $(A \rightarrow D)$ & $(\sim A \rightarrow D)$.

To say that explanatory priority is transitive would be to assert that it follows from (2*) and (3*) that the true counterfactuals of creaturely freedom would have been true no matter what we would have decided to do; in other words, it would be to say that from (2*) and (3*) we can derive

(6) $(A \rightarrow T)$ & $(\sim A \rightarrow T)$.

But it seems clear that we can't derive (6) from (2*) and (3*) alone. The first conjunct of (6) would present no obstacle to the Molinist, but the second surely would; why think it follows from (2*) and (3*)? Were the counterfactual relation transitive, we could derive that second conjunct of (6) from the second conjunct of (3*) and the first conjunct of (2*). But, again, the counterfactual connection *isn't* transitive, so that mode of argument is blocked. And since, as we saw in our discussion of Hasker's Hypothesis in the last chapter, $(\sim A \rightarrow T)$ is hardly the kind of premise a Molinist would be predisposed to accept, one could hardly expect her simply to embrace the second conjunct of (6) as an obvious truth.

   One could try to effect the move to (6) by supplementing (2*) and (3*) with other premises. That is, one might grant that, given (B), explanatory priority is not transitive, yet insist that premises unstated by Adams would be just as undeniable for the Molinist and do just as good a job as (4) in taking us to (6) and thus refuting Molinism. But what might these premises be? There are a couple of clear candidates. Were $(D \rightarrow \sim A)$ a premise to which the Molinist is committed, then this conditional, when combined with the second conjunct of (3*) and the first of (2*), would lead to (6). Since our assumption was that D and A are both true, however, no one, Molinist or not, could plausibly endorse $(D \rightarrow \sim A)$. Similarly, were the Molinist committed to

(7) $[(\sim A$ & $D) \rightarrow T]$,

the second conjunct of (6) would again clearly follow from the second conjunct of (3*) and (7). But a moment's reflection reminds us that (7) is not a premise one can pin to the Molinist without begging the question at issue. For the Molinist wants to insist that we do have counterfactual power over our counterfactuals of freedom; were we to act other than we actually do act in the situations in which God has decided to place us, the counterfactuals of creaturely freedom which are in fact true would have been false. To ask the Molinist simply to assume something on the order of (7) is to ask him simply to assume his position to be false. Needless to say, philosophical etiquette permits the Molinist to decline such a request.[10]

(B), then, seems to offer Adams little hope of refuting the Molinist. While it allows us a means of constructing readings of the first three premises that no reasonable Molinist would reject, it renders (4) indefensible, and seems to offer no alternative means of embarrassing the Molinist by warranting the move to (6).

5. Other Possibilities

Neither (A) nor (B), then, will do what Adams needs done. If he uses (A), (2) through (4) seem plausible, but (1) doesn't, at least not to one who shares the Molinist's orthodox inclinations. If Adams switches to (B), (1*), our replacement for (1), is virtually undeniable, but (4) no longer passes muster.

Are there other ways of understanding explanatory priority? Of course. Do any of them do any better (from Adams's point of view) than (A) or (B)? I don't think so. Of the various ways of understanding explanatory priority that I have considered, none succeeds in rendering each of the crucial premises of Adams's argument plausible from a Molinist perspective. Let me briefly mention three possibilities.

Given the failure of the causal and counterfactual accounts of explanatory priority thus far considered, one might attempt to understand explanatory priority in terms of some proposition's being *logically* prior to our choices and actions. Were one to construct such an account along the lines of (A) and (B), one might end up with

(C) x is explanatorily prior to my choices and actions $\equiv$ x is true and there is no choice or action z within my power such that my doing z would entail that x is false.

But (C) would do no better than (B) in supporting (4). For (C) tells us, in essence, that a proposition is explanatorily prior to my choices if it is logically compatible with any choice I might make. Since logical compatibility is not a transitive relation, there is no reason to think that explanatory priority,

---

[10] Actually, I doubt that anyone, Molinist or not, should feel much attraction toward (7). If our actual decisions and actions had been different, then T, which includes only true counterfactuals of creaturely freedom, could still have been true only if our decisions and actions had taken place in different situations from those which in fact obtained. But how could the situations in which we act have been different if D, God's creative decisions, had stayed the same? It seems, then, that $(\sim A \ \& \ T) \Rightarrow \sim D$. But from this it follows that $(\sim A \ \& \ D) \Rightarrow \sim T$. So (7) appears to be not just false, but necessarily false.

understood along the lines of (C), would be transitive. In other words, (4) would be false on this understanding of explanatory priority.

One inclined to analyze explanatory priority in terms of entailment might think that a stronger relation than logical compatibility is what is needed here. Perhaps to say that a truth is explanatorily prior to my decisions is to say that any action or decision within my power would entail that truth. Putting this more precisely, one might propose

(D) x is explanatorily prior to my choices and actions $\equiv$ x is true and, for any choice or action z within my power, my doing z would entail x.

On this account, though, neither (2) nor (3) remain reasonable. Surely it is logically possible that God reach the creative decisions he has in fact reached even had other counterfactuals of creaturely freedom been true. And, just as surely, our free decisions and actions are logically consistent with God's having made different creative decisions from those he has in fact made. So (D) is no improvement over our earlier attempts.

One might attempt to fashion more complicated analyses of explanatory priority based upon causal, counterfactual, or entailment relations, but I doubt that epicyclic adornment will aid Adams here. (In particular, I suspect that, where relatively simple explications fail to justify the claim that explanatory priority is transitive, more complicated transformations of them will not do the job any better.) One case, perhaps, is worthy of mention in this regard. Recall our discussion of the relation of bringing about in our examination of Hasker's argument in Chapter 6. On the surface, there might be some plausibility to using this notion to analyze the notion of explanatory priority: something is explanatorily prior to my actions, we might think, just in case I cannot bring about its falsity.[11] Hence, one might propose:

(E) x is explanatorily prior to my choices and actions $\equiv$ x is true and I don't have the power to bring it about that x is false.

[11] It is worth remembering that Adams would almost surely frown on attempts to import the notion of bringing about into the analysis of explanatory priority. After all, Adams proposed his argument in part as a means of escaping controversies concerning power entailment principles and the notion of bringing about. (See "Anti-Molinist Argument," pp. 348–349.) It would be odd indeed to attempt to bolster his argument by reintroducing that notion, since one would thereby reopen the door to precisely those disputes his argument was molded to banish. Indeed, Adams implies (at the top of p. 348) that the notion of bringing about ought to be analyzed in terms of explanatory priority, not the other way around.

Of course, (E) is less *an* account of explanatory priority than it is a blueprint for fashioning *many* accounts, one for each understanding of bringing about. Still, I doubt that any of these accounts will strengthen Adams's hand. Simpler versions would more or less mirror some of the explications already considered. More convoluted definitions of bringing about would yield correspondingly complicated accounts of explanatory priority. But I see no reason to think that any of these options would constitute real advances. Even if we take (BA_{12}), the notion of bringing about which, as we saw in Chapter 6, Hasker has tentatively endorsed, we wind up with a notion of explanatory priority that seems to fail the transitivity test.[12] Appeal to the notion of bringing about, then, seems unhelpful.

6. Why Adams's Argument May Be Doomed to Failure

Our efforts to isolate a notion of explanatory priority that will do what Adams needs done have thus far proved futile. By itself, of course, this fact proves little. Perhaps the correct account is somewhere in the neighborhood; perhaps my failure to spot it is nothing more than a sign of my limited philosophical talents. I suspect, though, that this is not the case. I suspect that my feeble philosophical faculties haven't found the right explication for Adams's purposes because there simply *isn't* any such account. And my suspicion here is based on the fact that our examination of (B) suggests that *any* attempt to resurrect Adams's argument by reinterpreting explanatory priority is doomed to failure.

---

[12] The apparent failure of (BA_{12}) to ensure transitivity is relevant to our appraisal of an analysis of explanatory priority recently proposed by Hasker. In "Explanatory Priority: Transitive and Unequivocal, A Response to William Craig," *Philosophy and Phenomenological Research* 57 (1997), 389–393, Hasker offers the following analysis of the general notion of explanatory priority:

    (F) p is explanatorily prior to $q \equiv p$ must be included in a complete explanation of why q obtains.

In explaining this account, Hasker continues: "Here 'explanation of why q obtains' is to be understood in the sense that p contributes to q's obtaining; it plays (or played) a role in bringing it about that q obtains." So (F) implies that p is explanatorily prior to q just in case p (along, perhaps, with other events or states of affairs) brings it about that q obtains. But this means that, if "bring about" is understood in Hasker's preferred, (BA_{12})-ish sense, (F) would appear not to guarantee transitivity, and so (4) again would fall. It is also worth mentioning that both (2) and (3) would seem eminently dubitable given a (BA_{12})-ish interpretation of (F).

Surely, one might respond, there *are* ways of understanding "included in a complete explanation" that *would* both yield an (F) which underwrites transitivity and render the denial of (2) or (3) unavailable. I suspect so. I suspect just as strongly, though, that no such account of explanatory priority will allow Adams to pin (1*) to the Molinist's lapel.

Adams's argument requires that both premises (2) through (4) and premise (1*) be ones that the Molinist cannot reasonably reject. Of course, (2) through (4) will be true only if it is also true that counterfactuals of creaturely freedom are explanatorily prior to our decisions and actions. As we saw in our discussion of (B), though, Molinists will insist that we have at least counterfactual power over true counterfactuals of creaturely freedom, and Adams at this point in his argument has no grounds for asking Molinists to ignore that thesis when considering whether or not they are indeed committed to the premises he is proposing.[13] It seems very likely to me, then, that, for (2) through (4) to turn out clearly true from the Molinist perspective, we need a sense of explanatory priority where counterfactuals of creaturely freedom can be explanatorily prior to my choices and actions *even though* I have counterfactual power over those counterfactuals; accounts of explanatory priority such as (B) or (C) which deny this possibility will offer the Molinist reasonable grounds to deny either (2), (3), or (4). But then, suppose that the consequent of (1*) is false—that is, suppose that there is a truth (call it X) strictly inconsistent with my refraining from freely doing A in C which, *in the sense needed to support (2) through (4)*, is explanatorily prior to my choices and actions. Why conclude from this that the antecedent of (1*) is false—that is, that I don't freely do A in C? On the understanding of explanatory priority in question, saying that X is explanatorily prior to my choices and actions is *fully compatible* with saying that X is under my counterfactual control. But if I do have counterfactual power over X, why think X's truth jeopardizes my freedom? So the antecedent of (1*) could still be true even under the supposition that its consequent is false. And from that, of course, it follows that (1*) itself can reasonably be viewed by the Molinist as a false conditional.

Hence, it appears likely that any account of explanatory priority which commits the Molinist to (2) through (4) is guaranteed to justify her viewing (1*) as false. And if this is so, then Adams's argument fails. Its semblance of persuasiveness stems from its implicit employment of different accounts of explanatory priority in its crucial premises. Once this reliance on equivocation is brought to the fore, the argument collapses.

---

[13] It should be noted that what Adams calls the First Stage of his argument (pp. 346–348) is of no assistance to him here. For that stage shows at most that the Molinist is committed to saying that there are senses of "bring about" in which we don't bring about the truth of counterfactuals of creaturely freedom about us. This, of course, the Molinist can say while still maintaining that we *do* have counterfactual power over some such counterfactuals of creaturely freedom.

7. The Vicious Circle and Equivocation

So much for Adams. But what about that monstrous little member of the Adams family I introduced a while back, the vicious circle argument, which I likened to a noose around the neck of the Molinist? Am I going to say the same thing about it that I said about Adams's argument—that it borrows whatever plausibility it has from an equivocal use of terms? That I know of no univocal understanding of explanatory priority which makes the argument a powerful one?

In a word: Yes. Again, I don't think I can *prove* this. But I do think that even our brief excursus into Adams's argument should make us at least *suspect* that there might be some equivocation going on here as well. And we can, I think, make these suspicions even more vigorous by reminding ourselves of the kind of priority which seems to be involved in each quadrant of the circle.

Consider first the claim that *I* ($C \rightarrow A$) is prior to *II* (God believes that $[C \rightarrow A]$). In some sense, this is clearly true. But in what sense? In the sense, I think, that *I* is what we might call *noetically prior* to *II*, where to say that *X* is noetically prior to *Y* is just to say that *Y* asserts that someone knows *X*. For God believes something, I take it, if and only if he knows it to be true, and we generally think that, for any person, a proposition's being true is part of what is involved in saying that the person knows that proposition. So, *I* is prior to *II* in this sense.

Is *II* (God believes that $[C \rightarrow A]$) prior to *III* (God decides to put Cuthbert in *C*) in this sense? No. Its priority is rather that *II* provides us with a partial *reason* for God's performing the action described in *III*. This reason, note, was neither necessary nor sufficient for God's act. God as a free creator could have decided *not* to put Cuthbert in *C* even though he knew that $C \rightarrow A$; and he could have decided to go ahead and put Cuthbert in *C* even had he known that $C \rightarrow A$ was *false*. Still, the Molinist at least does look upon *II* as being one of the factors influencing God's decision to put Cuthbert in *C*. And since we generally think of reasons as prior to actions, it is not at all odd to think of *II* as prior to *III* in this sense.

What of the claim that *III* (God decides to put Cuthbert in *C*) is prior to *IV* (Cuthbert does *A* in *C*)? Can this be understood in either of the ways we have already seen? I don't think so: *III* isn't noetically prior to *IV*, nor does it provide us part of the agent's reason for the action described in *IV*. No, the priority here is more that of an *enabling condition*: had God not decided to put Cuthbert in *C*, Cuthbert couldn't have been in *C*, and so (of course) couldn't have had doing *A* in *C* as one of his options.

Finally, consider *IV* (Cuthbert does *A* in *C*) and *I* ($C \rightarrow A$). Is there a sense in which Cuthbert's action is prior to the truth of the counterfactual? Well, given that, as we have seen, the truth of *I* is *counterfactually dependent* upon what Cuthbert does, I suppose we could view *I* as dependent upon the action described in *IV*, and, in this sense, could say that *IV* is prior to *I*. But, to all appearances, this will be a very different kind of priority from the three types already discussed. In fact, it hardly seems to be a relation of *explanatory* priority at all. For genuine explanatory priority, we have been assuming, is irreflexive and asymmetric; the relation of counterfactual dependence linking *IV* and *I* is neither.

So it surely looks as though we are dealing with more than one notion of priority in this argument. But that means that we don't really have a vicious circle or noose at all. The circle would be vicious if we had one kind of explanatory priority throughout and if this kind of explanatory priority were transitive, for then we would wind up saying that a proposition was explanatorily prior to itself. If we don't have a relation throughout the circle which is *univocal, transitive* and *explanatory*, there is no reason to think that any unsavory consequences follow.

8. Molinism and Priority

As noted above, given the Molinist's claim that natural knowledge is prior to middle knowledge, which is in turn prior to free knowledge, it is hardly unfair for critics of Molinism to focus upon the notion of priority (though, again, speaking of *explanatory* priority in this context might be a bit misleading). Even if one agrees that the criticisms discussed in this section have been guilty of equivocation, then, one might still be left with a nagging question: Just how does the Molinist understand this notion? Molina frequently refers to it as "priority in our way of conceiving it, with a basis in reality."[14] Can we contemporary Molinists be a bit more precise here?

It seems to me that our discussion of the Adams family of arguments might well open the door to at least one way of proceeding here. Consider again (B), the counterfactual account of priority discussed above. Such an account, it seems to me, allows us to draw the crucial Molinist distinction between God's prevolitional knowledge and his postvolitional knowledge. Any element of the former will be prior, in the sense offered by (B), to God's choices and actions; any element of the latter will not be so prior. By itself, then, (B) allows us to see how both natural and middle knowledge are prior to free knowledge.

[14] For Molina's own discussion of this phrase, see Disputation 53, part I, section 20, pp. 211–212.

What, though, about the further distinction within God's prevolitional knowledge between natural and middle knowledge? Does (B) provide us a means of viewing the former as prior to the latter? The answer, quite clearly, is no; God's natural knowledge will remain the same no matter what he does, but precisely the same is true of his middle knowledge. If we wish to explain how natural knowledge is prior to middle knowledge, then, we need to move beyond (B). But we needn't move much beyond it. For, though God's middle knowledge will as a matter of fact remain the same no matter what he does, this isn't a *necessary* truth. To put the same point more precisely: any element of God's middle knowledge will be true no matter what God does, but it is entirely possible for that element to be false and yet for God to choose and act. The same, of course, cannot be said for the elements of God's natural knowledge. Consider, then, the following amendment of (B):

(B*) x is prior to my choices and actions $\equiv$ x is true, and, *necessarily*, there is no choice or action within my power such that, were I so to choose or so to act, x would be false.

In the sense offered by (B*), any element of natural knowledge is prior to God's choices and actions, while no element of his middle knowledge is.

If we so wished, we could employ (B) and (B*) together to fashion a single account of priority, understood now as a relation between propositions, of the following sort:

(MP) x is prior to z $\equiv$ In either sense (B) or sense (B*), x is prior to God's choices and actions, and z is not prior to them.

In the sense offered by (MP), the Molinist can say that middle knowledge is prior to free knowledge, while natural knowledge is prior to both middle and free knowledge.

So the discussion of the Adams family of arguments can help us see one way of explicating the Molinist concept of priority. Of course, there is nothing sacrosanct about the language employed in (MP); there surely are other equivalent ways of expressing the distinction Molina had in mind when speaking of priority.[15] Still, the fact that there is at least this one way of doing so might

---

[15] Indeed, far from seeing (MP) as sacrosanct, some might see it as a rather hokey pastiche, a hodgepodge thrown together solely to give the results the Molinist wants, not a plausible analysis of an independently respectable concept of priority. I must confess to a degree of sympathy with such a reaction. Perhaps it is only in a somewhat artificial sense of priority that the Molinist can view natural knowledge as prior to middle knowledge, and middle knowledge as prior *in that same sense* to free knowledge. Still, a concept need not be seen as useless simply

be of assistance to those who find Molina's language, his "in our way of conceiving it but with a basis in reality," a touch too vague.

9. Conclusion to Part II

I have argued in this chapter that neither Adams's argument nor its vicious-explanatory-loop relative offers us any convincing reason to abandon the Molinist picture. As we have seen, similar evaluations seem warranted with respect to Thomistic objections, the "grounding" objection, and Hasker's argument against middle knowledge. Perhaps there are stronger reasons to abandon it, but, as I have already said, I don't know of any. And most critics, I think, would agree; if the arguments canvassed here fail, then Molinism stands unrefuted. But, as we saw in Chapter 3, the attractive features of Molinism and the defects of its competitors render it the position which, in the absence of clear and compelling arguments to the contrary, should be embraced by the libertarian traditionalist. In other words, the burden of proof is with the critics. As I have tried to show in the preceding four chapters, it is a burden they fail to discharge. And thus we can conclude that the orthodox Christian with libertarian leanings has a powerful basis for endorsing this picture of God's providential activity.

---

because of its artificiality. More importantly, the *crucial* distinction for the Molinist to make, I think, is between the prevolitional and the postvolitional, and this distinction, as we have seen, can easily and clearly be made by means of the (comparatively?) nonhokey (B).

PART III

SOME APPLICATIONS OF THE MOLINIST ACCOUNT

[8]

Papal Infallibility

We are all human, and in this Council as in all others, human imperfections may have their share. But our belief is precisely this—that the Holy Ghost directs, fashions and consumes these imperfections, and turns them to the service of truth. No one is a real Catholic who has not this faith, which is mine; and therefore I declare beforehand that whatever happens, I adhere, I submit; that I am happy thus to adhere—joyous thus to submit.
—Bishop Dupanloup of Orleans, one of the opponents of an official declaration of papal infallibility, prior to Vatican Council I

1. Shifting to Applied Molinism

If the defense of the theory of middle knowledge offered in the second part of this work has succeeded, then the time has come for us to move beyond the general objections to the Molinist account of providence which have thus far consumed so much of our energy. The major thrusts against middle knowledge have, I think, been parried successfully. Further discussion of such criticisms is surely appropriate, but I suspect that little will be gained and much might well be lost should Molinists concentrate exclusively on what is in large measure a merely defensive battle. Were the scholarly objections to the general Molinist account of providence more compelling, or were the orthodox Christian's concept of providence seemingly at odds with the Molinist suggestion, such an apologetic program might well be in order. But, as we have seen, the objections are not compelling, and the view of providence common among orthodox Christians simply is rough-hewn Molinism. This being the case, the time for an obsession with defense is past.

What is needed as a complement, I believe, is an attempt to apply the concept of middle knowledge to the many particular types of exercisings of divine providence that Molinists have claimed can be illuminated by such an application. In the past, such claims often took the form of literary promissory notes, which suggested that one *could* employ middle knowledge to analyze one or another element of providence (such as predestination, prayer, or prophecy), but which actually refrained from so employing it in a detailed or extended way.[1] The time for cashing in such notes has come. Only by applying middle knowledge to particular areas of providence can we reach a mature assessment of its usefulness as a concept in philosophical theology.

The four chapters that follow can be seen as early installments in the redemption plan proposed in the previous paragraph. My focus in this chapter is on a particular element of the Roman Catholic view of providence, the doctrine of papal infallibility. Chapter 9 looks at prophecy, while Chapters 10 and 11 examine issues connected with petitionary prayer. In each of these chapters, the aim is to investigate the ways in which, and the degree to which, adopting the Molinist picture allows one better to understand these specific areas of divine providential activity.

A word of explanation is probably in order before we proceed further. Even if one accepts my recommendation that Molinists focus upon particular doctrines, one might find my choice of infallibility a rather peculiar place to begin—rather like beginning a discussion of Great American Heroes by focusing on Richard Nixon. For it is no secret that many Christians, including some who at least call themselves Roman Catholics, reject the doctrine of papal infallibility. Even among those who accept it, it is sometimes treated as a bit of an embarrassment, an odd and obstreperous old uncle whose membership in the family is not denied but about whom well-mannered members maintain a decorous silence while in public. Given this state of affairs, why focus on infallibility?

Well, for a number of reasons. As a Roman Catholic, I feel a special obligation to examine those elements of providence that my faith recognizes but that Molinists of other denominations do not; papal infallibility would surely rank high on such a list. Second, insofar as the doctrine of infallibility continues to divide Christians, and insofar as that division may be based in part on philosophical (as opposed to historical, scriptural, and other such) objections to the doctrine, the cause of Christian unity may be advanced by looking at the doctrine philosophically. Third, many of those Christians who reject the notion of papal infallibility nevertheless endorse other notions (e.g., indefectibility, conciliar infallibility, inspiration, and the like) regarding God's guidance of his church which engender questions similar to those raised by infallibility. Since the notion of papal infallibility is, as these things go, a fairly simple and clearly delineated one, applying middle knowledge to it first may be seen as engaging in a controlled experiment, which should prove instructive for anyone interested in applying it to the comparatively murky

---

[1] For two such promissory notes, see Freddoso, "Introduction," p. 61, and my "Two Accounts of Providence," in Thomas V. Morris, ed., *Divine and Human Action* (Ithaca: Cornell University Press, 1988), p. 162.

issues mentioned above. Hence, a discussion of infallibility may prove eminently relevant even to those who reject the Roman Catholic belief. And finally, many of the issues surrounding a Molinist explication of the doctrine of infallibility will, as we shall see, also arise in Molinist explications of other dimensions of providence. For all these reasons, infallibility seems as good a place to start as any.

2. The Doctrine of Papal Infallibility

The doctrine of papal infallibility, though explicitly affirmed by theologians at least as far back as the thirteenth century, was first declared to be part of Catholic belief by the First Vatican Council.[2] The relevant section of the dogmatic constitution *Pastor Aeternus* reads as follows:

> Therefore, faithfully adhering to the tradition received from the beginning of the Christian faith, for the glory of God our Saviour, the exaltation of the Catholic Religion, and the salvation of Christian peoples, the Sacred Council approving, We teach and define that it is a dogma divinely revealed: that the Roman Pontiff, when he speaks *ex cathedra*, that is, when in discharge of the office of Pastor and Doctor of all Christians, by virtue of his supreme Apostolic authority he defines a doctrine regarding faith or morals to be held by the Universal Church, by the divine assistance promised to him in blessed Peter, is possessed of that infallibility with which the divine Redeemer willed that His Church should be endowed for defining doctrine regarding faith or morals: and that therefore such definitions of the Roman Pontiff are irreformable of themselves, and not from the consent of the Church.[3]

This doctrine was explicitly reaffirmed by the Second Vatican Council's dogmatic constitution *Lumen Gentium*:

> This infallibility with which the divine Redeemer willed His Church to be endowed in defining a doctrine of faith and morals extends as far as extends the deposit of divine revelation, which must be religiously guarded and faithfully expounded. This is the infallibility which the Roman Pontiff, the head of the college of bishops, enjoys in virtue of his office, when, as the supreme shepherd and teacher of all the faithful, who confirms his brethren in their faith (cf. Lk. 22:32), he proclaims by a definitive act some doctrine of faith or morals. Therefore his definitions, of themselves, and not from the consent of the

---

[2] For an informative (though hardly unbiased) look at the early history of the notion of infallibility, see Brian Tierney, *Origins of Papal Infallibility* (Leiden: E. J. Brill, 1972).

[3] Translation in Cuthbert Butler, *The Vatican Council* (London: Longmans, Green, 1930), vol. 2, p. 295. The statement by Bishop Dupanloup is quoted on p. 117 of vol. 1.

Church, are justly styled irreformable, for they are pronounced with the assistance of the Holy Spirit, an assistance promised to him in blessed Peter. Therefore, they need no approval of others, nor do they allow an appeal to any other judgment. For then the Roman Pontiff is not pronouncing judgment as a private person. Rather, as the supreme teacher of the universal Church, as one in whom the charism of the infallibility of the Church herself is individually present, he is expounding or defending a doctrine of Catholic faith.[4]

Several points are worth noting with regard to the doctrine these two statements promulgate. First, the pope is held to be infallible only when speaking ex cathedra—that is, only when speaking (as Vatican II puts it) "as the supreme shepherd and teacher of all the faithful." Popes can and do sometimes speak in other capacities (e.g., as private theologians), but when doing so are not said to be infallible. Furthermore, since one can speak ex cathedra only when one speaks, it follows that the pope's private, unexpressed opinions are a fortiori not said to be infallible. Second, papal pronouncements are held to be infallible only when they define a doctrine—only when they embody an intention on the part of the pope to decide a question once and for all. Even when speaking as pope, many popes have not spoken in this definitive fashion, and thus have not exercised their charism of infallibility. Third, the pope is declared to be infallible only with regard to faith and morals; though neither council declares him to be fallible in other areas, the suggestion that he is seems patent. Fourth, the charism of infallibility is said to be one which is given to the Church as a whole, not simply to the pope. Fifth, papal definitions which meet the conditions stipulated above are "irreformable of themselves": no council need approve them, and no successor to the papacy can abrogate them. Finally, the guarantor of papal (and, more generally, of Church) infallibility is held to be the Holy Spirit, though the manner in which he effects this guarantee is left unspecified.[5]

The doctrine of papal infallibility has, of course, been subject to numerous criticisms, most of which rest on theological or historical claims which one would expect others to be better equipped to adjudicate than are philosophers. But there is one type of objection to the doctrine that lies squarely within

[4] Translation in Walter M. Abbott, ed., *The Documents of Vatican II* (New York: Corpus Books, 1966), pp. 48–49.

[5] Many Catholic commentators on the doctrine of infallibility have suggested that much of the dispute over papal infallibility stems from misconceptions (by both proponents and opponents of the doctrine) concerning what the doctrine actually is. For example, one prominent Catholic theologian contends that, though the doctrine "is and will always remain a matter of much theological and pastoral importance," it is already becoming "much less an ecumenical problem" insofar as it is being "disengaged from exaggerations of papal authority." See Richard McBrien, *Catholicism*, study ed. (Minneapolis: Winston Press, 1981), p. 842.

the domain of philosophy—an objection that deals with the question of papal freedom.

3. Papal Infallibility or Papal Freedom?

According to Vatican I and Vatican II, the pope cannot err when he makes a pronouncement, provided that certain conditions are satisfied. But how exactly can this be if the pope is, like you and me, a free human being? Let us say that a pope who fulfills the various conditions laid down by the Councils (i.e, one who speaks publicly and definitively as pope on a question of faith or morals) speaks ex cathedra. Isn't a pope who speaks ex cathedra speaking freely? If so, then couldn't the pope who speaks ex cathedra resist the assistance of the Holy Spirit? And if he did, couldn't he fall into error even when speaking ex cathedra? So isn't it simply false to say that a pope who speaks ex cathedra speaks infallibly?

Though rarely articulated in so blunt a form, this objection, or something much like it, surely lies behind much of the opposition to the doctrine of papal infallibility. It is, of course, really an objection to *any* notion of Church infallibility: we can't obviate the problem raised by the Bishop of Rome's freedom simply by throwing in a few more, equally free bishops. Indeed, if the objection has force, it is not easy to see how even so amorphous a thesis as that of the Church's indefectibility can be maintained. If to err (or more precisely, the potential to err) is, so to speak, ineluctably human, then many divines (and not just those at the Vatican Councils) require forgiveness for having claimed a stronger form of providential guidance of the Church than reason can allow.

There is one obvious way to defuse this objection which I will mention only to dismiss. The objection presupposes that a person acts freely only if the full set of circumstances in which a person acts do not determine one particular course of action. If we dispense with this libertarian notion of freedom, the objection against papal infallibility can be dispensed with as well, for we could then say that the circumstances in which the pope acts are determinative of his action (most likely because the grace brought by the Spirit determines the action) even though the act performed is a free one. While it is, I suspect, true that we could meet the objection to papal infallibility in this way, we would in doing so be abandoning the notion of freedom that, as we have seen, is both very attractive to many if not most orthodox Christians and an essential part of the Molinist's defense of the traditional picture of providence. For libertarian traditionalists at least, the rock of infallibility claimed by Peter's successors would be ill-supported indeed were it grounded in the uncertain sand of compatibilism.

If we accept the libertarian notion of freedom presupposed by our objection to papal infallibility, it might appear that there are but two ways in which we might respond. On the one hand, we might endorse the objection—that is, we might say that the pope, being free, is not immune from error even when speaking ex cathedra. On the other hand, we might uphold papal infallibility by surrendering papal freedom. In other words, we might say that God guarantees that papal ex cathedra pronouncements are infallible by simply determining what it is that the pope pronounces in such situations.

Needless to say, neither of these alternatives will appear particularly appealing to the orthodox Catholic. The first response allows us to hold on to papal freedom, but only at the unacceptable cost of forcing us to reject outright the teaching of Vatican I and Vatican II. The second response allows us to hold on to papal infallibility, but only by saying that the pope isn't free when speaking ex cathedra. Not only does such a view seem somewhat implausible (or so it would surely appear, one would think, to the pope himself when in the act of speaking ex cathedra), but it also at least appears rather demeaning both to God and to the pope to suggest that the only way God can infallibly guide his Church is by playing Edgar Bergen to the pope's Charlie McCarthy. What the orthodox Catholic would like, clearly, is some way of holding on to *both* papal infallibility and papal freedom. But, in light of our objection, how *can* we hold on to both?

4. Rotundo to the Rescue?

It is here that the concept of middle knowledge seems to come to the rescue.[6] For if God has middle knowledge, why can't he arrange things in such a way that the pope always freely follows his guidance? How, one might ask, can he do so? By seeing to it that the *right* person *becomes* pope. If God has middle knowledge, then he knows how any candidate for the office would act—would *freely* act—if elected pope. Using this knowledge, God would then direct the cardinals to select as pope one of those men who God knows would freely cooperate with his guidance and thereby safeguard the church from error; he would also lead them away from selecting any of those men who he knows would not freely cooperate with his guidance and consequently lead the Church into error. By then guiding the man selected in the ways that, as his middle knowledge tells him, will elicit a free but positive

---

[6] My remarks here should not be taken to imply that we can solve this problem *only* if we say that God has middle knowledge. The point, rather, is that the Molinist seems to be able to offer a particularly attractive and plausible solution, one not available to those who deny God middle knowledge.

response from him, God can insure that the pope is infallible even though he respects his freedom. This respect for human freedom would presumably extend to the cardinals as well. God's direction of them toward certain candidates and away from others would most likely be accomplished, not by God's determining their actions, but by his arrangement of circumstances which he knows via middle knowledge will lead to the result he desires.

An example of how this might work will perhaps be of some help here in making the Molinist suggestion more concrete. Suppose that a conclave to elect a new pope has begun, and that two prime candidates for the office have emerged, Cardinal Elfreth and Cardinal Filbert. Suppose also that the choice between these two will be influenced enormously by the way in which an elderly and well-respected Italian cardinal (call him Cardinal Rotundo) decides to vote. Finally, suppose that among the infinite number of true propositions God knows via middle knowledge are the following two (where t represents the time of the conclave and h the history of the world prior to t):

(A)   If Elfreth were elected pope at time t in a world with history h, he would freely follow divine guidance and keep the Church safe from error.

(B)   If Filbert were elected pope at time t in a world with history h, he would freely reject divine guidance and proclaim ex cathedra a falsehood.[7]

Given this knowledge, God decides to act. While Rotundo is at prayer, God causes him to concentrate upon the various virtues of Elfreth. This leads him (as God knew it would) freely to come to the conclusion that Elfreth would make the better pope. Acting on this conviction, Rotundo enthusiastically throws his considerable weight behind Elfreth. As a result, Elfreth is indeed elected, and the Church is saved from the errors that Filbert would have proclaimed.

No doubt the election of a pope is not often as simple as in our example. Seldom are there only two viable candidates; rarely is there but one kingmaker

---

[7] In supposing (A) and (B) to be the counterfactuals which are guiding God, we are engaging in a considerable degree of simplification. For example, if (A) were true, God would presumably know it based on his knowledge of counterfactuals whose antecedents include stages of the world later than h and whose consequents identify specific free actions by Elfreth in those situations. For purposes of expository clarity, however, I have decided to focus the discussion around the simpler (A) and (B) rather than around the innumerable counterfactuals of creaturely and divine freedom upon which (A) and (B) would be based.

such as Rotundo; and only infrequently are people persuaded to a certain course of action in the rather blunt way we created for Rotundo. Even so, I think the essentials of the matter are captured adequately in our simplified case. And most essential of all, from the Molinist point of view, would be counterfactuals such as (A) and (B). Provided God has knowledge of true counterfactuals of each of these kinds, he can guide the conclave toward those who would freely serve the Church unerringly and away from those who would freely proclaim a falsehood.

5. Collapsing Counterfactuals

Although I believe that this Molinist answer to our problem with infallibility is on the right track, I fear that it may need to be shunted off to a siding for repairs before it can safely reach its intended destination. For there is a problem with this attempted solution: one of the counterfactuals upon which it is based seems to collapse.

Consider again the second of the two counterfactuals the truth of which we assumed would guide God's actions vis-à-vis the cardinals:

> (B)   If Filbert were elected pope at time t in a world with history h, he would freely reject divine guidance and proclaim ex cathedra a falsehood.

Letting E stand for "Filbert is elected Pope at t in a world with history h" and R for "Filbert freely rejects divine guidance and proclaims ex cathedra a falsehood," we can represent (B) as

> (B) $E \rightarrow R$.

The problem with (B) is simply this: if (B) is true, how could God possibly allow Filbert to be elected? Having established his Church in the way he has, and having allowed (indeed, guided) that Church through its two most recent councils to proclaim papal infallibility as a dogma, how could God then permit the cardinals to elect as pope a man who he knew with certainty would make an erroneous ex cathedra pronouncement? Isn't it impossible for God to allow Filbert's election if he knows that (B) is true?

What is being suggested here is that the truth of (B) entails the falsity of (B)'s antecedent—that is,

> (1) $(E \rightarrow R) \Rightarrow {\sim}E.$

If (1) is true, then (B) is what we might call a *collapsing counterfactual*—a counterfactual which entails that its own antecedent is false. Now, as we have seen, there seems to be a strong prima facie case for Molinists to view (B) as a collapsing counterfactual. Unfortunately, there would be something rather embarrassing in their doing so. For one can make a strong case for thinking that (B) is false if it collapses. Since the story told above as to how God might arrange for a free but infallible pope requires that (B) be true, that story would have to be amended if (B)'s falsity does follow from its collapsing.

Why, one might ask, think it does follow? Intuitively, because in saying that God couldn't allow Filbert to be elected if (B) were true, we seem to be saying that it is impossible for someone elected to the papacy to reject God's guidance and proclaim a heresy; but if we do hold this to be impossible, it is hard to see how we could also hold (B) to be true. Let us try to spell out these intuitions a bit more formally. Suppose that (B) collapses—that is, that (1) is true. Adding E to both the antecedent and the consequent of (1), we can derive

(2) $[E \,\&\, (E \to R)] \Rightarrow (\sim E \,\&\, E)$

from (1). Now, the standard analyses of counterfactuals maintain that a counterfactual is true in every world in which both its antecedent and its consequent are true, and though one might have cause to question whether this is a general truth (e.g., does it hold in cases where the antecedent and consequent are utterly unrelated?), there would seem to be little doubt of its applicability to (B). Hence, we seem to be well justified in asserting:

(3) $(E \,\&\, R) \Rightarrow [E \,\&\, (E \to R)]$.

From (3) and (2) it follows that

(4) $(E \,\&\, R) \Rightarrow (\sim E \,\&\, E)$,

which in turn entails

(5) $\sim \Diamond (E \,\&\, R)$

and the equivalent

(6) $E \Rightarrow \sim R$.

On reflection, we probably shouldn't be surprised by the fact that (5) and (6) follow from (1), for the very considerations which led us to think that (B) collapses should lead us just as readily to think that (5) and (6) are true. E, recall, is a *complete* antecedent, one that includes the entire history of the world prior to the time in question. How, one might ask, could there be a world with such a history—a history that includes God's establishment of the papacy and his councils' pronouncements on the charism of infallibility—in which one of the popes proclaims ex cathedra a heresy? So if we are at all inclined to concede that (B) collapses, the fact that (5) and (6) follow from that collapse should hardly strike us as unexpected.

But if (5) and (6) do follow from (1), it is hard to see how we can still hold (B) to be true. If Filbert's election to the papacy *entails* that he *doesn't* freely reject God's guidance and proclaim a heresy, how could his election *counterfactually imply* that he *does* so reject and proclaim? Admittedly, if E were impossible, there would be no difficulty in holding both (6) and (B) to be true. But there is no reason at all to think that E is impossible. If Filbert is perverse enough, it might perhaps just conceivably be the case that there is no feasible world (i.e., no world which God has the power to actualize) in which he is elected pope, simply because there is no such world in which he always freely refrains from proclaiming an error. (Were Filbert this obstinate type of character, we might say that he was *transworldly deprived* of the papacy.) Yet even if this were true, it would show only that there is no *feasible* world in which E is true; in no way would it challenge the obvious fact that there are *possible* worlds in which E is true. So, given that (6) is true, there doesn't seem to be any way in which (B) could also be true.

As we have already noted, the ramifications of (B)'s being false are serious indeed. For our story of how middle knowledge is supposed to be action-guiding for God, leaving him room for a pope who is both free and infallible, crumbles if (B) is false. That story, recall, requires both that there be true counterfactuals such as (A) and (B) which God knows via middle knowledge and that this knowledge guide him as he guides the cardinals. If (B) and other such counterfactuals are not true, then of course God cannot know them to be true via middle knowledge, and cannot employ his knowledge of them to lead the cardinals away from the Filberts of the world. In short, if (B)-type counterfactuals are false one and all, the Molinist answer to our problem with papal infallibility seems to dissolve.

As I see it, there are two ways Molinists might try to resurrect their solution. On the one hand, noticing that all our troubles seemed to arise when we granted that a counterfactual such as (B) collapses, they might question this assumption and attempt to rebuild the middle knowledge position on the foundation of a solid, noncollapsing (B). On the other hand, they might concede that (B) collapses, but suggest that there are other counterfactuals in the vicinity that don't collapse and that could thus serve the same action-guiding purpose that (B) served in our original story. Let us consider each of these alternatives in turn.

6. The Reconstruction of (B)?

To deny that (B) collapses is to say that (1) is false that is, that $(E \rightarrow R)$ doesn't entail $\sim E$. But if $(E \rightarrow R)$ doesn't entail $\sim E$, then it is possible that both $(E \rightarrow R)$ and E be true. Since $[(E \rightarrow R) \& E]$ entails R, it follows that $[(E \rightarrow R) \& E]$ is possible only if $[(E \rightarrow R) \& E \& R]$ is also possible. Therefore, to deny that (B) collapses is to maintain that it is possible that $[(E \rightarrow R) \& E \& R]$—in (other) words, that it is possible that Filbert be elected and proceed to proclaim ex cathedra a falsehood.

But if this is what the denial of (1) entails, then doesn't that denial ultimately amount to nothing less than a rejection of the doctrine of infallibility itself? Surely, one would think, the doctrine entails at least that no one in a world where God has allowed the doctrine of infallibility to be officially endorsed will as pope proclaim ex cathedra a falsehood. Since holding (1) to be false would commit us to endorsing a possibility excluded by the doctrine of infallibility, denying that (B) collapses would seem to be a fruitless means of attempting to defend that doctrine.

Of course, there are ways of making the means in question at least appear fruitful. For example, one could point out that denying (1) is compatible with affirming the similar but weaker conditional

$$(1^\star) \quad (E \rightarrow R) \rightarrow \sim E.$$

Now, one might continue, isn't $(1^\star)$ really all that we need to endorse infallibility? For $(1^\star)$ tells us that God as a matter of fact would not allow Filbert to be elected if he saw by his middle knowledge that Filbert would proclaim ex cathedra a falsehood. Presumably there would be many other true conditionals like $(1^\star)$ relating to other persons, times and histories. And the truth of all these conditionals might well underwrite the truth of even so broad a statement as

(7)   If a pope in a world such as ours (i.e., a world in which papal infallibility has been defined) says ex cathedra that x, then it is not the case that x is false.

Since (7) can be seen as simply stating in a nutshell the doctrine of infallibility, it might well appear that the doctrine is indeed defensible even if (1) is rejected.

Tempting as such a response might appear, I think it is susceptible to several serious objections. In rejecting (1), this response tacitly grants that it is possible that a pope make an erroneous ex cathedra pronouncement. Hence, while it can accept (7), it can view (7) as only a contingent truth; it must grant that there are possible worlds in which a pope who has been defined to be infallible makes an erroneous ex cathedra pronouncement. It seems to me exceedingly unlikely that many defenders of the doctrine would be willing to grant this possibility. Though they may well grant that there are possible worlds with fallible popes, they would insist that such worlds would have different histories from our own, and would not include the kind of biblical and later historical events upon which the doctrine of infallibility is grounded. In a world where that doctrine has been proclaimed, though, there simply is no possibility of a papal ex cathedra error. If there were, we might ask, what would be the point of the doctrine? If there are worlds with histories just like ours in which the pope makes an erroneous ex cathedra pronouncement, what confidence could we place in papal ex cathedra pronouncements in our own world? What confidence could we have that this isn't one of those possible worlds in which the pope goes awry?

Of course, if (1*) and other conditionals like it were known by us to be true, perhaps we would have a sufficient base for such confidence. But once we have rejected (1), what grounds do we have for thinking that (1*) is true? Proposition (1) seems to be supported by the belief that an all-good, non-deceiving God could not allow both that the doctrine of infallibility be proclaimed and that a pope make an ex cathedra error. Those who reject (1) would presumably deny that there is any such necessary connection between God's perfect nature and what he allows to happen in a world where infallibility has been defined. But if there is no such necessary connection, why think that even (1*) is true? If nothing in God's nature prevents him from putting a Filbert in Peter's chair, why should we believe that he hasn't done so?[28]

It seems clear, then, that the rejection of (1) leads inexorably toward a vitiation of the doctrine of infallibility. If we are to defend a robust understanding of the doctrine, I think we are going to have to do it while accepting

---

[x] We might appeal to revelation as a ground for endorsing (1*). But if we think that revelation doesn't give us sufficient reason to embrace (1), it is hard to see why we would think it offers us good reason to accept (1*).

(1)—that is, while acknowledging that counterfactuals such as (B) collapse, and thus offer us no help in reconciling papal infallibility with papal freedom.

7. An Alternative to (B)?

Suppose, then, that we grant that (B) collapses, and hence can't be known via middle knowledge to be true. In that case, the only clear way to repair our story reconciling infallibility and freedom would be to find a replacement for (B). That is, we must find a counterfactual that God could use in the action-guiding way we envisaged for (B), but that, unlike (B), can plausibly be held to be true by the defender of the doctrine.

It seems to me that a promising candidate is not all that hard to draft. For consider what happens to (B) if we alter its consequent to make it similar to the consequent of (A), but negate that consequent. The result would be:

> (B★) If Filbert were elected pope at time *t* in a world with history *h*, it is not the case that he would freely follow divine guidance and keep the Church safe from error.

Notice that, while the consequent of (B) entails that Filbert doesn't keep the Church free from error, the consequent of (B★) has no such implication; it entails only that Filbert doesn't *freely* keep the Church free from error. This distinction, I believe, is of crucial importance to the Molinist reconciliation of papal infallibility and papal freedom. For the upshot of this distinction is that, while (B) collapses, and thus is false, (B★) doesn't collapse, and thus could be one of the true counterfactuals that God's middle knowledge comprises.

Why think that (B★) doesn't collapse? Because the Molinist need not be a zealot with regard to the range of free actions. The core of the Molinist project in discussing infallibility is the attempt to show that papal freedom and papal infallibility are compatible—that there is no inconsistency in a pope's being both free and infallible. But nothing in this project (and, to the best of my knowledge, nothing in Church doctrine) commits the Molinist to thinking that a pope has to be both free and infallible. Thus, the Molinist should have no trouble granting that, in some possible worlds, the pope's infallibility is safeguarded at the expense of his freedom. But if this is so, then there is no reason to think that (B★) collapses. There are indeed worlds in which (B★) is true, Filbert is elected pope, and Filbert doesn't freely follow divine guidance concerning doctrinal proclamations. But these are not worlds in which Filbert makes an erroneous ex cathedra pronouncement. Rather, they are worlds in which Filbert's freedom to do so is somehow blocked—by some natural occurrence (such as death), by the free action(s) of some other created agent(s), or perhaps even by the direct action of God. Since Molinists have no reason that I can see to doubt that such worlds are possible, they have no reason to doubt the truth of a counterfactual such as (B★).[9]

If (B★) is true, though, it could well play just as important a role in guiding God's actions as we had earlier ascribed to (B). For though God does not have to permit his creatures the freedom in each instance to act in the manner they intend to act, it seems fair to assume that, other things being equal, God would prefer to respect his creature's freedom rather than to frustrate it. If we don't make such an assumption, reconciling God's creation of free creatures with his goodness would seem to be all but impossible. Hence, though God could protect the Church from error even with a Filbert as pope, it would seem to be more fitting for him to do so by guiding the Church toward an Elfreth. Given his knowledge of both (A) and (B★), then, it seems not at all unlikely (other things being equal—we are, remember, greatly simplifying things by considering only Elfreth and Filbert) that God would have ample reason to move Rotundo in just the way we described.

Indeed, one might go so far as to argue that God might not have a choice in the matter. For it could be that other elements in God's middle knowledge tell him that Elfreth would in *all* respects (not just concerning ex cathedra statements) be an exemplary pontiff, whereas Filbert would in all respects be a pope worthy of disdain. In that case, one might argue, God would have no choice but to lead the Church to Elfreth. If we let (M) stand for the conjunction of all the counterfactuals other than (A) and (B★) which make up God's middle knowledge, we can represent this argument as suggesting that

(8) $[(A) \& (B★) \& (M)] \Rightarrow {\sim}(\text{Filbert is elected pope at time } t \text{ in a world with history } h)$

is true.

Though I am not convinced that we should hastily accept the argument for (8)—after all, don't we often point with pride to God's ability to bring a bounty of unforeseen good out of willful wickedness?—I see no reason to doubt that some propositions of the form of (8) are true. In other words, the totality of God's middle knowledge may place limitations upon his actions

[9] One of the early proponents of the doctrine of infallibility, Guido Terreni, argued in much the way I have suggested here. As Brian Tierney notes, Terreni was convinced that if a pope "formed the intention of defining a false doctrine, . . . God would intervene to stop him from doing so. 'God would impede such a pope from his evil intention either by death or by the resistance of others or in other ways.'" See Tierney, *Origins of Papal Infallibility*, p. 250.

that individual elements of his middle knowledge do not place. Even if this
is so, though—indeed, even if (8) itself is true—the crucial distinction between propositions such as (B) and those such as (B*) remains. For as it is
only a conjunction of propositions in (8) which entails that the antecedent of
(B*) is false, the truth of (8) would give us no reason to think that (B*) itself
collapses. Hence, whether or not we think that there are true propositions
such as (8), the usefulness of propositions such as (B*) for reconciling papal
freedom and papal infallibility remains.

8. Objections

Before concluding, I would like briefly to consider a couple of objections
to our attempt to resurrect the Molinist reconciliation of papal freedom and
papal infallibility. The first objection focuses on the credentials of (B*) as a
candidate for an element in God's middle knowledge; the second asks whether
our solution has not come at the cost of too great a surrender of papal freedom.

Since it is commonly said that what God knows via his middle knowledge
are counterfactuals of freedom, one might question whether (B*) qualifies for
inclusion in middle knowledge. For (B*) doesn't say what Filbert would do;
all it tells us is that there is a free action he wouldn't perform. Therefore,
since it is doubtful that (B*) should be considered a counterfactual of creaturely freedom, it is doubtful that our strategy can succeed.

Perhaps it is sufficient in reply to point out that this objection relies upon
a rather coarse conception of middle knowledge. As we have seen, middle
knowledge is that part of God's knowledge which consists of contingent truths
that are at all times beyond God's power to control. Counterfactuals of creaturely freedom would undoubtedly be counted in this class, but there is no
reason to think that they exhaust this class. Hence, so long as a proposition
such as (B*) is true, contingent, and not such that its truth value is dependent
upon what God does, that proposition belongs to God's middle knowledge,
whether or not it qualifies as a counterfactual of creaturely freedom. Since
(B*) passes all three of the relevant tests, it clearly would be included in God's
middle knowledge.[10]

It may be worth pointing out in addition, though, that (B*) itself might
qualify as a counterfactual of creaturely freedom, depending upon precisely
how we define such counterfactuals. In any event, it is clear that (B*) might
be based upon some other counterfactual that undeniably is one of creaturely
freedom. For example, there could well be worlds in which Filbert is elected

[10] See Chapter 2, section 3.

and in which he freely undertakes to resist God's grace and to make a false ex cathedra pronouncement.[11] Though God or some other free being would in some way prevent this endeavor from flowering into an actual erroneous proclamation, the important point is that, since Filbert in such a world would indeed have acted freely in undertaking as he did, there clearly would be a counterfactual of creaturely freedom describing this action. So while (B*) will (if true) be part of God's middle knowledge whether or not it qualifies as a counterfactual of creaturely freedom, it may well at least have such a counterfactual lying behind it.

The tendency to equate middle knowledge with knowledge of counterfactuals of creaturely freedom, then, is a dangerous one, one which (as was argued in Chapter 2) we need strenuously to avoid. Indeed, if we extend our story of Filbert just a bit further, we can see that there may well be constituents of middle knowledge that are even more distant from counterfactuals of creaturely freedom than is (B*). Suppose God knew that, if Filbert were elected, he would indeed undertake to declare ex cathedra a falsehood. Let

$$(9) \quad E \rightarrow D$$

represent this counterfactual. Suppose God also knew that no free action on the part of any of his creatures (including Filbert) would block this Filbertian decision from issuing in an erroneous declaration. Let

$$(10) \quad (E \ \& \ D) \rightarrow B$$

represent this counterfactual. Given his knowledge of (9) and (10), God would also know that

$$(11) \quad E \rightarrow B.$$

And since (11) entails

[11] I use "undertake" in more or less the Chisholmian sense of the term. Hence, my undertaking to (say) raise my arm is to be distinguished from my raising my arm. Undertakings can plausibly be seen as events brought about by the agent which, if not checked, result in some sort of (usually) public action. (Thus, if my body is functioning properly, and if nothing and no one prevents my arm from moving, my undertaking to raise my arm will culminate in my raising my arm.) Undertakings can plausibly be seen as the final exercise of freedom on the part of the agent with respect to the action in question. That is, once the agent undertakes to perform a specific action, whether or not the action occurs is no longer up to the agent, but depends upon factors (e.g., the proper functioning of the agent's body, the intervention of other agents, and the like) *not* under the agent's control.

(12) $E \rightarrow (E \;\&\; B)$,

God would know (12) as well. But, as we have seen, it seems impossible that God allow a pope, in a world where infallibility has been declared, actually to proclaim ex cathedra a falsehood. If no other free creature would step in to block Filbert's undertaking from turning into an actual proclamation, then God would have no choice but to block Filbert from making the proclamation he intends to make. That is,

(13) $(E \;\&\; B) \Rightarrow G$,

where G stands for God's acting to block Filbert, is true. But from (12) and (13) it follows that

(14) $E \rightarrow G$.

So if things were as we depicted them in our story, (14) would also be true. Proposition (14), of course, is not a counterfactual of creaturely freedom, for its consequent describes what God does, not what one of his creatures does. Indeed, it seems odd to view (14) as a counterfactual of freedom at all, for the story as we have described it seems to be one in which God has no choice but to block Filbert, not one in which he freely elects to do so. Nevertheless, (14) would still qualify as an element in God's middle knowledge. It couldn't be included in God's natural knowledge (i.e., his knowledge of necessary truths) because (14) isn't necessary. And it couldn't be included in God's free knowledge (i.e., his knowledge of contingent truths whose truth is dependent upon his creative activity) because God could know that (14) is true prior to his deciding upon any creative activity whatsoever. As we saw, (14) follows from (9) through (13). But the first four of these five conditionals are either constituents of God's middle knowledge or entailments therefrom, and thus would be known prior to creation, while the last of the five is a necessary truth and thus would also be known prior to creation. So (14), too, would be known prior to creation. And since it is clearly a contingent truth, it would have to be counted as part of God's middle knowledge.

With a bit of ingenuity, I suspect, we could easily concoct other, even stranger candidates for inclusion in middle knowledge. But none of this, of course, is really necessary to respond to our first objection. So long as we realize that middle knowledge need not be limited to counterfactuals of creaturely freedom, we will have no problem acknowledging propositions such as (B*) as included in God's middle knowledge.

The second objection to our solution can be both stated and handled more briefly. One might charge that our attempt to defend both papal freedom and papal infallibility has resulted in too great a diminution of the former. For we have granted that God might maintain the infallibility of a pope only by stripping that pope of his freedom. In defending infallibility from the Scylla of its detractors, have we not in effect fallen into the Charybdis of divine determinism we had sought to evade?

I think not. All that we have granted is that there are possible worlds in which God maintains the infallibility of the pope by limiting the pope's freedom. But it hardly follows from this that papal freedom has thus been denied. In the first place, there is no reason at all to think that the kind of divine limitation on the pope that we are entertaining has in fact ever occurred. Indeed, if God has middle knowledge, one would expect that he would generally have more than enough Elfreths available to him, and hence little need to resort to a Filbert. More important, though, even if this type of divine activity has occurred, it hardly follows that the pope must henceforth be thought of as a robotic extension of his divine programmer. For the kind of divine intervention we have imagined, the kind that seems most likely to occur, is purely preventive in nature. Rather than determining the pope to speak in a particular way, it blocks him from following through on a decision he has come to freely. Hence, though the solution we have suggested clearly does countenance the possibility of God's circumscribing the pope's power in order to maintain papal infallibility, the charge that it constitutes too great an infringement of papal freedom seems to me unfounded.

9. Conclusion

In sum, then, I think at least this one promissory note has been redeemed: the concept of middle knowledge can indeed play an important role in defending the doctrine of papal infallibility. The role is, perhaps, a bit more difficult to play than many Molinists would have suspected, and the final production perhaps a bit less polished than we would have liked. Still, it seems to me that the contribution of the concept of middle knowledge in explicating this niche of the notion of providence is quite significant, and should give Molinists a degree of confidence that the concept will in fact exhibit the kind of fruitfulness they have envisaged. Let us now proceed to see if this confidence can be further bolstered by applying Molinism in two other areas, prophecy and prayer.[12]

[12] I am especially grateful to Michael Byron, whose penetrating comments on an earlier version of this chapter led me to make several alterations.

[9]

Prophecy

... about an hour later still another kept insisting, "Surely this man also was with him; for he is a Galilean." But Peter said, "Man, I do not know what you are talking about!" At that moment, while he was still speaking, the cock crowed. The Lord turned and looked at Peter. Then Peter remembered the word of the Lord, how he had said to him, "Before the cock crows today, you will deny me three times." And he went out and wept bitterly.

—Luke 22: 59–62

I. The Ground of Prophecy: Foreknowledge or Middle Knowledge?

If the conclusions of the previous chapter are accepted, one might naturally suspect that there is at least one related area in which the Molinist picture of providence can fruitfully be applied. For whether or not they believe the pope to be infallible, most orthodox Christians would surely want to insist that God is infallible, in the sense that no divine statement can possibly be mistaken. And this freedom from the possibility of error, the orthodox would insist, extends even to divine declarations about the future—even to divine prophecies.[1] If middle knowledge was of assistance in seeing how papal infallibility might function, then, it seems reasonable to think that it will also contribute to our understanding of prophecy.

In the end, I think this hunch is on target: middle knowledge is indeed of inestimable value to God in deciding when and how to convey to his creatures his knowledge of future events. On the other hand, it surely looks, at least at first glance, as though it is foreknowledge, not middle knowledge, which is fundamental to divine prophecy. Suppose, for example, that Jesus were to say that Peter will raise his arm at noon on a specific day. Suppose, furthermore,

[1] It is not my intention to claim that a necessary condition of something's properly being called a prophecy be that some event in the future be foretold. Clearly enough, though, some prophetic utterances do have this revelatory aspect. It is prophecy in this sense that is my focus in this chapter.

that in so saying, Jesus was intending to express the proposition that Peter will raise his arm at noon; he was not simply reading from a letter or play, testing his voice, or anything of that sort, but using the words in the ordinary declarative manner. Under such conditions, it seems clear that Jesus can be said to have *prophesied* that Peter will raise his arm at noon. And, of course, from the perspective of the orthodox Christian serious about divine infallibility and divine honesty, it follows from Jesus' divinity that whatever he prophesies comes to be. Hence,

(1)   Jesus prophesies that Peter will raise his arm at noon ⇒ Peter will raise his arm at noon.

But now let us ask: Why does Jesus make that prophecy about Peter? On what is the prophecy based? Why not make it about Andrew or Matthew instead? After all, just as (1) is true, so too are

(2)   Jesus prophesies that Andrew will raise his arm at noon ⇒ Andrew will raise his arm at noon

and

(3)   Jesus prophesies that Matthew will raise his arm at noon ⇒ Matthew will raise his arm at noon.

So why make the prophecy about one, but not the others? What is the ground for making such a prophecy?

A natural answer to make here is that Jesus' prophecy is based upon God's foreknowledge—or, less tendentiously, upon God's knowledge of those events that lie in our future. Knowing our future, God knows that Peter will raise his arm at noon, but that neither Andrew nor Matthew will. Hence, one might argue, it is God's knowledge of the future, not his middle knowledge, which guides Jesus' prophesying.

However, given our presentation of the Molinist account of providence, it surely looks as though something is amiss in thinking of prophecy as directed by foreknowledge. For on that Molinist account, recall, it is supposed to be middle knowledge that guides divine decisions, while foreknowledge arrives (so to speak) too late in the game to have any effect. Foreknowledge, for the Molinist, is *itself* an effect of God's creative act of will, and hence can hardly be seen as guiding that act. Since God's decision to issue that prophecy concerning Peter's arm-raising will be part of God's creative act of will, his foreknowledge of Peter's action cannot be that on which the prophecy is based.

At first glance, it seems easy to propose an alternative basis in God's middle knowledge for the prophecy concerning Peter. Suppose middle knowledge told God that Peter would raise his arm if placed in a certain set of circumstances (call them C). Suppose it also told him that, should he perform a particular creative act of will (call it V), Peter would indeed (as a result of the free actions of God, Peter, and others) find himself in C. Should God then decide to perform V, he would know that Peter would raise his arm; hence, he could decide to have Jesus prophesy the arm-raising. On the other hand, if God's middle knowledge told him that neither Andrew nor Matthew would (should God perform V) be placed in circumstances in which they would raise their arms, then God would see to it that Jesus prophesies no such action on their part. Thus, from a Molinist perspective, it appears that it is indeed middle knowledge, not foreknowledge, upon which God relies in issuing prophecies.

2. A Problem with Privileging Middle Knowledge

Thus far, the Molinist perspective appears to have handled our question concerning prophecy quite tidily. Indeed, the neatness of our solution should give us pause, for though the absence of clutter may in many areas be the sign of a well-ordered life, in philosophy it often points merely to a proficiency at sweeping things under the rug. Are there, in fact, reasons for a Molinist to be dissatisfied with our handling of prophecy?

I believe there are. For recall the story we told about how God's middle knowledge would guide him in prophesying Peter's arm-raising, but not those of Andrew and Matthew. The idea was that, by middle knowledge, God would know a conditional of the form

(4)   Peter is in circumstances $C \rightarrow$ Peter will raise his arm at noon.

He would then, having decided to put Peter in C, know that Peter will raise his arm; and, given this knowledge, Jesus could make the appropriate prophecy. Unfortunately, two problems seem evident with this suggestion.

First, hasn't our suggestion surreptitiously brought foreknowledge back on stage as at least a partial basis for prophecy? Isn't our picture one of God's middle knowledge leading to foreknowledge of the arm-raising, which foreknowledge in turn leads to the prophecy? And if this is so, then mustn't our claim that it is *only* middle knowledge, not foreknowledge, which provides the basis for divine prophecy be at least modified?

The second problem seems even more troubling. Consider the C mentioned in the antecedent of (4); what is it to include? What are the circumstances in which an action is performed? As we have seen, Molinists typically respond that the circumstances should be thought of as including the entire causal history of the world prior to the time specified by the consequent, along with whatever influences are acting on the agent at that time. But if the entire causal history of the world is included in C, then it would seem that C must include Jesus' prophesying that Peter will raise his arm.[2] And if it is so included, then Peter's being in C entails that Peter raises his arm, for from

(5)   Peter is in circumstances $C \Rightarrow$ Jesus prophesies that Peter will raise his arm at noon

and the indisputable

(1)   Jesus prophesies that Peter will raise his arm at noon $\Rightarrow$ Peter will raise his arm at noon

it indisputably follows that

(6)   Peter is in circumstances $C \Rightarrow$ Peter will raise his arm at noon.

The second problem with seeing middle knowledge as the foundation for prophecy now becomes evident. For if (6) is true, then (4) cannot be known by God via middle knowledge. Middle knowledge, recall, is supposed to be knowledge of contingent truths beyond God's control. If (6) is true, then (4) is a necessary, not a contingent, truth. But then (4) cannot be part of God's middle knowledge, and so cannot be the kind of conditional that guides God in prophesying Peter's arm-raising. After all, *anyone* who is in circumstances in which Jesus has prophesied an arm-raising is going to raise her arm. Knowledge of such trivial necessary truths is of little value to God in deciding when to make such a prophecy and when not to make it. So how does middle knowledge guide God in prophesying? If not counterfactuals such as (4), what counterfactuals *are* of practical assistance to him?

One response would be to suggest that (4) is not of assistance precisely because it is *not*, strictly speaking, a counterfactual of creaturely freedom. For its consequent says only that Peter will raise his arm at noon, not that he will

---

[2] Some with Molinist sympathies might deny this; see, for instance, Edward Wierenga, "Prophecy, Freedom, and the Necessity of the Past," in J. E. Tomberlin, ed., *Philosophical Perspectives*, vol. 5 (Atascadero, Calif.: Ridgeview, 1991), pp. 425–445. Most Molinists, though, would (and, I think, should) feel uneasy about adopting such a position.

do so freely. If we change (4) into a genuine counterfactual of creaturely freedom, we get

(4*)   Peter is in circumstances $C \rightarrow$ Peter will freely raise his arm at noon.

Does (4*) suffer the same fate as (4)? Is it, too, a necessary truth, and hence ineligible for inclusion in God's middle knowledge? No. For C specifies only that Jesus foretells that Peter will raise his arm, not that Jesus foretells that Peter will do so *freely*. Hence, the analogue to (6), namely

(6*)   Peter is in circumstances $C \Rightarrow$ Peter will freely raise his arm at noon

is plainly false. Similarly, the analogues to (4*) concerning Andrew and Matthew might also be false; in other words, it might be that God sees by his middle knowledge that neither Andrew nor Matthew would freely raise his arm if God prophesied such an event. This might not force God not to make such prophecies—after all, God surely has it within his power to cause Andrew or Matthew to raise his arm—but, given what Molinists might plausibly assume concerning God's general preference for exercising providential control without robbing his creatures of their freedom, it might well lead him not to issue such prophecies concerning Andrew and Matthew. And so there is no problem with (4*)'s being the counterfactual of creaturely freedom which guides God's prophetic action.[3]

Such a response is surely right as far as it goes; and, as we shall see, I think it is genuinely instructive. Still, there is something less than fully satisfactory about it. For such a response is clearly not available when the action foretold is foretold *as free*. Had Jesus said, not just that Peter would raise his arm, but that he would do so freely, then the set of circumstances in which Peter found himself would entail that he raise his arm freely, and so the analogue of (4*) would be a necessary truth, not something known by middle knowledge. Nor would such a response be available when the action foretold is one which is *essentially* free—for example, when what is foretold is a sin. And indeed, if we take what is perhaps the most famous instance of prophecy in Scripture, Jesus' prophecy of Peter's denials, we seem to have an action of just this sort; to deny another person seems to be something one does only if one is free.[4]

---

[3] The response offered here bears obvious similarities to the manner in which I attempted to reconcile papal infallibility with papal freedom in Chapter 8.

[4] Of course, someone could have caused Peter to say the words which he actually uttered to deny Jesus. Had Peter's utterance taken place in such a way, however, it would have been (at best) extremely misleading to say that Peter had denied Jesus.

If we henceforth allow C to stand for the circumstances in which Peter actually found himself, a set of circumstances which included Jesus' prophecy, we see that

(7)   Peter is in circumstances $C \rightarrow$ Peter will deny Jesus

could not be an element in God's middle knowledge which guided the prophecy, for the circumstances entail the action and hence render (7) necessary. So again, we are left without any evident role for middle knowledge to play in God's decision to prophesy.

The two problems we have identified here seem to me deep and difficult ones, and I am not sure that any simple Molinist solutions are available. And indeed, when we step back from the specifics of this example to consider the problem as a whole, perhaps the state of perplexity at which we have arrived should not surprise us. Prima facie, prophecy looks to be logically posterior to foreknowledge; God, it would seem, can foretell that something will happen only when he already sees that it will happen. But, on the Molinist picture, foreknowledge is in turn logically posterior to middle knowledge and God's decisions as to what actions he will perform. And among the actions God sometimes decides to perform are prophetic actions. So God's decision to make a particular prophecy would seem to be logically prior to his foreknowledge of the consequences of that action, a foreknowledge that results only when the decision is combined with middle knowledge. And so, for the Molinist, God's decision to perform a prophetic action appears to be both logically prior and logically posterior to his foreknowledge that the foretold event will occur.

There are a number of approaches that a Molinist might take to escape this uninhabitable corner. Clearly, any solution will be of one of two types: it will render a decision to prophesy solely logically prior to the foreknowledge of the events prophesied, or it will render such a decision solely logically posterior to that foreknowledge. Let us examine one solution of each type. We will then consider whether a third solution, which combines some of the advantages of the first two, might not be available.

3. The First Solution

Taking the example of Peter and his arm-raising to heart, one might claim that God never does and never can prophesy that a certain action will *freely* occur, but only that it will occur. The decision to prophesy could then be made logically prior to God's knowledge as to precisely how the prophecy will be fulfilled, freely or not freely; that foreknowledge will come about only after God consults counterfactuals such as (4★) which he knows via middle knowledge. But this foreknowledge has no bearing on the decision to prophesy; that decision is made prior, and in no sense posterior, to God's detailed and complete foreknowledge. And so the predicament outlined in the preceding section is eluded.

Though providing a neat solution to our problems, a solution that vindicates our earlier presentation of Molinism by exiling foreknowledge from the realm of the action-guiding part of God's knowledge, such an approach has a fundamental drawback: it seems unduly limiting of God's prophetic abilities. As the example of Peter's denying Jesus suggests, there appears to be good Scriptural evidence that God does sometimes decide to prophesy that an essentially free action will occur. To deny God such an ability would thus appear to be at odds with Scripture, and (to many theists) at odds with their intuitions as to the power of God, who they would think should have the ability to prophesy free actions as free. Hence, while this solution may be of some help to the Molinist in showing how middle knowledge guides some prophecies, it can hardly tell the whole story.

4. The Second Solution

Can the Molinist resolve the quandary concerning prophecy by taking the opposite approach—by suggesting that the decision to prophesy is logically posterior, not prior, to the foreknowledge that the relevant event will occur? Such an approach does seem to have some promise. Let $C^\star$ stand for the circumstances in which Peter found himself *not* including the prophecy; hence, $C^\star$, to be made eligible as an antecedent of a counterfactual of creaturely freedom, must be completed either by Jesus' act of prophecy or by his refraining from issuing such a prophecy.[5] Now, suppose God knew, given his

---

[5] Stating more precisely what $C^\star$ is to include is no simple matter. Presumably we cannot, for instance, say it includes all the states of affairs included by C with the exception of *Jesus' prophesying*, for then it would have to include such states of affairs as *God's knowing that Jesus prophesies Peter's denial*. Nor can we say that it includes all the states of affairs included by C except those whose actuality is entailed by the fact that Jesus prophesies, for then it would have to include all those states of affairs upon which Jesus' prophesying supervenes—states of affairs such as *Jesus' saying the Aramaic equivalent of "You will deny me" at t, Jesus' intending to express a proposition by uttering certain Aramaic words at t*, etc.—and these states of affairs together would give us a set of circumstances the actuality of which would still entail Peter's denial. The general problem of how to excise one element from a larger set of circumstances is an important and difficult one for which I have no general solution. For this case, though, it *may* be sufficient to think of $C^\star$ as excluding the initial event involved in Jesus' act of prophesying (i.e., his decision, or volition, or undertaking to prophesy) along with the later events that flow from that initial event.

middle knowledge, that his decision to prophesy Peter's denial would make
no difference as to whether or not Peter denies Jesus. That is, suppose God
knew that both

(8)   (Peter is in circumstances $C^\star$ and Jesus prophesies that Peter will deny
       him) $\Rightarrow$ Peter will deny Jesus

and

(9)   (Peter is in circumstances $C^\star$ and it is not the case that Jesus prophesies
       that Peter will deny him) $\rightarrow$ Peter will deny Jesus.

Since (9) is a counterfactual of creaturely freedom, God would know by
middle knowledge that both (8) and (9) are true. But since (8) and (9) together
entail

(10)   Peter is in circumstances $C^\star$ $\rightarrow$ Peter will deny Jesus

God would know (10) by middle knowledge as well. Suppose that, seeing
that (10) is true, God decides to act so as to put Peter in $C^\star$. This would
immediately provide God with the foreknowledge that Peter will deny Jesus.
Given this foreknowledge, God then decides that Jesus will foretell Peter's
freely denying him.

Clearly, such an approach has many attractive features. By suggesting how
counterfactuals such as (9) and (10) might play a part in God's decision to
prophesy, it allows the kind of action-guiding role for middle knowledge that
Molinists would like to see. Furthermore, it escapes from the kind of divine
hand-tying that seemed to weaken our earlier solution; if God's prophecy is
truly irrelevant to Peter's action, then there is no reason why God cannot
prophecy even such an essentially free action. Finally, it clearly allows us to
escape from the paradox that seemed to beset the Molinist picture of prophecy, for it insists that the divine decision to prophesy Peter's denial is made
only after, not before, God foresees that denial.

Despite these virtues, elements of this second solution remain disturbing.
For example, isn't the first of our two problems with seeing middle knowledge
as guiding prophecy—namely, that it covertly makes foreknowledge part of
God's basis for action—left untouched by the second solution? Indeed, isn't
that problem actually exacerbated by this solution? For it offers us a fragmented picture of divine action which traditional Molinists would surely find
troubling. As we saw in Chapter 2, Molina himself offers a simple picture of
the logical ordering of God's knowledge, whereby natural knowledge is aug-

mented by middle knowledge which is augmented by a single free act of the divine will, thereby producing complete foreknowledge. But our second solution complicates this picture immensely. For it suggests that natural knowledge [of (8)] and middle knowledge [of (9) and (10)] is augmented by a divine decision (to put Peter in C^*), yielding foreknowledge (that Peter will deny Jesus), which foreknowledge in turn leads to a logically *later* divine decision (to prophesy Peter's denial). Such a picture may not be at odds with anything essential to Molinism, but it surely is one that many Molinists would find unsettling.

I shall return to this problem in the next section to suggest a way in which this unease might be diminished. For now, though, let us turn to another, and arguably more significant, difficulty with our second solution—namely, that, like our first solution, it seems to have, at best, only a limited application. It suggests that middle knowledge may be of assistance to God in deciding to prophesy in those cases in which the prophecy will make no difference. But why think that God is limited to issuing prophecies only in such cases? Couldn't it be the case that some divine prophecies play a nonsuperfluous causal role in the coming to be of those prophesied events? Fictional cases of this sort are well known; for example, Oedipus almost surely would not have killed his father and married his mother had not the gods foretold (and humans subsequently tried to prevent) these very occurrences. But why think such cases are exclusively fictional? On the contrary, isn't there some plausibility in thinking that the real-life case of Peter's denying Jesus was precisely such an incident? True, if Peter is free, Jesus' words cannot have causally determined him to act as he did. But might it not be that Jesus' prophecy gave the thought within Peter's mind of denying Jesus a kind of plausibility that it otherwise would not have had—made it, in the Jamesian sense, a live option—and thereby set the stage for the denial, a denial which simply wouldn't have been made had the option of denial not been made live by Jesus' words? Whether or not we read the case of Peter in this way, it surely seems possible that some prophesied event be such that the prophecy itself causally contributes to its occurrence. And for such instances of prophecy, our second solution seems to offer no help in understanding the role middle knowledge would play in God's decision to prophesy.

Fortunately for the Molinist, I think one can rescue the second solution from this objection by noting that the path by which a prophecy might causally contribute to the occurrence of that which is prophesied can be severed in such a way as to give us an action-guiding counterfactual of creaturely freedom. For instance, in the story of Peter told in the last paragraph, Jesus' prophecy causally contributes only in a remote way to Peter's denial—that is, only by causing Peter to believe that Jesus has prophesied his denial. Might we not argue that it is this belief-state which is truly relevant to Peter's denial, and that this belief-state could have been caused in any number of ways—by demonic activity, by neural malfunctioning, etc.? Of course, God knows that, necessarily, if this belief state is caused by Jesus' actually having prophesied that Peter will deny him, then Peter will deny him. So, letting C^{**} stand for C^* *minus* Peter's either being or not being in this belief-state, God knows that

> (11)   (Peter is in circumstances C^{**}; Peter believes that Jesus prophesies that Peter will deny him; and Jesus prophesies that Peter will deny him, thereby causing Peter's belief) $\Rightarrow$ Peter will deny Jesus.

But perhaps God also knows that, if Jesus were *not* to make this prophecy, but Peter were in some aberrant way to come to believe that he *had*, Peter would still deny him. In other words,

> (12)   (Peter is in circumstances C^{**}; Peter believes that Jesus prophesies that Peter will deny him; and it is not the case that Jesus prophesies that Peter will deny him, thereby causing Peter's belief) $\rightarrow$ Peter will deny Jesus.

Proposition (12), of course, would not be a necessary truth, for the conjuncts in the antecedent do not entail (either individually or collectively) that Peter deny Jesus. Hence, (12) would be known by God via middle knowledge. But now the characteristic move of the second solution can again be made. For (11) and (12) together entail

> (13)   (Peter is in circumstances C^{**}, and Peter believes that Jesus prophesies that Peter will deny him) $\rightarrow$ Peter will deny Jesus.[6]

Since (13) is a contingent truth which follows logically from a conjunction which God would know via middle knowledge, (13) too would be part of God's middle knowledge. Given his knowledge of (13), God could decide both to place Peter in C^{**} and to bring it about that Peter believes that Jesus makes the relevant prophecy. This decision on God's part will provide him with the foreknowledge that Peter will deny Jesus. God could then decide to have Jesus make the relevant prophecy. So, even though the prophecy would

---

[6] In a sense, the move from (11) and (12) to (13) just *is* the move from (8) and (9) to (10) over again. For (12) and (13) are simply equivalents of (9) and (10) with the antecedents written more expansively, while (11) is very close (though not identical) to (8).

be the cause of Peter's belief, God's decision to make the prophecy would still be guided by his middle knowledge; and the decision to prophesy would still be solely posterior to God's foreknowledge of the prophesied event.

Ingenious and helpful as this attempt to rescue the second solution may be, I fear that it is not a complete success. For it succeeds only if we can indeed claim that God knows a counterfactual such as (12) by middle knowledge. But since the antecedent of (12) fails to specify how it is that Peter comes to have his belief, that antecedent is incomplete; hence, (12) is not itself a genuine counterfactual of creaturely freedom.[7] Of course, it could still be part of God's middle knowledge—for example, if it were logically implied by true counterfactuals of creaturely freedom. And this could indeed be the case. It could be that, for any possible aberrant way in which Peter might come to have the belief in C^{**} that Jesus has prophesied his denial, God sees by middle knowledge that, if Peter were to come to have the belief in that way, he would deny Jesus. If all these counterfactuals meshed in this way, God could indeed know by middle knowledge that (12) was true, and so our rescue mission on the second solution would be triumphant. But suppose that the relevant counterfactuals *don't* harmonize in this way. Suppose, for instance, that

(14)   (Peter is in circumstances C^{**}; Peter believes that Jesus prophesies that Peter will deny him; it is not the case that Jesus prophesies that Peter will deny him; and Peter's belief is caused by demonic action A) $\rightarrow$ Peter will deny Jesus

is *true*, but

(15)   (Peter is in circumstances C^{**}; Peter believes that Jesus prophesies that Peter will deny him; it is not the case that Jesus prophesies that Peter will deny him; and Peter's belief is caused by neural malfunction B) $\rightarrow$ Peter will deny Jesus

is *false*. In that case, God's knowledge of counterfactuals of creaturely freedom would seemingly not provide God with (12) as part of his middle knowledge; and so the rescue mission on our second solution would falter.

Some Molinists, I suspect, would look upon the degree of faltering here as so slight as not to be bothersome. For even if, as libertarians, we cannot insist that the relevant counterfactuals would *have* to harmonize in the desired man-

---

[7] Obviously, C^{**}, which [in order to see (12) and (13) as possibly both true] we are thinking of as compatible with Peter's belief's being caused in various different ways, cannot itself specify the cause of that belief.

ner—we cannot, for example, say that the truth of (15) *follows* from the truth of (14)—we can maintain that it would be very *odd* for one but not the other to be true. After all, Peter is placed in phenomenologically indistinguishable situations in (14) and (15); would it not be strange *in excelsis* if *which* aberrant cause of his belief occurred made a difference to his action, given that he is totally ignorant of that cause in either case? Perhaps God would not be able to use his middle knowledge to guide his prophetic activity if the relevant counterfactuals failed to mesh. But such a situation would be so bizarre to begin with that the Molinist shouldn't be worried by this fact.

One problem remains: Why should we think it so bizarre or unusual for the relevant counterfactuals to be disharmonious? God, of course, has no say in which counterfactuals of creaturely freedom are true. Though any of an infinite number of possible combinations of such counterfactuals—that is, an infinite number of what were called *creaturely world-types* in Chapter 2—could be true, God simply finds, prior to creation, that one such combination is true. Why should we think that God is lucky enough to be presented with a completely harmonious world-type? The inharmonious world-types—ones that, say, include (14) but not (15)—seem every bit as logically possible as the harmonious ones. So the odds would seem to be just as good that God will be presented with an inharmonious world-type as with a harmonious one. Do we really want to tie God's prophetic activity to his good fortune in having been presented with a harmonious world-type? Do we not, rather, want to say that prophecy would be possible for God, and would be guided by God's middle knowledge, regardless of which kind of world-type presented itself to him?

Fortunately for the second solution, a final response to this final objection seems available. For even if God is presented with an inharmonious world-type, there may well be harmonious enclaves within it. That is, it may well be that, though for *some* creatures he might create in some circumstances, the counterfactuals about those creatures fail to mesh in the appropriate way, and thus would block his middle knowledge from guiding his prophetic activity, there are *other* creatures he might create (and/or other circumstances) where the counterfactuals *do* harmonize in such a way as to open the door for middle-knowledge-guided prophecy. If God were to realize that the true world-type were of this sort, and were he to wish to employ prophecy in his governance of the world, he might well be inclined to create only those free beings who inhabit the harmonious enclaves of the world-type. For instance, seeing that (14) is true but (15) false might give God a reason not to create Peter, or at least not both to create him in C** and to bring it about that Peter believes that Jesus prophesies Peter's denial; on the other hand, seeing that both (14) and (15) are true might, other things being equal, give God some inclination toward bringing Peter into existence, perhaps in C^{**}. So the fact that God might just as likely be presented with an inharmonious as with a harmonious world-type gives us no real argument against the second solution.

5. Transforming the Second Solution: The Best of Both Worlds?

Let us return now to the initial problem mentioned both with our attempt to see prophecy grounded in middle knowledge and with what we have called the second solution. That problem, recall, is that, by seeing God's decision to put Peter in C^* as logically prior to his foreknowledge that Peter will deny Jesus, which foreknowledge in turn is logically prior to God's decision to prophesy that Peter will deny Jesus, we not only restore foreknowledge to an action-guiding role Molinists are reluctant to accord it, but also fragment what should be a single, simple act of the divine will.

Perhaps the first thing to note is that both the restoration of foreknowledge and the fragmentation of God's will would appear to be essential to any solution of the second of the two types mentioned at the end of section 2. For solutions of that type simply *are* ones which view a decision to prophesy as logically posterior to the foreknowledge of what is prophesied. Since that foreknowledge will surely be posterior to at least some divine decisions (e.g., the decision to create the beings involved in the prophesied event), fragmentation of the divine action seems inevitable if we adopt a solution of the second type.

If God's act of will is not to be fragmented, then, no solution of the second type would seem to be acceptable. Yet it is fairly simple to transform our second solution into one of the first type, one in which God's decision to prophesy is solely logically prior to the foreknowledge of the events prophesied. All that we need do is think of God's creative decision as directed more at a whole world rather than at particular occurrences in that world. For example, rather than thinking of God as first willing to put Peter in C^*, then knowing that Peter will deny Jesus, and then willing to prophesy the denial, we need to think of God as prevolitionally recognizing via middle knowledge that, *if* he willed to put Peter in C^*, Peter would deny Jesus, and God could, if he so willed, prophesy that denial. On the basis of this (and other) prevolitional knowledge, God could then perform a single act of will that would have among its results both Peter's being in C^* and Jesus' prophesying the denial; and only logically posterior to this single act of will would God have foreknowledge.

So our second solution, transformed into a solution of the first type, seems to solve our remaining problem, for it gives us a God whose middle knowledge guides his single act of world-actualizing will, an act that logically precedes and in no respect depends upon his foreknowledge. While I suppose a Molinist untroubled by the elevation of foreknowledge and the fragmentation of the divine will presupposed by the second solution might see no need to transform it into the third kind of solution proposed here, such a Molinist would undoubtedly face some embarrassing questions. Does it not, one might ask, seem more becoming for a provident God to postpone making *any* decisions regarding divine activity until he has made *all* such decisions? If fragmentation *can* so easily be avoided, why not avoid it? Answering such questions would surely not be easy. For most Molinists, then, the transformed solution will no doubt seem the most appealing.

6. Conclusion

Our attempt to find a way in which middle knowledge might guide God's prophetic activity seems to me to have been, on the whole, a success. Some of God's prophesying, according to the first solution to our problem with seeing middle knowledge as guiding prophecy, might be guided by his deciding, logically prior to any foreknowledge on his part, to bring about certain events, and to prophesy that those events will occur, though not that creaturely freedom will be involved in their occurrence. Other prophesying, the second solution suggested, might take place as a result of God's having decided, on the basis of his knowledge of counterfactuals of creaturely freedom that harmonize appropriately, to place a creature in a situation in which, as God foresees logically prior to the decision to prophesy, the creature will act in a particular way.

To be sure, each of these first two solutions has its drawbacks: the first is limited to the prophesying of actions that are not prophesied as free, while the second seems illicitly both to elevate foreknowledge to an action-guiding status and to fragment the creative act of the divine will. Nevertheless, neither of these drawbacks seems to me to be fatal. The first solution, though of limited application, may well be completely correct within that limited range, while the elevation of foreknowledge and the fragmentation of God's will entailed by the second solution can easily be eliminated by transforming that solution to one of the third type proposed in section 5.

Of course, in evaluating the strengths and weaknesses of the Molinist understanding of prophecy, one must keep in mind the available alternatives which might be offered by rival accounts of providence. We have already seen the perplexities facing the openist who wishes to take prophecy seriously.[8] Thomists would undoubtedly have an easier time; still, I suspect that

---

[8] See Chapter 3, section 6.

a thorough Thomistic account of prophecy would serve only to highlight the implausible picture of freedom upon which that account is constructed. Hence, though making no claims to prescience, I do feel warranted in predicting that most orthodox Christians, having made the appropriate comparisons with rival views of prophecy, will find the Molinist picture the most attractive.

But if God sees all counterfactuals, then by placing Judas in his path who is responsible for Christ's betrayal?

Unanswered Prayers

> When considering the problem of the usefulness of prayer, one must re-
> member that divine providence not only disposes what effects will take
> place, but also the manner in which they will take place, and which actions
> will cause them. . . . [W]e do not pray in order to change the decree of
> divine providence, rather we pray in order to impetrate those things which
> God has determined would be obtained only through our prayers.
> —St. Thomas Aquinas, *Summa Theologiae*, 2a2ae, 83, 2

1. Questions Concerning Prayer

According to the notion of providence outlined above, God is to be
thought of as intimately involved with the lives of his creatures. Part of this
involvement, as we have seen, has to do with God's speaking to us—via
prophetic utterances, inspired writings, infallible papal or conciliar pronouncements, and the like. But, of course, creatures are not solely the *recipients* of
communication bridging the gap between the creator and the creature; often
enough, we are the *initiators*, and God (we hope) is the recipient.[1] To put
this in less academic language: We pray, and God (we trust) hears us. And as
the quotation from Aquinas suggests, our prayers may often play essential roles
in God's overall providential plan.

Prayer, of course, comes in a wide variety of forms. At times our prayer is
simply an expression of praise, an explicit articulation of and celebration in
God's glory. At other times, we pray to thank God, either for the general
gifts of life and love which we constantly enjoy, or for more specific blessings
which we feel God in his providence has bestowed upon us. And we often
pray that God forgive us for what we have done, or what we have failed to

---

[1] To speak of ourselves as initiators would be misleading if we were to think of our prayers
as arising solely from ourselves. Most reflective Christians would surely concede that the very
impetus toward prayer is of divine origin. Insofar as this impetus is nondetermining, though,
speaking of ourselves as initiating acts of prayer is probably harmless—at least, as long as we
remind ourselves that our action, in this as in every case, is essentially reactive.

do. Sometimes, though, we pray to ask God for certain things.[2] It is this type of prayer—petitionary prayer—which is my focus both in this chapter and in the next.

Prayer of any form raises a number of interesting questions, and this is especially true with respect to petitionary prayer. For example, for what, we might ask, is it appropriate to pray? Should we pray for specific goods, or only for divine blessings of whatever sort God thinks best? If specifying goods is acceptable, may we pray for what we might call *external* (or *material* or *temporal*) goods, such as health or wealth? If so, is it appropriate to pray for such goods both for oneself and for others? Or is it proper, or at least better, to seek such goods only for others? And what about (arguably) less important external goods? Is praying that one's favorite football team win their upcoming game acceptable? Or is praying for *any* sort of external or material good, regardless of its significance, somehow misguided? Should our prayer rather be directed toward *internal* or *spiritual* goods—the development of virtue, the gift of grace, final salvation, and the like? Furthermore, to whom should our prayers for goods (of whatever sort) be addressed? To God? To Christ? To the Virgin Mary? To angels and saints generally?[3]

These are but a few of the questions that arise when we begin to think carefully about the topic of petitionary prayer. Theists, of course, would not answer all such questions with a single voice. Indeed, even among Christians, there would be considerable disagreement over the questions listed above. Some of these disputes, I suspect, are utterly irresolvable. Others may be adjudicable (to a greater or lesser degree), but only by appeal to evidence and arguments which are largely non-philosophical in character. To expect philosophers in general, or advocates of the Molinist picture of providence in particular, to contribute significantly to most of these debates is to expect far too much.

Still, I think there are at least a couple of issues relating to petitionary prayer where the Molinist outlook may well be able to shed some light. First, why is it that our petitions so often appear to go unanswered? And second, does it make sense to pray for things to have happened? The first of these questions is our focus in this chapter; Chapter 11 then addresses the second. As we shall see, though completely satisfying answers to these questions (especially the first) might well be unattainable, a Molinist perspective

---

[2] One needn't think of the forms of prayer mentioned here as exclusive. For example, to ask God for forgiveness is clearly to petition God for something.

[3] It should come as no shock to readers to hear that many of these questions, along with others, are discussed with characteristic ingenuity and insight by Aquinas. See especially *Summa Theologiae*, 2a2ae, question 83.

appears at least to soften the shadow of perplexity which often surrounds such questions.

2. The Problem

Central to the Christian view of a provident God is the conviction that God does not leave his children to fend for themselves. A provident creator cares for his creatures. Thus, the biblical story of creation shows us a world in which God is very much present to his creatures, a world in which God sees to it that all of their needs are satisfied, and abundantly so. Indeed, even after the sin of Adam and Eve, the punishments required by divine justice are tempered by the continuing gifts flowing from divine love; it is God, after all, who not only speaks to his disobedient (and almost comically buck-passing) children, but provides them with clothing to hide their newly-discovered nakedness. And all of this, note, God does without being asked.

If Scripture from the very start emphasizes God's kindness to his creatures even in the absence of petitionary prayer, it is no less explicit in the conviction that our requests for divine help will always be answered. A classic statement for Christians of this conviction is found in the gospel of Matthew (7:7-11), where Jesus assures us:

> Ask, and it will be given you; search, and you will find; knock, and the door will be opened for you. For everyone who asks receives, and everyone who searches finds, and for everyone who knocks, the door will be opened. Is there anyone among you who, if your child asks for bread, will give a stone? Or if the child asks for a fish, will give a snake? If you then, who are evil, know how to give good gifts to your children, how much more will your Father in heaven give good things to those who ask him!

Other passages may add nuance to this message—for example, Luke 11: 5–8 suggests that persistence may be crucial to prayer's efficacy—but they don't seem to negate the basic message that God hears our pleas and responds to them.

Yet, as we know, sometimes there doesn't seem to be a response. We pray for rain in a time of drought—and the drought continues. We pray for healing in a time of sickness—and we receive yet greater agony and, finally, death. We pray for peace—yet violence increases. The list of prayers which seem to have been in vain is an endless one, and each of us, I suspect, contributes to it. For many of us, God's apparent failure to respond, his seeming abandonment of his children, can be the harshest test of our faith, a test which some of us (like Job) endure, but which others (like many victims of the Holocaust) do not.[4]

As Christians, then, we seem to be confronted with a genuine puzzle: given repeated Scriptural assurances that God hears our petitions, how are we to account for, or understand, the fact that our prayers often seem to go unanswered? One response, of course, would be to say that we *can't* account for or understand this fact, and shouldn't expect to do so. God's ways are not our ways, we will be reminded; to presume to comprehend why he acts as he does is to show a confidence in human intellectual powers which is unbecoming in a Christian. There is undoubtedly a core of truth in this type of response. Still, I think that few of us can deem it fully satisfying. For the problem we have confronted is one, not simply of a mystery, but of what (at least at first glance) might look like a contradiction in Christian belief. Just as few of us would find it appropriate for the Christian community to turn a blind eye toward other apparent inconsistencies in Christianity (concerning such issues as evil, the Incarnation, or the Trinity), so I think most of us will insist that something more needs to be said here as well. Even if we can't *completely* understand why prayers often appear to go unanswered, is there *anything* we can say which can at least dispel the scent of contradiction?[5]

---

[4] An especially vivid picture of the abandonment felt by many Holocaust survivors is offered in Elie Wiesel, *Night* (New York: Bantam Books, 1960).

[5] The situation with regard to unanswered prayers can profitably be compared to that concerning the problem of evil. Some atheologians claim that there is a contradiction in the notion of a God of the Christian description creating a world containing evil. In response to such a claim, some theists have tried to offer a *defense*—i.e., they have tried to show that there is no contradiction involved, for there are reasons God *might* have for creating a world containing evil. Other theists have offered *theodicies*—i.e., attempts to explain what reasons God *actually does* have for permitting evil to exist.

Furthermore, it is crucial to note that defenses can differ enormously in terms of plausibility. What we might call a *minimal* or *mere* defense relies on a premise which we believe is both possibly true and actually false. Such a defense, though adequate to refute the charge of simple contradiction, may really do little more than show that the atheologian's argument is enthymematically imprecise. Offering a mere defense, then, may be rather like your saying, in response to my claim that your having put arsenic in my tea is incompatible with your loving me, "Not at all! For it's possible that I believe that arsenic is good for you. I *don't*, as a matter of fact, believe that. But I could have. So, don't worry, there's no inconsistency of the sort you feared!" Needless to say, such a response would not put my mind (or stomach) at rest. For much the same reason, a mere defense should not be expected truly to satisfy most atheologians. What the typical atheologian is looking for, it seems, is at least what we might call a *tenable* defense—one whose premises are all, not merely possible, but at least plausible. And the more plausible, one would think, the better.

It seems to me that what we should be seeking with regard to unanswered prayers is more analogous to a tenable defense than to either a theodicy or a mere defense. Our goal should be to show that there is no contradiction in God's not giving us that for which we pray

3. Molinism to the Rescue?

It seems to me that there are at least a couple of contributions the Molinist can make in this regard. The first is a very simple point that stems from the libertarian view of freedom upon which Molinism is based. Often, what we pray for depends upon the free actions of other people. A mother, for example, may pray that her son turn from a life of sin to a life of holiness, as St. Monica prayed for the conversion of her son Augustine. But if we view such conversion as involving a free act on the part of the convert, we must realize that it is not solely up to God whether or not the prayer is answered, in the sense that the desired change of life comes to fruition. God may do all he can—indeed, may do more than he would have done in the absence of the prayer—and yet find his best efforts rebuffed by his free creature. When we recall how often the objects of our prayer depend in one way or another on the free actions of other people, the fact that our prayers sometimes appear to be in vain becomes at least a tad less surprising.

Though helpful, this point can hardly be the whole story. In most cases, one might think, God would be able to bring about the required free actions by directly or indirectly affecting the agent's cognitive and conative states so as to actualize a situation in which the person freely acts in the desired manner. Furthermore, many of the gifts for which we petition God seem in no essential way dependent upon free creaturely activity. Suppose that my child is dying of cancer, and I pray that God intervene to spare her life. God could conceivably intervene by eliciting a free response from one of his creatures—say, by arranging things so that one of my child's doctors reads of a new treatment for this form of cancer, a treatment which the doctor subsequently uses successfully. But as Christians, we know that such mediated intervention is not God's only option. If he wishes, he can cure my daughter on his own. When miraculous or other direct divine activity can by itself answer our prayers, appeals to the limitations that human freedom places upon God seem misdirected.

It is here that Molinism can promote a second and more powerful suggestion, one which is surely familiar to many ordinary believers with no knowl-

---

because we can think of reasons God *might* have for doing so, and, whether or not these *actually are* God's reasons, it is at least *plausible* to think that they are.

The distinction between a defense and a theodicy comes from Henry Schuurman via Plantinga; see Alvin Plantinga, *The Nature of Necessity* (Oxford: Clarendon Press, 1974), p. 192. For a discussion by one prominent atheologian of the "middle ground" between a theodicy and a defense, see David Lewis, "Evil for Freedom's Sake?" *Philosophical Papers* 22 (1993), 151–152.

edge of Molinism. Recall the end of the passage from Matthew quoted above, in which Jesus assures his listeners that the Father will "give good things to those who ask him." Recall also the common saying that we should be careful what we pray for, because we might get it. Or think of Oscar Wilde's variation on the same theme: "When the gods wish to punish us they answer our prayers."[6]   Surely such passages are suggestive of at least a partial explanation as to why some prayers seem to go unanswered. Perhaps we need to see that the "good" in the last line of the quotation from Matthew is not superfluous. Perhaps God *does* always give us the *good* things we request. Perhaps the prayers he doesn't answer are cases where what we have prayed for *wouldn't* have been good, for ourselves or for others.[7] And perhaps God can see that this is so precisely because of his middle knowledge.

Suppose we take Cuthbert the prospective iguana-buyer as our example once again. Imagine Cuthbert on his way to the pet shop, where he intends to buy an iguana as a birthday present for his wife. We may assume that Cuthbert's aim in doing so is to please his wife and demonstrate his devotion to her, thereby strengthening their (to his mind unaccountably) fragile marriage. Knowing that the pet shop is sometimes unable to keep up with the demand for iguanas, and realizing that, should they be out of these lovable lizards, he would be forced to settle for a more conventional gift (say, flowers and candy), Cuthbert prays as he walks, "O God, please let there be an iguana for sale at the pet shop!"

God, of course, hears Cuthbert's plea. But God knows much more about the overall situation than Cuthbert does. In particular, if he has middle knowledge, then God knows how things would turn out if there were to be an iguana at the pet shop and if Cuthbert were to purchase it for his wife. And perhaps what God knows is that things would turn out rather miserably for Cuthbert and others. Perhaps his wife, heeding the admonition never to look a gift iguana in the mouth, would run screaming from the room at the first sight of her scaly present. Perhaps she would take this latest eccentricity on the part of her husband as the last straw, declare their marriage at an end, and leave their home that very day. Perhaps Cuthbert's employer, who happens also to be his father-in-law, would tell Cuthbert a few days later that he had best look elsewhere for work. Perhaps Cuthbert's parents, their hopes that

---

[6] Oscar Wilde, *An Ideal Husband* (London: Methuen, 1899), Act II, p. 84.

[7] It is interesting to note that some petitionary prayers employed for liturgical purposes explicitly ask that God answer our prayers by providing what really is best for us, not necessarily what we think is best for us. For example, the Anglican evensong service incorporates a prayer of St. John Chrysostom, which asks, "Fulfil now, O Lord, the desires and petitions of thy servants, as may be most expedient for them." See *The Book of Common Prayer* (1662; Cambridge: Cambridge University Press, 1968), p. 26.

marriage would bring a semblance of normalcy to Cuthbert's life now dashed, would simply give up, and inform him that they wish to have nothing more to do with him. And perhaps Cuthbert himself would respond to all of these events by sinking into a deep and lasting despair, one element of which is his abandonment of belief in God.

If God were to know all this via middle knowledge, it seems reasonable to conclude that he would see that letting there be an iguana in the shop would not be doing Cuthbert a favor. Cuthbert may think that the iguana would bring him much good, but God knows otherwise: that for which Cuthbert prays would in fact ultimately bring him to ruin. Knowing this, God, not wishing to act like one of Oscar's grouchy gods, might well do his best to see to it that there is no iguana in the shop when Cuthbert arrives.[8] If he can then steer Cuthbert toward those flowers and candy, he might be able to do him some genuine good.

Now, some might argue that God's possession of middle knowledge is not actually essential to such an attempt to account for unanswered prayers. Even if God doesn't know what *would* have happened had Cuthbert purchased the iguana, he might well know what *probably* would have happened had Cuthbert so acted. Perhaps he knew that the probability of Cuthbert's wife's leaving him should he present her with the iguana was .7, that the likelihood of his boss's firing him in the wake of his wife's action was .8, and that the chance that Cuthbert would give up his belief in God should he lose his wife and job was .9. Given such knowledge of probabilities, God would still have sufficient reason to separate Cuthbert from the iguanas of the world. True, God wouldn't know *for sure* that the iguana would presage disaster for Cuthbert, but he would know that the chances are high enough to warrant his seeing to it that no iguana is present when Cuthbert enters the pet shop.

Our discussion in Chapter 3 of the "open" alternative to the traditional concept of providence should make it clear why I find this suggestion misguided. God's action would presumably be directed by his knowledge as to the ramifications of his action, not simply in the short run, but in the long

---

[8] Of course, it is conceivable that God fail in this endeavor—or, to put this more accurately, it is possible that God might see that there is no acceptable way for him to render the pet shop iguana-free. The normal ways of doing so—e.g., seeing to it that the owner decides not to stock lizards any longer, or bringing it about that all the iguanas are purchased prior to Cuthbert's arrival—would involve free creaturely actions which might prove infeasible for God to actualize. To be sure, God could effect the iguanectomy in more heavy-handed ways (e.g., by directly causing every iguana in the shop to explode moments before Cuthbert appears on the scene), but perhaps he sees that all such approaches would have repercussions even messier than those Cuthbert's purchase of the iguana would initiate.

run as well; an action might well have wonderful short-term ramifications, but disastrous long-term ones. As we saw earlier, though, a God who knows only probabilities concerning how his creatures will freely act is bound to suffer from a severe case of myopia. Perhaps he could foresee fairly accurately how his creatures would freely react in the short run to any course of action he might take, but, since multiplied probabilities swiftly approach zero, the long-run consequences of his action will be all but utterly opaque to him.[9] One could evade this point by charging that the probabilities God is aware of are exceedingly high, but, as we saw, there is no reason whatsoever to think that this is the case, and the wiser advocates of the "open" alternative (such as Hasker) deny it. A God with only probabilistic knowledge, it seems to me, would basically be at a loss to tell what kind of response to Cuthbert's prayer would lead to the best result. Only if God has middle knowledge can he act with confidence and assurance.

4. Suspicions of Superfluity

Appealing as these Molinist responses to our problem might appear, there is, I think, a difficulty with them which many readers have probably already discerned and which can no longer be kept offstage.[10] For the heart of the second Molinist response outlined above seems to be that sometimes God doesn't give us that for which we pray because he sees that it wouldn't be good for us. In those cases where it *would* be good for us, the implication seems to be, he does give us the object of our prayer.[11] In other words, the Molinist seems to be assuming the truth of some such principle as:

---

[9] Indeed, even the moderately short-run consequences will often be such that God will be pretty much at a loss to say how they will turn out. For example, even if the probabilities concerning Cuthbert were as high as we assigned them in the previous paragraph, the probability that Cuthbert would lose his faith should he purchase the iguana could easily be right around .5.

[10] The problem has been much discussed. See especially Eleonore Stump, "Petitionary Prayer," *American Philosophical Quarterly* 16 (1979), 81–91, which contains both a first-rate (albeit non-Molinist!) discussion of the problem and numerous helpful bibliographical references. See also the response to Stump's article by Joshua Hoffman, "On Petitionary Prayer," *Faith and Philosophy* 2 (1985), 21–29, as well as (in the same issue of the same journal) Stump's response to Hoffman's response ("Hoffman on Petitionary Prayer," pp. 30–37) and Hoffman's response to Stump's response to Hoffman's response to Stump's article ("Reply to Eleonore Stump," pp. 38–42).

[11] Some sort of ceteris paribus clause is presumably needed here to cover cases where, though giving us what we pray for would be good for us, God could effect an even better outcome by not giving us what we pray for. To avoid inessential complications, I have ignored the need for such a clause in the statements of (1) and (2).

(1)   For any X, if we pray for X, then God gives us X if and only if he sees (via middle knowledge) that X would be good for us (and for all concerned).[12]

Yet, we might wonder, isn't there another true principle in the neighborhood that diminishes the apparent significance of (1)? Recall again the biblical story of creation, and our suggestion that this story shows (among many other things) how a provident God takes care of his creatures even in the absence of their petitioning him for specific goods. If God is truly provident in the way Christians have traditionally affirmed, then won't he do what is good for us *regardless* of whether or not we ask him to do so? Isn't his providential care for his creatures *always* in evidence, not simply an effect triggered by our supplicatory activity? To put this more formally, isn't the following principle just as plausible as (1):

(2)   For any X, if we *don't* pray for X, then God gives us X if and only if he sees (via middle knowledge) that X would be good for us (and for all concerned).

And now the problem becomes obvious. So long as our focus was solely on (1), the efficacy of prayer seemed a reasonable position. But once we see that (2) is true as well, doesn't petitionary prayer appear to be rather pointless? Propositions (1) and (2) together seem to imply that prayer doesn't make any difference at all. God will give us X just in case he sees that X is good for us; whether we pray that he give us X seems utterly irrelevant with regard to God's action. Molinism attempted to show why God might *sometimes* not respond to our prayers. Yet what it has really shown is that God *never* responds to our prayers. What he "responds" to is only his knowledge of which actions on his part would lead to better results. Molinism has thus rendered petitionary prayer utterly superfluous—hardly, one would think, a result that the Molinist intended.

5. Prayer as Consciousness-Raising?

One way to respond to a prickly objection is to embrace it while denying its prickliness, and some Christians of a more liberal bent might attempt so to handle this objection. That is, they might agree that, in a sense, petitionary prayer *is* utterly superfluous, that it *does* make no difference at all. But, they

---

[12] I assume here that God's concern would be with what is in everyone's best interest, not merely with what's in the best interest of those doing the praying.

might caution us, we need to understand in *what* way prayer is superfluous or ineffectual. What the considerations of the last section show, they might continue, is that petitionary prayer is utterly superfluous *with respect to God's activity*. Whether we pray or not makes no difference at all to God; he will do what is good for us regardless. But it hardly follows that prayer is superfluous in every sense. Prayer may make no difference to God, but it makes a big difference to us. Properly understood, the aim of our prayer should be not to elicit a response from God, but to elicit a response from us.

How can prayer make a difference to us? What kind of response should it elicit? The possibilities here are many and obvious. Prayer, one might argue, helps us to recognize more clearly our needs and the needs of others. It strengthens in us a feeling of gratitude when those needs are met, a recognition that God is taking care of us. When those needs are not met, it emboldens us to act so as to meet them. It goads us out of our lethargy and leads us to put into practice the faith we profess. In these and many other ways, prayer may raise our consciousness and foster Christian action. While utterly irrelevant to God's activity, it may well be crucial to ours.[13]

Such a position toward prayer is hardly unknown. It is evident in the works of literary figures, such as the nineteenth-century British novelist George Meredith ("Who rises from prayer a better man, his prayer is answered").[14] It is also at least suggested in the writings of certain philosophers and theologians.[15] Indeed, the general attitude that prayer benefits the one who prays directly, rather than through God's hearing the prayer and responding to it, seems close in spirit to the widespread belief among even secular authorities that activities such as meditation can have dramatic and direct effects on the psychological and physical well-being of the meditator.

To deny that there is some truth to this account of prayer seems to me implausible. Prayer, I think, does and should have the direct effect upon us which is being suggested here. But it is crucial to avoid a false dichotomy. Our choices are not between (a) prayer affects *only* God and (b) prayer affects *only* us. There is obviously the third possibility—that (c) prayer affects *both*

---

[13] As Trenton Merricks has pointed out to me, the position articulated here wouldn't really meet the superfluity objection if none of the goods obtained through prayer were not essentially tied to the act of praying. If, for example, all the consciousness-raising prayer brings about in us could be brought about directly by God even in the absence of our prayer, then prayer would still appear to be superfluous. Hence, the advocate of the consciousness-raising solution needs to see at least some of the relevant goods as unobtainable except through prayer.

[14] George Meredith, *The Ordeal of Richard Feverel* (New York: Macmillan, 1926), p. 86.

[15] See, for example, Richard P. McBrien, *Catholicism*, study ed. (Minneapolis: Winston Press, 1981), pp. 331–333. See also Charles Sanders Peirce, *Collected Papers* (Cambridge: Belknap Press of Harvard University Press, 1960), 6.515–6.518.

God *and* us. And this, it seems to me, is surely the view that the vast majority of Christians, both past and present, would endorse. Our prayer *should* serve to augment our knowledge, our gratitude, and our action. But it should also do more than this. It should make a difference to God; it should be at least a factor in his decisions as to how he will act; and sometimes, his actions can and should be seen as responses to our prayers. Petitionary prayer is more than individualistic meditative therapy; it is the act of speaking to another person who can help us.

Clearly, there are dangers and perplexities aplenty here. The Christian presumably wants to avoid turning prayers into magical incantations that render God subject to our control. We may well want to insist that we can have no *causal* effect upon God, and so we may not want to understand our prayers reaching God in a manner analogous to the way in which our requests for aid reach another human person. Similarly, if wedded to the belief that there can be no change in God, we may need to exercise care in understanding how God can be said to respond to our prayer. Nevertheless, that a Christian should endeavor to understand petitionary prayer as something more than consciousness-raising seems evident to me. So this first attempt to deal with the apparent superfluity of prayer cannot, I think, be seen as a suitable solution to the problem.

6. Prayer as Circumstance-Changing?

If we wish to move beyond consciousness-raising and think of prayer as making a difference to God's activity, one direction seems to me clearly suggested by Molinism—a direction which needn't force one to reject (1) or (2). Suppose we agree with the claim that God will do what is good for us whether or not we direct petitions toward him. It still might be that our decisions have an impact on what God decides to do. Why? To put it simply: Because what is good for God's creatures will in part be a function of the *circumstances* in which they find themselves, and petitionary prayer *changes the circumstances*.[16]

It would be easy to embellish the story of Cuthbert to illustrate this point, but let us allow Cuthbert and his iguana a brief respite and instead look at what I take to be an actual instance of prayer's affecting God's activity. The example I have in mind is a Scriptural one—the story of the cure of the lame man in the third chapter of Acts, verses 1–10.

---

[16] Prayer does not, of course, change the circumstances in which the prayer itself is offered. Rather, the prayer, by becoming part of the causal history of the world, becomes part of the circumstances in which future actions take place. In a sense, then, it might be more accurate to say that prayer helps to create those circumstances than to say that it changes them.

One day Peter and John were going up to the temple at the hour of prayer, at three o'clock in the afternoon. And a man lame from birth was being carried in. People would lay him daily at the gate of the temple called the Beautiful Gate so that he could ask for alms from those entering the temple. When he saw Peter and John about to go into the temple, he asked them for alms. Peter looked intently at him, as did John, and said, "Look at us." And he fixed his attention on them, expecting to receive something from them. But Peter said, "I have no silver or gold, but what I have I give you; in the name of Jesus Christ of Nazareth, stand up and walk." And he took him by the right hand and raised him up; and immediately his feet and ankles were made strong. Jumping up, he stood and began to walk, and he entered the temple with them, walking and leaping and praising God. All the people saw him walking and praising God, and they recognized him as the one who used to sit and ask for alms at the Beautiful Gate of the temple; and they were filled with wonder and amazement at what had happened to him.

Three points should be noted concerning this passage. First, what we have reported here is clearly a miraculous cure—a case of God's direct intervention into the usual course of nature. Only a reader crippled by naturalistic prejudice could think of the cure in any other way. Second, and just as clearly, the cure is a response by God to Peter's activity. To think of Peter's words as _making no difference_—to think that God would have cured the lame man at this time no matter what Peter had done—seems to me to misread the story completely. Finally, though Peter's actual words have the grammatical form of a command, I think they are best read as embodying an implicit prayer on his part that God cure the lame man. Peter makes it abundantly clear later in this chapter that we are to think of the cure as effected not by _his_ power, but by _God's_—a judgment with which the lame man (who praises God, not Peter) evidently concurs. Thus, the cure is to be seen as a miraculous action on God's part performed in response to Peter's prayer.[17]

On these three points, I think, most discerning readers of the passage would be in accord.[18] But, as Molinists, we might well be able to go further. We

---

[17] In Mark 9:28–29, Jesus tells his disciples that their failure to cure a possessed boy was due to their failure to pray. One might infer that the kind of prayer Jesus means here is the kind we are ascribing to Peter.

[18] Actually, I think that _all_ discerning readers would agree on the first two points (that the cure is miraculous, and that it occurs in response to Peter's words). Scott Davison has convinced me, though, that one might more reasonably dissent from the third point (that Peter's words constitute an implicit prayer that God cure the lame man). One could, for instance, think of Peter as simply acting rashly in speaking as he does to the lame man; alternatively, one might claim that the Holy Spirit directly inspired Peter to command the lame man to stand up and walk, with no petitionary prayer of any sort accompanying this command. Any such interpretation, though, seems to me to be far less plausible than the one offered above.

might be able to throw at least some light on how we can think of prayer as making a difference to a God who is always exercising his full providential care for us.

Consider the situation in which Peter is placed in this story. It seems plausible to think that this situation (call it S) is such as to leave Peter free. Though his act of calling upon God to cure the lame man (call this act by Peter P) seems natural and laudable under these circumstances, by no means does it appear to be necessitated by them. As we know from the story, God responds to Peter's prayer by immediately healing the lame man; call this specific act on God's part A. And, as the following passages in Acts relate, this divine action has a noteworthy positive effect, not simply on the lame man, but on many of those who witnessed his cure: many of them become followers of Christ in the wake of this incident, and many others, we might surmise, are at least led to take Peter's message more seriously.

So we seem to have many free actions described here—by Peter, by God, by the lame man, and by the onlookers. Of course, if Molinism is true, none of the actions his free creatures perform would have taken God by surprise. By middle knowledge, he would have known how they would freely react to the situations in which they were placed. In particular, God would have known how the lame man and the onlookers would react to God's curing the lame man in the wake of Peter's prayer. That is, he would have known by middle knowledge such counterfactuals of creaturely freedom as:

(3)　　$(S \ \& \ P \ \& \ A) \rightarrow$ The lame man freely praises God

(4)　　$(S \ \& \ P \ \& \ A) \rightarrow$ Onlooker X listens to Peter more seriously

and

(5)　　$(S \ \& \ P \ \& \ A) \rightarrow$ Onlooker Y becomes a Christian.

Consider, on the other hand, what might well have happened had God *not* responded to Peter by curing the lame man. Quite possibly, the lame man would have turned away from God, or from Christ; quite possibly, onlookers such as X and Y would have concluded that Peter and his words about Christ

---

Should readers disagree with me on this point, I would remind them that the story from Acts is being used purely as an example here, and that nothing really hinges on whether or not Peter's action actually did involve an implicit petition. Those who think that it did not can simply think of our petition-involving example as a fictional rather than (as I view it) a historical one.

were not worthy of their serious attention. So, again via middle knowledge, God might well have known prevolitionally such counterfactuals of creaturely freedom as

(6) $(S \& P \& \sim A) \rightarrow$ The lame man turns from God

(7) $(S \& P \& \sim A) \rightarrow$ Onlooker X decides to ignore Peter

and

(8) $(S \& P \& \sim A) \rightarrow$ Onlooker Y decides not to follow Christ.

Such a reading of the situation seems not at all improbable. But if things were this way—if God knew all these counterfactuals of creaturely freedom, as well as similar ones concerning the longer-term ramifications of his diverse courses of action—it seems to me that they might well have provided God with a powerful reason to respond to Peter's request by curing the lame man, because he saw that doing so would lead to many good consequences, while failing to do so would lead to many bad ones. And since there is no reason to think that these good consequences would have resulted had God cured the lame man in the absence of Peter's prayer, it makes sense to think that Peter's prayer may well have made the difference in this situation (by, in effect, changing the situation).[19]

The point here can, I think, profitably be viewed from a slightly different perspective. If what we have suggested is correct, then the counterfactuals of creaturely freedom mentioned above would seem to provide the basis for the truth of certain counterfactuals of divine freedom—namely,

(9) $(S \& P) \rightarrow A$

---

[19] Thinking about what would have happened had Peter *not* prayed should remind us that (3) through (8) are only *some* of the relevant counterfactuals of creaturely freedom here. Presumably, other such counterfactuals which God would have known would include

(3*) $(S \& \sim P \& A) \rightarrow$ The lame man doesn't freely praise God
(4*) $(S \& \sim P \& A) \rightarrow$ Onlooker X doesn't listen to Peter more seriously
(5*) $(S \& \sim P \& A) \rightarrow$ Onlooker Y doesn't decide to become a Christian
(6*) $(S \& \sim P \& \sim A) \rightarrow$ The lame man doesn't freely praise God
(7*) $(S \& \sim P \& \sim A) \rightarrow$ Onlooker X doesn't listen to Peter more seriously
(8*) $(S \& \sim P \& \sim A) \rightarrow$ Onlooker Y doesn't decide to become a Christian

Just as (3) through (8) provide the basis for the counterfactual of divine freedom labeled (9) in the next paragraph, so (3*) through (8*) would provide the basis for (10).

according to flint. God does not know
his own divine counterfactuals.

and

$$(10) \quad (S \mathbin{\&} \sim P) \to \sim A.\,[20]$$

Such counterfactuals, though true, will not be prevolitional (since God is presumably free to respond to Peter's prayer by doing A or by doing something else), and hence will be part, not of God's middle knowledge, but rather of his free knowledge.

We can also now see, I think, how, from a Molinist perspective, Peter's prayer can be thought of as making a difference even if we don't think of that prayer as having any causal effect upon God, or as leading to any real change in God. For God's decisions as to how to act will be based upon his middle knowledge of how Peter and others would freely act in various circumstances, not upon his free knowledge as to how they will act. Since his middle knowledge is not caused by Peter's action, and since God's decision to cure the lame man in the wake of Peter's prayer is part of the one all-encompassing creative decision that God makes, Peter's act of praying neither causes God to know anything about Peter nor effects any change in God's intentions. Still, that Peter's prayer makes a difference follows, it seems to me, from the truth of (9) and (10) and the relevant counterfactuals of creaturely freedom. Since there is good reason to think that Peter would have been in S even had he not prayed—that is, good reason to think that

[20] In calling these counterfactuals of divine freedom, we may be speaking a bit loosely. For, just as counterfactuals of creaturely freedom are best thought of as including *all* the circumstances of action in the antecedent, so one might feel that counterfactuals of divine freedom should state only what God would do given the *totality* of his middle knowledge. Still, I don't think any real harm is done by speaking of (9) and (10) as counterfactuals of divine freedom, for, if they are true, they would seem in all probability to follow from counterfactuals that meet the stricter standard noted above. Take (10) as an example. If the antecedent of (10) were true, then, since Peter actually did pray in S, the complete set of truths God knew via middle knowledge—the world-type—would have been at least slightly different. If we let WT stand for the true world type, then

(a) $(S \mathbin{\&} \sim P) \to WT\star$

is true, where $WT\star$ is distinct from WT. If the conditions are as we have speculated, though, it seems likely that God, had he known prior to creation that $WT\star$ were the true world-type, would have put Peter in S, but would have reacted to his failure to pray by failing to cure the lame man. That is, both

(b) $WT\star \to (S \mathbin{\&} \sim P)$

and

(c) $WT\star \to \sim A$

seem to be warranted. Since (10) follows immediately from (a), (b), and (c), and since (b) and (c) are counterfactuals of divine freedom which fit the strict standard, there seems to be little harm in honoring their implications such as (10) with the same name.

$$(11) \quad \sim P \to S$$

is true—and since it follows from (11) and (10) that

$$(12) \quad \sim P \to \sim A,$$

we can truthfully say that, had Peter not prayed for the lame man's cure, he wouldn't have been cured.[21] In other words, Peter had counterfactual power over A, power which he exercised by praying.[22]

7. Conclusion

It appears, then, that Molinism may well be of some help in understanding why it is that our prayers sometimes appear to go unanswered. At times, what we pray for may depend upon others' free actions, actions which are not in fact forthcoming. At other times, it may be that God sees via his middle knowledge that we would not benefit should he grant us that for which we have prayed, and so, being a loving father, he doesn't give us that which would ultimately harm us. Nor should God's activity in the wake of prayer

[21] Even if one were (somewhat implausibly, I think) to deny (11), the case for (12) would not necessarily be weakened. Suppose one felt that God wouldn't have allowed Peter to be in S if he saw that Peter wouldn't pray for the lame man's cure in that situation. That is, suppose one embraced

$$(11^*) \quad \sim P \to \sim S$$

instead of (11). Still, it seems unlikely that God would have performed the very act of healing the lame man which he did perform had Peter not been in S and had he not prayed for that cure. That is,

$$(11^{**}) \quad (\sim P \ \& \ \sim S) \to \sim A$$

seems quite probable. So, since (12) still follows from (11*) and (11**), Peter's counterfactual power over A would seem to remain intact even if (11) were rejected. Of course, the case for such power would not remain if (11**) were to be rejected as well. But that is as it should be. If (11*) is true but (11**) false, then we *shouldn't* think of Peter's praying as making a difference with regard to A. Needless to say, though, the fact that Peter's praying *could* have been inconsequential gives us scant reason to think it *actually* made no difference.

[22] One might wonder whether, given that Peter has this counterfactual power over God's activity, we can speak of God as *replying* to Peter's prayer by curing the lame man. It seems to me that counterfactual power, though necessary, might well not be sufficient for that action to be seen as a reply. Still, my guess is that whatever additional conditions are required are satisfied in this case, and hence that the cure should be viewed as a reply. It *is* a guess, though, since I am not sure precisely what those additional conditions would be. For a discussion of this issue, see William Alston, "Divine-Human Dialogue and the Nature of God," in *Divine Nature and Human Language* (Ithaca: Cornell University Press, 1989), pp. 144–161, especially 156–157. Readers should note, though, that Alston is apparently thinking of *reply* in a less metaphorical sense than I am employing it here.

be seen as utterly independent of those prayers, for what is good for God's creatures is in part dependent upon the circumstances in which they are placed, and prayer affects those circumstances.

Needless to say, there are many questions concerning unanswered prayer which remain. What we have sketched are *possible* reasons why our prayers may at times seem to fail. There are undoubtedly other possible explanations that might occur to us. Whether any of these are the *actual* reasons for God's apparent nonresponsiveness is, I think, beyond our ability to know. Still, if we can see why a loving Father *might* refrain from giving us that for which we pray, and especially if that possible explanation is not a ridiculous or far-fetched one, then our uncertainty concerning God's actual reasons need not prove a crippling one. Since the possible explanations a Molinist can offer here are, I think, eminently plausible ones, and since middle knowledge is essential at least to the second of those two explanations, it seems to me that Molinism is of real value when applied to this topic.

where does faith fit in to this?

Does it seem possible that God provide the world with what is needed?

Praying for Things
to Have Happened

O. J.: I'm Praying That You Didn't Do It
—Sign seen outside the house of O. J. Simpson
   shortly after the murder of his former wife.[1]

1. The Problem

Generally, petitionary prayer is future-oriented. Though we may thank God for what he has done for us in the past, and praise him for what he is in the present, we usually ask God to help us in the future. We ask God that marriage vows newly made be kept; that this child being baptized have a rich and fruitful life; that this loved one approaching death be granted eternal life in heaven. Sometimes, of course, the future dimension of the object of our petition shades over into the present. In praying that God give me strength against a particular temptation, I may well be seeking such aid, not only for the long-term or even near-term future, but for the very moment of prayer as well. Nevertheless, that our petitions are usually directed at future events seems fairly clear.

Sometimes, though, it seems natural to pray concerning, not future or even present events, but past events. Think, for example, of the mother whose (rather foolhardy) child is late one Sunday night returning from a (rather foolhardy) mountain-climbing expedition. Suppose this mother, whose pre-occupation with more rational activities (say, attending Philadelphia Phillies baseball games) had filled her weekend, hears on the Sunday evening news that the area in which her child was climbing was hit by a record-setting blizzard Saturday morning, and that there is great concern for the survival of

---

[1] Curiously, the commentator who reported this incident on National Public Radio on June 22, 1994, interpreted the sign as part of an endeavor to *change* the past, and thus as an indication of the irrationality surrounding the Simpson case. My thanks to Trenton Merricks for calling this report to my attention.

those who were outdoors at the time. Would it not be natural for her to pray for the safety of her daughter? And would it not be natural for her to phrase this petition in the form of a prayer that certain things not *have happened*? ("O God, please let my daughter not have been harmed by the storm!")[2]

Such a prayer, an instance of what Michael Dummett calls *retrospective prayer*,[3] would not strike most Christians as odd or unusual. Indeed, most of us Christians have probably offered such a prayer at one time or another ourselves, and not felt philosophically indisposed in doing so. Of course, were we certain concerning the occurrence of the past event in question, things might be different. (Praying that World War III be prevented, most of us would agree, is beyond reproach; praying that World War I be prevented would surely raise more than a few eyebrows.)[4] Where we are genuinely unsure whether the prayed-for event occurs, though, praying often seems appropriate, whether the event be in the future or in the past.[5]

Yet, when we look at the matter more critically, we can easily begin to wonder whether this indifference to tense is so innocent as it seems. As lib–

---

[2] Michael Kremer has pointed out to me that such prayers could be interpreted as disguised prospective ones; e.g., the mother might really be praying that she see her daughter alive and well again. Such interpretations, though perhaps appropriate in certain contexts, seem to me generally strained and often utterly implausible. Suppose that the mother in our example were to discover that her daughter had indeed died in the storm. Could her subsequent prayer, "O God, please let her not have suffered long," seriously be interpreted as directed toward the *future*?

[3] Michael Dummett, "Bringing About the Past," in *Truth and Other Enigmas* (Cambridge: Harvard University Press, 1978), p. 335.

[4] If I am convinced that something did happen, praying that it not happen seems odd. But what about praying that it did happen when I am convinced that it did happen? Things seem less clear here. At the end of Book 9 of the *Confessions*, Augustine asks his readers to pray for the repose of the soul of his mother. Are those of us who know her as *Saint* Monica, and thus are convinced that she received the beatific vision, absolved of all responsibility to do as Augustine asks? Is it perhaps possible that Monica attained sanctity at least in part as a result of the prayers offered for her in response to Augustine's entreaty, including prayers offered by those who already believed in her sanctity? Monica's prayers are often, and I think rightly, viewed as partly responsible for her son's salvation; might it not also be true that the prayers of her son and his readers are partly responsible for her salvation? These questions, and others to which they lead, deserve much more time than I can allot them here. (So do other, closely related ones—e.g., Is all prayer for the dead properly understood as prayer that the dead have *been aided* in a certain way *while still alive*, and hence is all such prayer reasonable only insofar as retrospective prayer more generally is reasonable?) What seems obvious, though, is that the answers are not as obvious as one might have thought.

[5] For much-discussed presentations of this view, see both Dummett, "Bringing About the Past," and C. S. Lewis, *Miracles* (New York: Macmillan, 1947), pp. 185–186. For an oft-cited and vigorous attack on the view, see Peter Geach, "Praying for Things to Happen," in *God and the Soul* (London: Routledge & Kegan Paul, 1969), pp. 86–99.

ertarians, we believe that the future is open in a sense that the past is not. Actions we perform now can have a causal impact upon what happens in the future. The past, however, is closed; it is over and done with; it is completely immune to any interference by our current activities. As philosophers, of course, we will be cognizant of the distinction between hard facts and soft facts, and thus realize that certain propositions which appear to be about the past—for example, "It was true five years ago that I will vote in the Presidential election of 2012"—may really be as much or more about the future, and thus are arguably not exempt from our causal impact. But the kinds of past facts concerning which people are inclined to pray are not at all the "funny" kind of facts which have given rise to the hard/soft distinction. They seem to be facts (such as that child's surviving the blizzard) which are about as hard as they come. Perhaps our prayers, like Peter's prayer concerning the lame beggar, can have an impact on the future, but isn't it preposterous to think that they can causally affect the (hard) past? In short, however natural retrospective prayer may appear, isn't such activity essentially irrational?

Most of us will no doubt feel some force to such an objection. Still, the mention of Peter and his prayer concerning the lame man should serve to remind us that, for the Molinist at least, there may be a way to rescue retrospective petitionary prayer from the fate of the philosophically incorrect. For, as we saw in Chapter 10, the Molinist typically will view Peter's prayer as making a difference even though it *doesn't* have a causal impact upon God. Nor is there anything peculiar about Peter in this regard. If the Molinist is right, *no* petitionary prayer of *any* sort has any causal effect upon God. If I pray that some future event occur (say, that the Phillies win the World Series next year), my prayer has no causal impact upon God whatsoever. It might still make a difference, but if so, that difference needs to be explicated in terms of middle knowledge and divine decisions which are causally prior to my praying. But if this is the account the Molinist offers of *prospective* petitionary prayer, why not offer the same account of *retrospective* petitionary prayer? Why not say that prayers concerning the past are efficacious in the same noncausal way as are prayers concerning the future? Why not, in brief, claim that prayer may afford us, not *causal*, but *counterfactual* power over the past?

Molinism thus appears to open the door to a solution to our problem. But whether it is a door we can enter safely remains to be seen. To suggest that I have counterfactual power over the past would be to assert that there is some true proposition strictly about the past and some action I now have the power to perform such that, if I were to perform that action, that true proposition would not have been true. The counterfactual involved in such an assertion is what is generally referred to as a back-tracking counterfactual, and the claim that there are true conditionals of this sort is viewed by many philosophers as suspect at best.[6] While a wholesale skepticism concerning such counterfactuals seems to me unwarranted, it might be prudent for the Molinist to grant that, given the strength of our intuition regarding the fixity of the hard past, the burden of proof in this case lies with the advocate of counterfactual power over the past.[7] Our question, then, is this: Can one build a strong case from a solid Molinist foundation for the claim that we have the type of counterfactual power over the past which would justify retrospective prayer?

2. Alvin's Ants

The suggestion that we may have counterfactual power over the past has been put forward in recent days by Alvin Plantinga, in a paper entitled "On Ockham's Way Out."[8] While denying that we have causal power over the past, Plantinga contends that there is no obstacle to thinking of ourselves as having counterfactual power even over hard facts about the past. Plantinga's example concerns Paul (who may or may not be related, perhaps even by identity, to Jones the Mower made famous by Nelson Pike[9]) and a certain army of arthropods:

> Let's suppose that a colony of carpenter ants moved into Paul's yard last Saturday. Since this colony hasn't yet had a chance to get properly established, its new home is still a bit fragile. In particular, if the ants were to remain and Paul were to mow his lawn this afternoon, the colony would be destroyed. Although nothing remarkable about these ants is visible to the naked eye, God, for reasons of his own, intends that the colony be preserved. Now as a matter of fact, Paul will not mow his lawn this afternoon. God, who is essentially omniscient, knew

---

[6] For the principal reasons for such skepticism, see David Lewis, "Counterfactual Dependence and Time's Arrow," *Nous* 13 (1979), 455–476; reprinted, along with three postscripts, in both David Lewis, *Philosophical Papers*, vol. 2 (Oxford: Oxford University Press, 1986), and Frank Jackson, ed., *Conditionals* (Oxford: Oxford University Press, 1991).

[7] For a persuasive argument to this effect, see Linda Trinkaus Zagzebski, *The Dilemma of Freedom and Foreknowledge* (New York: Oxford University Press, 1991), pp. 98–106.

[8] Alvin Plantinga, "On Ockham's Way Out," *Faith and Philosophy* 3 (1986), 235–269; reprinted in Thomas V. Morris, ed., *The Concept of God* (New York: Oxford University Press, 1987), pp. 171–200. Page references are to the reprinted version. Readers should note that, though the concept of counterfactual power over the past is clearly one that Plantinga is endorsing, the terminology stems not from him but (I think) from William Hasker. See his *God, Time, and Knowledge* (Ithaca: Cornell University Press, 1989), chap. 6, as well as his earlier "Foreknowledge and Necessity," *Faith and Philosophy* 2 (1985), 121–157.

[9] Nelson Pike, "Divine Omniscience and Voluntary Action," *Philosophical Review* 74 (1965), 27–46.

in advance, of course, that Paul will not mow his lawn this afternoon; but if he had foreknown instead that Paul would mow this afternoon, then he would have prevented the ants from moving in. The facts of the matter, therefore, are these: if Paul were to mow his lawn this afternoon, then God would have foreknown that Paul would mow his lawn this afternoon; and if God had fore-known that Paul would mow this afternoon, then God would have prevented the ants from moving in. So if Paul were to mow his lawn this afternoon, then the ants would not have moved in last Saturday. But it is within Paul's power to mow this afternoon. There is therefore an action he can perform such that if he were to perform it, then the proposition

(A)   That colony of carpenter ants moved into Paul's yard last Saturday.

would have been false. But what I have called 'the facts of the matter' certainly seem to be possible; it is therefore possible that there be an agent who has the power to perform an action which is such that, if he were to perform it, then (A) would have been false.[10]

The central argument Plantinga is presenting here might be expressed as follows. Since God is omniscient, it follows that

(1)   Paul mows → God foreknows that Paul mows.

Given God's intention that the colony of carpenter ants be preserved, it is also true that

(2)   God foreknows that Paul mows → God prevents the carpenter ants from moving in.

But, of course, if God prevents the ants from moving in, then they didn't move in last Saturday. So,

(3)   God prevents the carpenter ants from moving in → ~(A).

And from (1) through (3), Plantinga claims, we can infer

(4)   Paul mows → ~(A).

Therefore, Paul has the power to do something—namely, mow his lawn—such that, were he to do it, then something which as a matter of fact *is* a

---

[10] Plantinga, "On Ockham's Way Out," pp. 189–190. What I have labeled (A) is Plantinga's (34).

truth about the hard past—namely, (A)—would *not* have been a truth about the past. In other words, Paul has *counterfactual power* over the past.

If this idea of counterfactual power over the past makes sense, then so does the idea of praying for things to have happened. Suppose that we alter Plantinga's example just a bit. Suppose that Paul's wife Paula, while away from home last weekend (searching for that benighted mountaineer), hears on the news that there was a massive carpenter ant invasion in parts of her hometown on Saturday. Knowing that their lawn is in bad enough shape as it is (or was), Paula considers praying that their lawn was one of those spared. She *considers* doing so—but that is all; no actual prayer for the safety of her lawn comes forth from Paula. Foreseeing this failure to pray by Paula, God allows the ants to enter their yard. However, had he foreseen that Paula *would* pray, God in his goodness would have seen to it that the ants avoid Paul and Paula's property.

Using this altered example, we can construct an argument parallel to Plantinga's—and, not surprisingly, reminiscent of our reasoning in Chapter 10 concerning Peter and the lame man—to show that Paula's prayer would have made a difference with respect to the ants' having invaded her lawn. Given God's omniscience, it follows that

    (5)   Paula prays that their lawn have been spared → God foreknows that Paula prays that their lawn have been spared.

As we have described the case, it is also true that

    (6)   God foreknows that Paula prays that their lawn have been spared → God prevents the carpenter ants from moving in.

But, of course,

    (3)   God prevents the carpenter ants from moving in → ~(A).

So, from (5), (6), and (3) we could derive

    (7)   Paula prays that their lawn have been spared → ~(A).

Paula, then, has counterfactual power over the past; that is, she has the power to do something (pray) such that, had she done it, a fact about the past (that the ants moved in) would not have been a fact about the past. Paula's decision not to pray, then, can appropriately be seen as making a difference with respect

[handwritten marginal note:] None of these effect apart that has taken place but a past that is yet to take place.

to (A)'s having been true. Thus, her praying that the carpenter ants not have invaded would have been anything but irrational.

If the notion of this type of counterfactual power over the past makes sense, then, our problem seems solved: Retrospective prayer turns out to be philosophically beyond reproach. And since Plantinga's story and our variation on it make the notion of counterfactual power over the past seem plausible enough, at least for one with Molinist sympathies, one might think that we are indeed out of the woods on this one.

3. Counterfactual Power: Some Causes for Concern

My fear, though, is that these woods are darker and deeper than our discussion thus far has acknowledged. For, despite its surface plausibility, Plantinga's argument for the conclusion that Paul could have counterfactual power over the past should give a Molinist concern for at least three reasons.

First, the argument as presented offers a picture of divine action that appears misleading from the Molinist perspective. From that perspective, recall, God's activity in the world is guided by his middle knowledge, while his foreknowledge, which simply follows from that activity and middle knowledge, plays no action-guiding role whatsoever. As Plantinga presents things here, though, foreknowledge at least appears to be that upon which God is relying in reaching his creative decisions, while middle knowledge seems to be entirely absent from the process. Consider again (2). What it seems to be telling us is that God's decision to prevent the carpenter ants from moving in would have followed from his foreknowledge that Paul would mow. And this, the Molinist will insist, is mistaken; it is middle knowledge, not foreknowledge, that guides divine activity.

This first concern needs to be taken seriously, for it is not unknown for philosophers to give to foreknowledge roles which, if Molinism is correct, are properly ascribed only to middle knowledge.[11] Still, it is important to note that Plantinga's argument, though silent regarding middle knowledge, need not be seen as rejecting it. Proposition (2) may, at first glance, appear to place foreknowledge in a role the Molinist would deny it, but the simple affirmation of such a counterfactual need not have so dire an implication. For despite its appearance, (2) needn't be seen as a conditional that displays God's *reason* for acting. Couldn't (2) be a truth which simply follows from other counterfactuals of freedom, both creaturely and divine?[12]

---

[11] See, for example, Dummett, "Bringing About the Past," pp. 336–338.

[12] It is helpful in this context to recall some of the conditionals which we suggested in

Plantinga's argument, then, is not necessarily weakened by the fact that middle knowledge doesn't play a starring role in that argument, for it could conceivably hold an essential, though off-screen, position. Molinists may prefer that God's middle knowledge be given top billing in arguments that rely upon it, but they ought not to inflate such presentational predilections into substantive objections.

A second cause for concern centers on the fact that Plantinga's argument appears to rely upon a fallacious rule of inference. For that argument is most plausibly read as suggesting that (4) follows directly from (1) through (3) via transitivity. Since transitivity is not a valid rule of inference for counterfactuals, it follows that the argument Plantinga offers us is invalid.

This second concern, like the first, points, I think, to a genuine expository infelicity in Plantinga's discussion. But, as in the first case, we ought not assume that this weakness of presentation points to a serious weakness in the argument. Though Plantinga makes it look as though (4) is derived via transitivity, one can in fact derive it in perfectly legitimate ways. For example, since what God foreknows cannot be untrue, it follows that

(8)   God foreknows that Paul mows $\rightarrow$ Paul mows.

From (1), (8), and (2), it follows via the valid inferential principle *If $(X \rightarrow Y)$, $(Y \rightarrow X)$, and $(Y \rightarrow Z)$, then $(X \rightarrow Z)$* that

(9)   Paul mows $\rightarrow$ God prevents the carpenter ants from moving in.

But then, since (3) is not only a truth, but a necessary truth—that is, since

(10)   God prevents the carpenter ants from moving in $\Rightarrow$ $\sim$(A)

Chapter 10 might be true concerning Peter and the lame man. In particular, consider
(12) $\sim P \rightarrow \sim A$,
the claim that, if Peter hadn't prayed, God wouldn't have cured the lame man. As we saw, the situation described in Acts seems to warrant our viewing this conditional as true. By itself, this conditional *might* be taken to imply that God's actions are in part guided by Peter's actions, or perhaps by his foreknowledge of Peter's actions. That is, (12), like (2) in the present chapter, *appears* to leave no role for middle knowledge. But, of course, we know that the appearance here is misleading with regard to (12), for we were able to make a case for its truth only by assuming that counterfactuals of creaturely freedom such as (3) through (8), along with counterfactuals of divine freedom such as (9) and (10), were true. Despite its appearance, then, (12) shouldn't be seen as a conditional that displays God's reason for acting. But then, why think (2) should be so viewed? Couldn't (2), too, be a truth that simply follows from other counterfactuals of freedom?

is true—we can derive (4) from (9) and (10) via the valid inferential principle *If (X → Y) and (Y ⇒ Z), then (X → Z)*. So, appearances to the contrary notwithstanding, Plantinga's line of reasoning is not in fact invalid.[13]

A final concern the Molinist might have is that Plantinga's argument obscures the fact that actions are always performed in a specific set of circumstances. As we have seen, Molinists believe that the antecedents of counterfactuals of creaturely freedom specify such circumstances, which are to be thought of as including the complete causal history of the world prior to the time in question, along with all simultaneous exercises of causal power by other agents. In Plantinga's argument, though, Paul's mowing appears to be taking place in a circumstantial vacuum. There is no mention in any of the premises or in the conclusion of the circumstances conditioning Paul's action.

Now, one might feel that this was a mere oversight on Plantinga's part, and that we could, if we so desired, simply plug the relevant circumstances into the premises and conclusions with no adverse effect. When we try to do so, though, we quickly discover that things are not so simple. Let C stand for the circumstances in which Paul found himself. As usual, C is to be thought of as including the complete causal history of the world prior to the time in question. Were we simply to include reference to C in the premises and conclusion of Plantinga's argument, we would end up with the following:

(1*) (Paul mows in C) → (God foreknows that Paul mows in C).

(2*) (God foreknows that Paul mows in C) → (God prevents the carpenter ants from moving in).

(3) (God prevents the carpenter ants from moving in) → ∼(A).

∴ (4*) (Paul mows in C) → ∼(A).

Though superficially similar to Plantinga's actual argument, this line of reasoning suffers from the malady of being palpably unsound. Recall that C is supposed to include all exercises of causal power prior to the time of Paul's action. But then C includes the fact that the ants moved in last Saturday. So C by itself entails that (A) is true. Hence, (4*) could be true only if it were impossible that Paul mow in C. Since it *isn't* impossible that he mow, something is obviously amiss with this argument.

---

[13] One might also validly derive (4) by thinking of the antecedents of (2) and (3) as tacitly including the statement that Paul mows. Plantinga has informed me that this is, in fact, how he thought of the argument as proceeding.

The source of the problem is easy to pinpoint: since (1*) and (3) are both necessary truths, it must be (2*) which is mucking up the works. And so indeed it is; (2*) is not only false, but necessarily false. For if God foreknows that Paul mows in C, then, given that C includes the fact that the ants moved in, God foreknows that Paul mows in the wake of the ants' moving in. But then God knows that the ants did move in, and so will hardly act so as to bring it about that they didn't move in.

If we wish to incorporate reference to the circumstances of action in Plantinga's argument, then, it can't be reference to the complete set of circumstances that *actually* obtained, but rather to some other set of circumstances. If these circumstances were to include the ants' having moved in, though, we would have made no progress, for our conclusion would still be clearly false. So, we might think, the circumstances need to include the statement that the ants *didn't* move in. Indeed, if our replacement for (2*) is to come out true, one might argue, the circumstances need to entail that God prevented their moving in. Perhaps, then, there is some such set of circumstances C* entailing the falsity of (A) which will do the trick. If so, our circumstance-incorporating variation on Plantinga's argument would look like this:

(1**) (Paul mows in C*) → (God foreknows that Paul mows in C*).

(2**) (God foreknows that Paul mows in C*) → (God prevents the carpenter ants from moving in).

(3) (God prevents the carpenter ants from moving in) → ~(A).

∴(4**) (Paul mows in C*) → ~(A).

This argument has the advantage of being both valid and sound. Given the restrictions we set up for C*, each of the three premises is not only true, but necessary; and since transitivity holds for strict implications, it is clear that the derivation of (4**) is indeed valid. Unfortunately, this argument fails to show that Paul has counterfactual power over the past. For Paul is actually in C, not in C*. The fact that he could do something in circumstances that don't actually obtain which would counterfactually imply that (A) is false no more shows that Paul has counterfactual power over (A) than the fact that I could buy the Sears Tower had I inherited a billion dollars last year shows that I have counterfactual power over my not owning the Sears Tower.

If we wish to leave the reference to the complete circumstances in the argument, we clearly need to supplement the argument if it is to be used to support the possibility of our having counterfactual power over the past. One, and perhaps the only, way to do this would be to add a premise at the start of the argument stating that, had Paul mowed, C^* would have been the circumstances in which he was mowing. That is,

(11)   Paul mows → C^*.[14]

When combined with (1^{**}) through (3), this would allow us to derive

(4)   Paul mows → ~(A)

as our conclusion, and this conclusion, of course, would allow us to say that Paul has counterfactual power over (A).

The problem with this supplemented argument, though, is that it appears tantamount to begging the question. The point of the argument, after all, is to *show* that it is possible that an agent such as Paul has the power to do something such that, were he to do it, the past would have been different than it in fact was. But if we use (11) as a premise in our argument, then we are simply assuming that which we were attempting to show. For to assume both that (11) is true and that Paul has the power to mow just is to assume that Paul has the power to do something such that, were he to do it, the past would have been different than it in fact was (C^* rather than C would have obtained). So I don't think we make any headway in demonstrating the possibility of counterfactual power over the past by bringing (11) into the discussion.

The ramifications of this result should not be minimized. Making no reference to the complete set of circumstances in which Paul acts, which at first appeared to be merely an accidental oversight by Plantinga, now at least appears to be essential to his argument's viability. In a sense, this should not surprise us; after all, *most* (if not *all*) back-tracking counterfactuals can be held true only if their antecedents are not held to be complete. Still, to the Molinist who feels that reference to circumstances cannot be so easily dismissed, and who grants (as we did implicitly at the end of section 1) that the sort of controversial counterfactuals required for counterfactual power over the past should be endorsed only insofar as we can see them as grounded in full-fledged counterfactuals of creaturely freedom, the fact that the argument Plantinga

---

[14] Strictly speaking, (11) should be stated as "Paul mows → C^* *obtains*." To simplify the presentation just a tad, though, I will generally refrain from writing the "obtains" in such cases.

actually presents seems resistant to such grounding should lead to a significant degree of dissatisfaction with it.

4. An Alternative to Counterfactual Power over the Past?

To the extent that one is dissatisfied with Plantinga's argument concerning Paul, of course, one will also be dissatisfied with our parallel argument concerning Paula, and consequently still skeptical about the practice of praying for things to have happened. A natural strategy to blunt such skepticism would be to find some other way of arguing for the possibility of counterfactual power over the past, and this is a strategy I will in fact pursue in the next section. But before doing so, it might be instructive to consider whether there might not be another way for the Molinist to go here. Is there, perhaps, an alternative to counterfactual power which allows a connection between our current activities and past events sufficient to make retrospective prayer reasonable?

One possibility is suggested by Freddoso in a footnote to the introduction to his translation of Molina.[15] Let C continue to stand for the set of circumstances in which Paul (in Plantinga's story) finds himself—a set of circumstances which includes the fact that the ants moved into his yard last Saturday. Since we are looking here for an alternative to counterfactual power over the past, let us assume that Paul lacks such power, and hence assume that were Paul to mow, he would do so in C. In other words, let us assume that the counterfactual *Paul mows* → *Paul mows in C* is true. Now, if Paul were to mow in these circumstances, then clearly the counterfactual of creaturely freedom stating that he would mow if in C would be true. Thus,

$$(12) \quad (\text{Paul mows in } C) \rightarrow (C \rightarrow \text{Paul mows}).$$

So, given that Paul is free either to mow or not to mow in C, and given that, were he not to mow, $(C \rightarrow \text{Paul mows})$ would have been false, it follows that Paul has counterfactual power over this counterfactual of creaturely freedom. But God, of course, has middle knowledge of all true counterfactuals of creaturely freedom. So we also know that

$$(13) \quad (C \rightarrow \text{Paul mows}) \rightarrow [\text{God has middle knowledge that } (C \rightarrow \text{Paul mows})].$$

---

[15] Freddoso, "Introduction," p. 59, n. 80.

Indeed, since (13) is *necessarily* true (because it is impossible that God be ignorant of a true counterfactual of creaturely freedom), we can conclude from (12) and (13) that

(14)   (Paul mows in C) → [God has middle knowledge that (C → Paul mows)].

Of course, Paul doesn't actually mow in C, and, since (C → Paul mows) is in fact false, God doesn't have middle knowledge of it. Hence, we are justified in concluding that Paul has counterfactual power over God's middle knowledge. That is, he has the power to perform an action such that, were he so to act, then God's middle knowledge would have been other than it in fact is. Even if counterfactual power over the past were dubious from a Molinist perspective, counterfactual power over God's middle knowledge would be undeniable.

Now in Plantinga's story, recall, God wants the colony of carpenter ants to survive. Had he known by middle knowledge, then, that Paul would mow if placed in C, God would presumably have seen to it that Paul is not placed in C. There are various ways in which he might have done this, but one way would be to prevent the ants from moving in last Saturday. So it may well be true that

(15)   [God has middle knowledge that (C → Paul mows)] → God prevents the carpenter ants from moving in.

Since, as we have already seen,

(3)   God prevents the carpenter ants from moving in → ~(A)

is true, and (more importantly) necessarily true, we could deduce from (15) and (3) that

(16)   [God has middle knowledge that (C → Paul mows)] → ~(A).

So the truth of (A) depends counterfactually upon what it is God knows via middle knowledge.

Now, one who questioned our working assumption of this section (i.e., that we have no counterfactual power over the past) might think that from (14) and (16) one could reach the kind of conclusion Plantinga reached. That is, one might be tempted to propose the following argument.

That paul doesn't Perform C does not mean he has power over.

(14) (Paul mows in C) $\rightarrow$ [God has middle knowledge that ($C \rightarrow$ Paul mows)].

(16) [God has middle knowledge that ($C \rightarrow$ Paul mows)] $\rightarrow \sim$(A).

$\therefore$(4★) (Paul mows in C) $\rightarrow \sim$(A).

But this, of course, would be to make the mistake once again of thinking that the counterfactual relation is transitive. Nor can we derive (4★) by way of the valid inference schemes we suggested warranted Plantinga's derivation of (4) from (1) through (3).[16] Indeed, there *can* be no way in which we can properly get to (4★), for, as we noted in our earlier discussion of Plantinga's argument, (4★) is quite evidently false. Since C includes the fact that the carpenter ants *did* move in last Saturday, Paul's mowing *in* C will in fact entail that (A) is *true*. So (4★) is not simply false, but necessarily false. Hence, we *shouldn't* be able to derive it from two truths such as (14) and (16).

Looking at the matter from this decidedly Molinist perspective, then, seems to offer us no reason to question our working assumption that Paul has no counterfactual power over the past. What we seem justified in saying, rather, is only this: Paul has the power to do something (mow in C) such that, were he to do it, God's middle knowledge would have been different; and had God's middle knowledge been different in that way, God would have prevented the ants from moving in, thereby both rendering (A) false and changing the situation in which Paul as a matter of fact found himself.

Now, were one so inclined, one might still think of Paul as having a kind of power over the past, though a kind even weaker than the counterfactual power Plantinga has in mind. Following a hint from Freddoso, one might

---

[16] Were it the case that

(15★)   [God has middle knowledge that ($C \rightarrow$ Paul mows)] $\rightarrow$ Paul mows in C,

(4★) would follow from (14), (15★), and (16) via the valid inferential principle *If* $(X \rightarrow Y)$, $(Y \rightarrow X)$, and $(Y \rightarrow Z)$, then $(X \rightarrow Z)$. But (15★) isn't true if (16) is. For the latter tells us that (A) would have been false had God known by middle knowledge that ($C \rightarrow$ Paul mows). But if (A) would have been false, then C, which includes (A), wouldn't have obtained, so Paul, of course, wouldn't have mowed in C. Similarly, were (16) a necessary truth, then (4★) would follow from (14) and (16) via the valid inferential rule *If* $(X \rightarrow Y)$ *and* $(Y \Rightarrow Z)$, *then* $(X \rightarrow Z)$. But (16) surely is *not* a necessary truth. Given his middle knowledge that ($C \rightarrow$ Paul mows), God surely could have achieved his purposes by doing many things other than prevent the ants from moving in. (For instance, he might simply have prevented *Paul* from moving in; indeed, he might have decided not to create Paul at all.) So we can't get to (4★) in this way either.

even distinguish between *strong* and *weak* counterfactual power.[17] Strong counterfactual power would be what we have heretofore been calling simply counterfactual power—the type of power Plantinga is ascribing to Paul. This kind of power, one might say, can be understood in the following way:

> S has *strong counterfactual power* over truth V iff for some X,
> (i) S has the power to cause it to be the case that X, and
> (ii) $X \rightarrow \sim V$.

Weak counterfactual power, on the other hand, would refer to the kind of relationship between Paul and the ants' entry which we have suggested Molinists could endorse. More formally, we might say:

> S has *weak counterfactual power* over truth V iff for some Y,
> (i) S has strong counterfactual power over Y, and
> (ii) $\sim Y \rightarrow \sim V$.

As Molinists, then, even were we to deny that Paul has strong counterfactual power over the past, we ought still to affirm that he has strong counterfactual power over God's middle knowledge. And if he does, then he may well have weak counterfactual power over the past.

Many Molinists (myself and Freddoso included) might well be somewhat perturbed by the language involved here. After all, if the ants would still have moved in no matter *what* Paul were to do, isn't it (at best) misleading to speak of him as having *any* sense of power over the truth of (A)? But suppose we put our stylistic qualms to the side and agree to abide by the terminology introduced above. The important question seems to be this: Is weak counterfactual power over the past enough to justify the practice of praying for things to have happened?

I am not sure, but I fear that it is not. Consider again the case of Paula, Paul's wife, who considers praying that their lawn have been exempt from the carpenter ant invasion. If our suspicion that there is no strong counterfactual power over the past is correct, then our earlier way of justifying her past-directed prayer can no longer be maintained. For

(7)   Paula prays that her lawn have been spared $\rightarrow \sim$(A).

---

[17] See again Freddoso, "Introduction," p. 59, n. 80. It should be noted that Freddoso does not commit himself to the claim that we have only weak counterfactual power over the past. Furthermore, Freddoso himself uses the terminology of weak and strong *counterfactual dependence*, not weak and strong *power*.

would no longer be tenable. And if (A) would have been true *whether or not* Paula prayed, it is at least difficult to see her failure to pray as making any difference.

This, of course, is not to say that the Molinist should reject the notion of weak counterfactual power. Indeed, given the reasoning outlined above, a Molinist denial of our weak counterfactual power over the past seems simply indefensible. Furthermore, there may well be contexts in which it is valuable to point to the distinction between weak and strong counterfactual power. My suspicion, though, is that this is not one of those contexts. If we have *only* weak counterfactual power over the past, the practice of praying for things to have happened appears insupportable.

5. Strong Counterfactual Power Resurrected

If we are to defend this practice, then, it seems that we need to find some way to justify the claim that we can have strong counterfactual power over the past. But how, we might wonder, can we do so? Plantinga's argument, as we saw, seems difficult to formulate once we try to incorporate reference to the circumstances of action in it, while our Molinist successor to his argument warrants only the claim that we have weak counterfactual power over the past. Is there a way to resuscitate one or both of these arguments?

Perhaps. In each of these arguments, we suggested, the circumstances in which an action occurs ought not to be ignored. Furthermore, we argued, circumstances are to be thought of in the rich Molinist sense as including the complete causal history of the world, for only counterfactuals that include such complete circumstances in their antecedents qualify as counterfactuals of creaturely freedom. Though both of these points seem to me nonnegotiable, perhaps they have blinded us to a fact we have already seen—that middle knowledge is not *simply* knowledge of counterfactuals of creaturely freedom. Some of the counterfactuals God knows via middle knowledge have antecedents that are *not* complete.

Recall our discussion of prophecy in Chapter 9. As we noted there, if Jesus' prophecy of Peter's denial is to be thought of as included in the circumstances in which Peter acts, then those circumstances by themselves entail that Peter denies Jesus; hence, a counterfactual whose antecedent includes those circumstances and whose consequent specifies Peter's denial would not be a contingent truth, and so would not be part of God's middle knowledge. If we wish to view middle knowledge as guiding God's decisions concerning prophetic action, then, we need to concentrate not on counterfactuals with *complete* antecedents, but on ones with *incomplete* antecedents which can plausibly be seen as following from those with complete antecedents. As we saw, at least in the case of Peter and Jesus' prophecy, a strong case can be made for thinking both that there are such counterfactuals and that God can use these components of his middle knowledge in an action-guiding way.

In the case of prophecy, the incomplete circumstances upon which we focused excluded from the complete set of circumstances those facts that might be thought of as making no difference to the action performed. Perhaps what we need to do is to see if similar restrictions on circumstances can help us justify the possibility of strong counterfactual power over the past and thereby undergird past-directed prayer.

Consider once again the case of Paula's failing to pray that her lawn have been kept free of the ants—that is, failing to pray that (A) be false. Paula's situation, we noted, is one of uncertainty concerning (A). Indeed, though many factors play a role in her free decision not to pray—her existing, her being free, her desire to have an ant-free lawn, her belief that there is a God who sometimes answers prayers, her having developed a degree of laxity concerning prayer, her uncertainty concerning whether her lawn was invaded, and the like—(A)'s being true or false does not seem to be such a factor. (A), we know, is actually true—the ants *did* move in—but Paula, unaware of this fact, considers praying that it be false before deciding not to do so. Had (A) been false, there is no reason to think Paula's action would have been different in the slightest.

Suppose, then, that we divide the circumstances in which Paula finds herself into two categories. First, consider only that subset of the circumstances which are *counterfactually relevant* to her free activity. Paula's beliefs about God, her desires for a healthy lawn, her laziness, and so on, are plausible candidates for membership in this subset (call it S), for it is reasonable to think that her activity wouldn't have been exactly the same had they not been present. Second, consider all those parts of the circumstances which are *counterfactually irrelevant* to Paula's freely acting as she does. Facts such as that someone in China lit a cigarette five seconds prior to the time in question, or that a certain iguana 8,000 miles away from Paula is opening its eyes at the time of her action, would presumably be part of this subset (call it T). And, as we have seen, so (apparently) would the fact that the ants moved into Paula's yard last Saturday. (A), then, is presumably also in T.

Together, S and T make up the complete set of circumstances in which Paula was placed. As we know, this was a set of circumstances in which she decided not to pray that God spare her lawn. So

(17)   [(Paula is in S) and T] → Paula doesn't pray that their lawn have been spared

is a true conditional with a complete antecedent; hence, God would know (17) by middle knowledge. Suppose, though, that *T hadn't* obtained. Would

(18)   [(Paula is in S) and ~T] → Paula doesn't pray that their lawn have been spared

also be an element of God's middle knowledge? It seems to me that it would. *T* could have failed to obtain in many different ways. It would not have obtained had that Chinese smoker not lit up, or had that iguana not opened its eyes, or had the ants not moved into Paula's yard last Saturday. But whichever way *T* failed to obtain—that is, whichever non-*T* way we choose to supplement *S* so as to form a complete set of circumstances for Paula—it seems that Paula still would not have prayed, given our assumption that *T* includes only circumstances irrelevant to her action.[18] So there are, it would seem, infinitely many harmonizing counterfactuals of creaturely freedom which together entail (18). Proposition (18), then, would also seem to be part of God's middle knowledge.

If (17) and (18) are both part of middle knowledge, though, a solution to our problem finally appears in sight. For (17) and (18) together entail

(19)   (Paula is in S) → Paula doesn't pray that their lawn have been spared.

---

[18] If counterfactual irrelevance is thought of in the most straightforward way, as what we might call *individual* irrelevance, then (18) could conceivably be false even though (17) was true. To say that, for example, the iguana's eye opening is *individually irrelevant* to Paula's action is to say that, had the iguana *not* opened its eyes, but everything else remained the same (as much as possible), Paula still wouldn't have prayed. If *T* is thought of as containing circumstances which are irrelevant only in this sense, then (17) clearly does not entail (18). For it is possible that, if Paula were in *S* and *T* had not obtained, then no element of *T* would have obtained. And it is also possible that, if Paula were in *S* and no element of *T* had obtained, then Paula *would* have prayed. But then, of course, it follows that (18) could have been false.

There are two responses one might make here. The first would be to leave the concept of irrelevance alone, concede that (18) could be false though (17) was true, but note that, since the counterfactuals involved in such a scene are clearly rather bizarre (e.g., Paula *wouldn't* have prayed if the iguana hadn't opened its eyes, *wouldn't* have prayed if the Chinese smoker hadn't lit up, but *would* have prayed if the iguana hadn't opened its eyes *and* the Chinese smoker hadn't lit up), Paula would have no reason to suspect that they were true, and hence no good reason (assuming the soundness of the rest of our argument) not to engage in retrospective prayer. The second response would be to tinker with the concept of relevance so as to guarantee the move from (17) to (18). We might, for example, say that a circumstance *Y* was *collectively irrelevant* to Paula's action just in case (i) *Y* is individually irrelevant to Paula's action (in the sense noted above), and (ii) for any set of circumstances $Z_1, \ldots, Z_n$, if each of Z_1 through Z_n is independently irrelevant to Paula's action, then $(Y \vee Z_1 \vee \ldots \vee Z_n)$ is independently irrelevant to her action. If we specified that *T* includes only those circumstances that are collectively irrelevant to her action, then (18) could hardly be denied.

Since (19) is a contingent truth entailed by two elements of God's middle knowledge, it too must be part of God's middle knowledge. Suppose that we henceforth abbreviate (19) as

(19) $S \rightarrow$ Paula doesn't pray.

As we have seen,

(20) $(S \rightarrow$ Paula doesn't pray) $\Rightarrow$ [God has middle knowledge that $(S \rightarrow$ Paula doesn't pray)].

Suppose, though, that (19) had been false. Suppose it had been the case that Paula would have prayed had she been in S, so, that

(21) $S \rightarrow$ Paula prays

had been true. Presumably God would have known (21) had it been true. And, had it been true, it presumably would have followed from a group of harmonizing complete counterfactuals of creaturely freedom, just as we have seen that (19) does actually so follow. So we seem justified in asserting that

(22) $(S \rightarrow$ Paula prays) $\Rightarrow$ [God has middle knowledge that $(S \rightarrow$ Paula prays)].

Of course, we also know that

(23)   (Paula prays in S) $\rightarrow$ $(S \rightarrow$ Paula prays).

And from (23) and (22) it follows that

(24)   (Paula prays in S) $\rightarrow$ [God has middle knowledge that $(S \rightarrow$ Paula prays)].

Now, if God had known that Paula would pray if placed in S, perhaps he would have seen via middle knowledge that much good would result were he to place her in S and answer her prayer by seeing to it that the ants avoided her lawn. That is, it might well be true that both

(25)   [God has middle knowledge that $(S \rightarrow$ Paula prays)] $\rightarrow$ Paula prays in S

and

> (26)   [God has middle knowledge that $(S \rightarrow$ Paula prays)] $\rightarrow$ God prevents
>   the carpenter ants from moving in.

But (24), (25), and (26) together entail

> (27)   (Paula prays in S) $\rightarrow$ God prevents the carpenter ants from moving in.

Since

> (3)   God prevents the carpenter ants from moving in $\rightarrow \sim(A)$

is a necessary truth, it would then follow from (27) and (3) that

> (28)   (Paula prays in S) $\rightarrow \sim(A)$.

And (28), of course, is precisely the type of conclusion we need. For it tells us that Paula has strong counterfactual power over the past: there is an action Paula has the power to perform (namely, pray) in the (incomplete) circumstances she is in (namely, S) such that, were she to perform that action, the ants would not have moved into her yard. Paula's retrospective prayer, then, really would have made a difference with regard to how things went last Saturday.

6. A Pair of Objections

Let us briefly consider two objections to this line of reasoning. The first of these objections contends that the argument offered above for (28) is faulty, while the second objection grants the soundness but questions the relevance of the argument.

Our first objection goes as follows. The argument offered for (28) depends upon the claim that (A) is counterfactually irrelevant to Paula's activity. But couldn't this claim be false? Might there not be some bizarre counterfactual connection between the ants and Paula such that, had they *not* moved in last Saturday, she *wouldn't* have acted as she in fact did? If so, then (A) would have to rank as one of the relevant circumstances—as part of S—and so the argument to (28) would be blocked.

We Molinists, of course, are in no position to deny the possibility of bizarre counterfactual connections. So we have little choice but to concede the possibility that (A) is counterfactually relevant to Paula's action. It seems to me, though, that such a possibility does little to undermine the case being made here for the legitimacy of retrospective prayer. For even if the counterfactuals concerning Paula and the ants were bizarre in the way described, all of us (including Paula) would surely be ignorant of this fact. Only if one knew, or reasonably believed, that someone's counterfactuals were bizarre could one know, or reasonably believe, that her retrospective prayer could make no difference. Since hardly anyone can know, or reasonably believe, this about anyone, the rationality of such prayer seems untouched by this first objection.

Our second objection grants that the argument for (28) succeeds, but denies that its success establishes the rationality of retrospective prayer. Since (28) makes reference only to *incomplete* circumstances, it doesn't change the fact that Paula is actually in *complete* circumstances, circumstances which would have obtained no matter what she had done. Hence, attempting to influence the past via prayer remains irrational even if the argument for (28) is accepted.[19]

As I see it, this objection amounts to little more than begging the question, for it asks us to assume that circumstances that are complete are ipso facto beyond one's counterfactual power. Furthermore, the assumption in question is in fact untenable if, as the objection grants, the argument for (28) is sound. For, in the case of Paula, that assumption would lead us to say that, had Paula prayed, she would have prayed in C, the complete set of circumstances composed of S and T. Consider, then, what follows if we make this assumption:

(29)	Paula prays $\rightarrow$ Paula prays in C	[assumption for *reductio*]
(30)	Paula prays in $C \Rightarrow$ Paula prays in S	[necessary truth]
(31)	Paula prays $\rightarrow$ Paula prays in S	(29), (30)
(32)	Paula prays in $S \rightarrow$ Paula prays	[necessary truth]
(28)	Paula prays in $S \rightarrow \sim(A)$	[argument in text]
(33)	Paula prays $\rightarrow \sim(A)$	(31),(32), (28)
(34)	$\sim(A) \Rightarrow \sim$(Paula prays in C)	[necessary truth]
(35)	Paula prays $\rightarrow \sim$(Paula prays in C)	(33), (34)

Given that it is possible that Paula prays, (29) and (35) cannot both be true. But the only contingent premises needed to derive (35) were (29) itself and (28). So (29) and (28) cannot both be true. Now the objector, we have been supposing, grants that we have a solid Molinist argument for (28). On the other hand, we have no real argument for (29). So, unless some problem with the argument for (28) can be uncovered, we have good reason to reject (29).

---

[19] I am indebted to William Ramsey for pointing out to me the significance of this type of objection.

In other words, one who accepts our argument has no choice but to grant that completeness does not entail fixity; had Paula prayed, the complete circumstances in which she prayed would have been different from those which in fact obtained.

7. Conclusion

Praying for things to have happened, then, seems to be defensible. Of course, the argument we have given for this conclusion depends essentially on Molinist assumptions concerning God's middle knowledge. So perhaps our conclusion should be stated more as a hypothetical: *If* Molinism is defensible, then so is the practice of praying for things to have happened. Some with Geachian qualms concerning retrospective prayer will no doubt see this as but one more reason to steer clear of Molinism. But, as I noted at the start of our discussion, I think that few believers find universal skepticism regarding such prayer to be attractive. For those in the majority here, the fact that Molinism allows us to justify such activity will surely count as a point in its favor. For those already convinced of the truth of Molinism, its ability to defend praying for things to have happened will most likely be seen as but one more illustration of the theory's fecundity.

Conclusion

The kind reader who has stuck with this lengthy work to this point deserves, it seems to me, a final word or two from the author—a brief recapitulation of what has been done, an acknowledgment of what remains to be
done, and some indication (to the extent that an author is in a position to
offer such) of the overall significance of the work.

Our investigation has shown, I think, that a very powerful case can be built
for seeing the Molinist account of divine providence as one that is excep-
tionally attractive from the standpoint of the orthodox Christian. As we saw
in Part I, such Christians are typically drawn toward both a strong traditional
notion of providence and an uncompromisingly libertarian view of freedom.
For the libertarian traditionalist, though, the vision of a God employing his
prevolitional knowledge of counterfactuals of creaturely freedom to fashion a
world that manifests his providential care for his children without in the
slightest diminishing their full libertarian freedom seems the natural picture of
providence to embrace, and this of course is what Molinism uniquely offers.
Indeed, given the various infelicities we identified at the start of Part II with
the three major alternatives (eternity, Thomist, and "open") to the theory of
middle knowledge, it seems clear that the libertarian traditionalist has excep-
tionally strong motivation to endorse the Molinist outlook unless and until
extremely potent objections to that outlook can be identified. As we saw
through the remainder of Part II, though, the arguments against Molinism
that have in fact been raised fail to provide significant reason to reject that
view. Furthermore, as we saw in Part III, adopting the Molinist stance enables
us better to understand certain dimensions of divine providential activity (concerning infallibility, prophecy, and prayer), and the success of these endeavors
to apply the Molinist outlook serves further to confirm the attractiveness of
that approach.

I suffer under no illusion that all, or even most, readers will close the covers
of this book as avowed Molinists. That is probably as it should be. Intellectual
journeys rarely take travelers onto the road to Damascus; swift conversions to
any philosophical or theological position are likely to be ill-considered and

frail. Still, if those readers loyal to the tenets of orthodox Christianity leave this work with some sense of the appeal that the theory of middle knowledge should offer to believers with their religious outlook, with a recognition of the enormous problems facing us if we abandon that Molinist position, and with a willingness to view Molinism as at least the prime contender for their support, my goals in writing this book will have been largely achieved.

It should go without saying that more needs to be done before any of us should form any adamantine conclusions concerning the Molinist picture of providence. Experience suggests that responses to alleged refutations of middle knowledge will lead critics to fashion revisions to their prior arguments. While I have little doubt that no such argument will succeed, the discussion has hardly reached a stage where one can confidently view as minuscule the likelihood that a genuinely new anti-Molinist argument will be offered. Hence, Molinists will surely need to continue to devote some of their resources to defense for some time to come. More important, though, the endeavor to apply the Molinist account—to see whether and how that account enriches (or, conceivably, distorts) our understanding of particular dimensions of God's providential activity—is still in its infancy. More undoubtedly needs to be said on infallibility, prophecy, and prayer. And much more surely needs to be done on many other topics, from predestination and biblical inspiration to omnipotence and Christology. Until such investigations are pursued, our assessment of Molinism must surely be somewhat provisional.

I am not, let me be clear, adopting or advocating a position of neutrality. The evidence examined in this book, it seems to me, offers us more than sufficient reason to accept the Molinist outlook and to feel confident that Molinism will prove both resilient in the face of future attacks and enlightening in the case of further applications. My point is only that the discussion of these issues has not reached a stage where confidence on any side can reasonably be unbridled. All of us engaged in this dispute should occasionally remind ourselves of the genuine epistemic possibility, however slight we might think it, that our opponents are correct. Intellectual humility is a virtue which few of us academics are in any danger of over-developing.

Such humility may have a further and more significant benefit: it may serve to remind us of the secondary (or perhaps even tertiary) significance of so many of our philosophical endeavors. This is not to say that such endeavors are not worth pursuing; obviously, something can be of secondary (or even tertiary) importance and still be quite important. But such subordinate concerns ought not blind us to what is of primary importance. It is perhaps fitting that we conclude this point, and this book, with the words (on a closely related topic) of Molina:

Therefore, with not a worry at all about the divine foreknowledge, let us, in accord with the advice of St. Peter [2 Pet. 1:10], busy ourselves so that by good works we might do what we are called to do. For just as the devil, who has understood far better than we have that God foreknows all things, caring not a bit about the divine foreknowledge, leaves no stone unturned and carefully roams about and circles the earth, seeking whom he might devour, so too let us, freed from every care about the divine foreknowledge, diligently work out our salvation, relying on God's help; for in this way it will come to pass that without any doubt we will attain eternal happiness. And in this regard it should be sufficient for each of us to keep in mind that God is God, that is, infinite wisdom, goodness, etc., in order that in these matters, which are beyond the understanding of many, we might commit ourselves firmly to God's goodness and providence and busy ourselves to the extent of our power with those things that it is our responsibility, with God's help, to look after most diligently.[1]

[1] Molina, Disputation 52, section 39 (p. 195).

Index